JESUS WAS A LIBERAL

ALSO BY SCOTTY MCLENNAN

Finding Your Religion: When the Faith You Grew Up with Has Lost Its Meaning

Church on Sunday, Work on Monday: The Challenge of Fusing Christian Values with Business Life, coauthored with Laura Nash

JESUS WAS A LIBERAL

RECLAIMING
CHRISTIANITY
FOR ALL

Rev. Scotty McLennan

palgrave
macmillan

First published in hardcover in 2009 by
PALGRAVE MACMILLAN®
in the United States—a division of St. Martin's Press LLC,
175 Fifth Avenue, New York, NY 10010.

Where this book is distributed in the UK, Europe and the rest of the world,
this is by Palgrave Macmillan, a division of Macmillan Publishers Limited,
registered in England, company number 785998, of Houndmills,
Basingstoke, Hampshire RG21 6XS.

Palgrave Macmillan is the global academic imprint of the above companies
and has companies and representatives throughout the world.

Palgrave® and Macmillan® are registered trademarks in the United States,
the United Kingdom, Europe and other countries.

ISBN: 978–0–230–10340–5

Library of Congress Cataloging-in-Publication Data is available from the
Library of Congress.

A catalogue record of the book is available from the British Library.

Design by Newgen Imaging Systems (P) Ltd., Chennai, India.

First PALGRAVE MACMILLAN paperback edition: December 2010

10 9 8 7 6 5 4 3 2 1

Printed in the United States of America.

CONTENTS

*To Ellen—love of my life, best friend,
and luminous critic*

PREFACE

What *Is* Liberal Christianity?

"**W**asn't Jesus a liberal?" asked an evangelical Southern Baptist preacher named Gary Vance before the 2004 U.S. election.[1] A year later he wrote: "I was saddened by the responses from the Religious Right." They made "bitter and vitriolic diatribes that questioned my credibility as a minister and my standing in the Kingdom of God."[2] The values he referred to as "dictionary definitions" of liberalism included belief in progress, tolerance, individual freedom, and the essential goodness of humanity.

Indeed, I believe that Jesus was a religious liberal. He came with a fresh new progressive vision, proclaiming again and again, "You have heard that it was said to those of ancient times... but I say to you..."[3] Instead of an eye for an eye, he asked us to turn the other cheek.[4] Instead of loving just our neighbors, we were called upon to love our enemies too.[5] He spoke of a new testament, distinct from the old testament that came before.[6] When the apostle Paul described Jesus's new testament, he explained that it was "not of letter but of spirit; for the letter kills, but the spirit gives life."[7] Jesus was not a fundamentalist in the sense of being a biblical literalist. He would break one of the Ten Commandments when he thought it was the most humane thing to do, as when he worked, healing people, on the Sabbath.[8] As he clearly said, "The Sabbath was made for humankind, and not humankind for the Sabbath."[9]

I'm a liberal Christian. So are a large number of American Christians, according to sociologists of religion.[10] We've also been called "progressive Christians," and we're generally found in mainline (as distinct from evangelical) churches. Unfortunately, we're often either forgotten or maligned in the current culture wars and public debates between the religious right and the secular left.

We are the religious left. But what do we stand for? Not all of us share exactly the same perspective, of course (nor would we all accept each description in the next paragraph), but we tend to be identifiable by many of the following principles.

The Bible is meant to be read largely metaphorically and allegorically, rather than literally. Science and religion are compatible; we are committed to the use of logic, reason, and the scientific method. Doubt is the handmaiden of faith. Love is the primary Christian value, and it is directly related to the promotion of liberty and justice in society at large. All people are inherently equal and worthy of dignity and respect. Free religious expression should be governmentally protected, but no particular tradition should be established as the state religion. There are many roads to the top of the spiritual mountain, and Christianity is only one of them. Interfaith understanding and tolerance are critical. We see Jesus primarily as a spiritual and ethical teacher and less as being identical with God. Living a fulfilled and ethical life here and now is more important than speculating on what happens to us after we die. Nonviolence is strongly preferred in relationships between human beings, groups, and nations. Women and men must play an equal role in religious leadership. And in terms of current American hot-button issues, we tend to be pro-choice on abortion and in favor of marriages for same-sex couples.

Most of us would consider the following people as within the circle of liberal Christianity: theologians Paul Tillich and Hans Kung, civil rights leader Martin Luther King Jr., biblical scholars Marcus Borg and John Dominic Crossan, scholars of religion Diana Eck and Harvey Cox, anti-war activist William Sloane Coffin Jr., authors Annie Dillard and Anne Lamott, Pastor Harry Emerson Fosdick, Sister Joan Chittister, and missionary Albert Schweitzer.

We have not always been treated well by conservative Christians, to say the least. This is true well beyond the American context. Historically, some of our forebearers, like Michael Servetus in the sixteenth century, were denounced as heretics and burned at the stake, and others were coerced by the church's Inquisition into renouncing their scientific discoveries, such as Galileo in the seventeenth century. Some, like philosopher John Locke, fared better and had considerable influence on the liberal Christian founders of the United States of America in the eighteenth century, including Thomas Jefferson, Benjamin Franklin, and John and

Abigail Adams. Yet even liberal Christians of the nineteenth century in America, like Ralph Waldo Emerson and Susan B. Anthony, met with strong public outcries of disgust for their religious beliefs. With the rise of fundamentalism in the twentieth century, liberals were often condemned as "enemies of the cross of Christ" and accused of apostasy.[11]

Ironically, however, strong denunciation of liberal Christianity is coming from another quarter in the early twenty-first century: from public atheists in Europe and America—such as scientists Richard Dawkins and Sam Harris, philosopher Daniel Dennett, and journalist Christopher Hitchens—who publish best-selling books with such titles as *The God Delusion*,[12] *The End of Faith*,[13] *Breaking the Spell*,[14] and *God Is Not Great*.[15]

Today, the estimated 60 million liberal Christians in America[16] are caught in the crossfire between the secular left and the religious right. While outspoken atheists like Richard Dawkins call God a delusion and back up their claim with compelling arguments, well-known conservatives like Ann Coulter, author of *Godless: The Church of Liberalism,* take aim with damning charges: "Everything liberals believe is in elegant opposition to basic Biblical precepts."[17] What's a liberal Christian to do?

We liberal Christians know in our hearts that there is much more to life than seems to meet the rational eye of atheists; yet, we find it hard to support supernatural claims about religion that fly in the face of scientific evidence. We also know that there is much more to our personal spirituality than Christian conservatives seem to think there is; yet, we have trouble mustering a response that is convincing to the religious right.

The result is that we frequently find ourselves without compelling answers—both for those who challenge our beliefs and even for our own questions about theological and social issues. Many of us choose either to lie low, sitting quietly in our pews at church or in private prayer at home, or to engage in political action without mentioning our faith.

I've written this book for us as liberal Christians—but also for all those interested in learning more about this type of Christianity that so impressed world leaders such as Mohandas Gandhi and Martin Luther King Jr. My goal is to bring new light and life to the perspective of this kind of Christianity and, in doing so, to help liberal Christian readers find their vision and voice, as well as open a dialogue with others. I hope you'll find here fresh, intelligent answers to what a progressive Christian faith is all about and why it is not only relevant but also vitally important in today's world. I also want to provide a meaningful overview of the Christian tradition that demonstrates how Christians can be logical, rational, and scientific within it, as well as metaphoric, poetic, and mythological.

This book is a result of the many conversations I have had over the past eight years with the congregation at Stanford University's Memorial Church and as a result of my work as the dean for religious life at Stanford. Both the church community and sincere students of many traditions are trying to make sense out of their faith. The doubts, the struggles, and the commitments that are evident in our discussions together have had a profound influence on my own spiritual life, my ministry, and the formulation of many ideas in this book. After my Sunday sermons at Memorial Church a couple of times a month, I have "talk-backs" that attract twenty or thirty people who spend about forty-five minutes discussing the questions that have arisen from what I've said from the pulpit. These talk-backs are intimate and fascinating discussions with agnostics and atheists as well as with assured Christians. They include more older adults than students, and they always affect how I think about future sermons, many of which have inspired what I've written in this book. As dean for religious life, I'm also regularly faced with tough questions from students whose world is being broadened—and whose faith is being challenged—not only by their formal education but also by the never-ending stream of information and diversity of beliefs that we all encounter in today's global environment. I'm very grateful for all of these opportunities for dialogue at Stanford, including with the two associate deans for religious life and members of Stanford Associated Religions groups, who in turn have helped to shape this book.

I didn't grow up as a liberal Christian. In my home church in the conservative Midwest, I'd learned to fear hell if I didn't follow the straight and narrow. My Sunday school teachers taught that non-Christians are condemned because they don't accept Jesus uniquely as their Lord and Savior. As a child, I'd found my religion constricting and life-denying. In college, I began to know Jesus in an utterly different way. In my university chapel, I experienced the living Jesus as welcoming, accepting, and joyous. My university chaplain helped me take wing into an open, progressive Christianity. I'd been raised to believe that religion required me to have "blind faith"—that to believe, I must take a "leap of faith" beyond what I knew to be true logically, scientifically, and historically. During my college years, I began to understand that my faith allowed me to integrate *all* that I knew to be true—rationally and poetically, concretely and mythically. I thankfully realized then that Jesus came so that I might have life in greater abundance than I had ever known. I came to love this "new" Jesus, who was so different from the one I'd been brought up to believe in. He was poet, wisdom teacher, and hope builder, just as surely as he was pragmatist, humanist, and iconoclast. This Jesus—a liberator, not a constrictor or ideologue—has inspired leaders of many generations to work to change the world.

This book intends to speak as powerfully to doubters as to those who sit comfortably in the pews of mainline churches. As a liberal Christian who has made the journey from conservative Christianity through atheism, I'm particularly concerned not only with defending liberal Christianity and supporting liberal Christians in their beliefs, but also with demonstrating how liberal Christianity can provide intelligent responses in increasingly turbulent and extreme times.

This book should help those of you who are liberal Christians to understand how to approach the Bible, pursue a personal spiritual life, negotiate Christian doctrine, celebrate the Christian year, and participate joyfully in Christian liturgical life—in ways that feed intellectual as well as spiritual needs. The Bible translation that I'll use most often is the New Revised Standard Version (NRSV) of 1989. That's because it stands in a direct line from the King James Version of 1611 but is written in accessible modern English and takes advantage of recent advances in historical, archaeological, and linguistic knowledge; it also uses gender-inclusive language wherever possible.[18] Here's some of what I hope to accomplish in these pages:

- Demonstrate that liberal Christianity can be a bulwark against religious violence, bigotry, and hatred
- Provide clear definitions for liberals of terms like faith, God, Jesus, and the church
- Tackle the hot-button topics of abortion, same-sex marriage, and intelligent design from a liberal Christian perspective
- Examine social issues such as war, poverty, bigotry, and environmental destruction
- Reclaim the word "liberal" in its commitment to rationality, tolerance, and dialogue.

I encourage you as reader to approach the chapters in this book in your own way—sequentially or independently, choosing to read whatever areas pique your interest. I have no intention to proselytize or convert. I hope bridges will be built to conservative Christians as well as to secular humanists. Liberal Christians are tired of being either ignored or condemned by association with our brothers and sisters at one end or the other of the spectrum. In fact, we share many positive values with evangelical Christians as well as with philosophical atheists like those who have written the recent best sellers. I would like to be in dialogue with people of other religious traditions as well. I hope you will come to see how living a liberal Christian life can radically transform and renew a person by redefining what it means to be liberated and playful, inclusive and egalitarian, loving and hopeful, nonviolent and humane, courageous and strong, happy and fulfilled. This book is an invitation to appreciate the joy, freedom, tolerance, and abundance of liberal Christianity.

PART ONE

How a Liberal Christian Looks at Religion

ONE

SOME LIBERAL PERSPECTIVES

Jesus, Science, Abortion, and Same-Sex Marriage

All who are led by the Spirit of God are children of God.

—*Romans 8:14*

Do not put the Lord your God to the test.

—*Matthew 4:7*

For everything there is a season...a time to be born.

—*Ecclesiastes 3:1–2*

Love is patient; love is kind...It does not insist on its own way.

—*I Corinthians 13:4–5*

A PERSPECTIVE ON JESUS

A Hindu priest with whom I spent a college-era summer in India used to speak of avatars: people with clear mystical awareness who have direct knowledge of the infinite spirit that infuses the universe. In other words, they have true God-consciousness. Avatars, he said, help the rest of us see what God is like in human form. They are sons or daughters of God in a uniquely pure way.

The priest's avatar was Ramakrishna, a nineteenth-century saint who inspired an order and mission in India that has come to be known in America as the Vedanta Society. At the end of the summer, when I expressed a strong interest in becoming a Hindu, the Hindu priest said no. Ramakrishna, he said, taught that avatars have had different impacts from culture to culture and era to era. Yet, ultimately—although they use different names and different religious methodologies—they all point to the same God. So Ramakrishna advised seekers not to look outside their own tradition, but to follow the path they know best with wholehearted devotion. Ramakrishna counseled, "A Christian should follow Christianity, a Muslim should follow Islam, and so on."

The priest directed me back to the Christianity with which I had grown up. He insisted that Jesus was my avatar, not Ramakrishna nor the Buddha nor anyone else. It was in Jesus's footsteps that I should walk to know God better. That didn't mean I should bring along all my prior assumptions about Jesus being the only way to God for all people. I needed to develop a wider view of Christianity that included respect not only for other religions but also for everything I'd come to know scientifically, logically, and rationally.

When I returned to the United States, I discovered and joined the Unitarian Universalist denomination. Rooted in liberal Christianity, it is wide open to the religions of the world as well as to those who do not accept the label "religious." In seminary, I learned about the sermon that Unitarian minister Ralph Waldo Emerson preached in 1838 to the graduates of the Harvard Divinity School. Jesus's role as avatar came through loud and clear in that magnificent address:

> Jesus Christ belonged to the true race of prophets. He saw with open eye the mystery of the soul. Drawn by its severe harmony, ravished with its beauty, he lived in it, and had his being there...He saw that God incarnates himself in man...He said, in this jubilee of sublime emotion, "I am divine. Through me, God acts; through me, speaks. Would you see God, see me; or, see thee, when thou thinkest as I now think."[1]

That's how I'm drawn to be a follower of Jesus in the liberal Christian tradition. I'm also struck by how Jesus of Nazareth, more than two thousand years after his birth, continues to astonish and inspire so many people. His teachings are dramatic and surprising and challenging. He insists that we love our enemies, not just our friends, and that we pray for those who persecute us, forgiving their trespasses. He uncomfortably confronts us with our own hypocrisy: "First take the log out of your own eye, and then you will see clearly to take the speck out of your neighbor's eye." He also provides comforting assurance that we can let go of our material insecurities: "Do not worry about your life, what you will eat or what you will drink, or about your body, what you will wear...Look at the birds of the air; they neither sow nor reap...[and] the lilies of the field, how they grow; they neither toil nor spin." These lessons are but a fraction of what he taught in one sermon—the "Sermon on the Mount,"[2] which Gandhi called us to drink deeply of and Martin Luther King Jr. credited as foundational to the modern American civil rights movement.

Genuine transformation is possible by trying to live in his ways. We can follow Jesus individually, with our studies, meditations, and private prayers, and by living according to his teachings. We can also follow Jesus by becoming part of the Body of Christ, a community of believers gathered together in church. But what do we really know about Jesus?

First of all, we can fairly say that he was a real historical figure. The facts concerning his life and work are so abundant that even atheist Richard Dawkins in his book *The God Delusion* concedes that Jesus "probably" did exist.[3] Today, most people's understanding of Jesus is drawn not from the various contemporaneous Roman, Jewish, and pagan sources, but from the collection of writings that we now know as the New Testament. Current scholarship views most of the books of the New Testament as having been written between 50 and 100 A.D., starting a generation after the death of Jesus, around 30 A.D. The earliest materials are the letters of Paul, written in the 50s, while the Gospel of John may have been as late as 100 A.D.[4]

Modern biblical scholars have used a variety of tools to try to generate solid data about the Jesus of history. For example, conservative N. T. Wright explains that "the scientific method of hypothesis and verification" is central to this work.[5] Liberal John Dominic Crossan describes three critical sources for locating the historical Jesus: literary and textual analysis of the New Testament and other Christian documents, use of non-Christian texts to understand the Greco-Roman and Jewish context of the time, and cross-cultural anthropology.[6] Liberal Marcus Borg also refers to the role of archaeology in this enterprise.[7]

According to a number of scholars, we can feel confident now about making the following six claims for the historical Jesus:

1. Jesus was a first-century Palestinian Jew. He acted and taught within Judaism in a particular eastern Mediterranean outpost of the Roman Empire.[8] Jews were convinced that their god was the one true god, and that the gods of other nations and cultures were mere human creations or idols. Jews also believed they were elect among all the nations as the chosen people of this one and only god.[9] Jesus was certainly involved in critiquing his own tradition, but his criticism was always from the inside. Rather than calling for his people to abandon Judaism for a new and different religion, he was asking them to become the true people of the one true God. Jesus wanted Israel reconstituted—nothing more and nothing less.[10]

2. Jesus was a prophet of Israel. I don't mean the type of prophet who primarily foretold the future, but one who called the Jewish people (and sometimes other nations) to account, speaking on behalf of God.[11] Jesus referred to himself as a prophet, acted like a prophet, and didn't correct other people when they referred to him as a prophet.[12] Early in his public career, he seems to have been in the circle of another prophet, John the Baptist.[13]

3. Jesus announced the coming of the kingdom of God. John baptized Jesus when he was about thirty,[14] and his public ministry lasted only a few years at the most before the Romans executed him. During this time his primary mission appears to have been announcing that the "kingdom of God" was breaking into the world, like light coming through a crack in the wall of a dark room, and eventually would achieve the total transformation of all that was known. This wasn't a matter of military rebellion against the Romans, as many Jews of the time were hoping. Instead, Jesus seemed to mean that God's rule was coming to replace that of all political authorities.[15]

In order to begin living in relation to the emerging, in-breaking kingdom of God, Jesus called for a radical equality. Class, rank, and gender were to be commingled. Eating together was central to Jesus's mode of operation, and he invited everyone to the same table—women and men, slaves and free people, socially privileged and socially excluded, ritually pure and ritually impure.[16] A world with God totally in charge, rather than a Caesar or a Herod, requires social justice. The poor become rich and the hungry are fed.[17]

4. Jesus was a political radical. He came from the marginalized peasant class in a marginalized village in Galilee, a region north of Jerusalem that was undergoing rapid social change at the time. His hometown of Nazareth was just a few miles from the largest city of Galilee,

Sepphoris, which was also the political center for King Herod. So Jesus could easily compare huge differences in wealth and culture within Judaism. His preaching and actions demonstrated an unusual sensitivity to the poor and the oppressed.[18]

When Jesus arrived in Jerusalem at the time of the Passover, near the end of his life, he went to the temple and violently disrupted its fiscal, sacrificial, and liturgical operations,[19] as reported in all four gospels.[20] He threw over the tables of the moneychangers and ran them out of the temple. He also threw over the seats of people selling animals to be sacrificed. The account in John 2:15 has him using a whip to drive out not only the moneychangers and sellers, but also large sacrificial animals like sheep and oxen. This was likely the immediate reason for his arrest and execution, since neither Jewish nor Roman authorities could tolerate this kind of dramatic disorder at the very center of the capital's life during this busy holiday season.[21]

5. *Jesus was a healer.* This activity also had political and social implications. He ministered to those who were rejected by society—the lepers, the insane, and the disabled—and gave them back some degree of control over their own lives.

John Dominic Crossan claims that Jesus didn't actually cure illnesses like leprosy or correct physical conditions like lameness. Instead, Jesus healed in the sense of removing the personal and social stigmas of uncleanliness, isolation, and rejection associated with these conditions. He opened his arms and brought the sick and the handicapped back into the community from which they'd been excluded, making the world humanly habitable and hospitable again for them. This didn't endear him to those in authority, but it made him very popular among the dispossessed.[22]

For Jesus, living in expectation of the coming kingdom of God was a matter of action and a way of life, not just a matter of words. Marcus Borg points out that Jesus explicitly connected healing with the coming kingdom of God as a time of deliverance.[23] N. T. Wright reminds us that this activity was a major part of Jesus's public work and that it included the healing of societies and institutions, along with psychological healing, healing of memories, and a wide range of other phenomena.[24]

6. *Jesus was a wisdom teacher.* As he described how to live in relation to the incipient kingdom of God, Jesus's teachings became a kind of

wisdom, and they felt subversive and challenging, rather than conventional.[25] He used aphorisms and parables to prod others to see the world in a radically new way. The kingdom of God demanded a new social and ethical vision, with compassion and love at its core:[26] "Blessed are you who are poor, for yours is the kingdom of God." "Be merciful, just as your Father is merciful." "Do not judge, and you will not be judged."[27]

So, this is all well and good. But the critical question for many people is this: "Was Jesus the Son of God?" For liberal Christians, the question of whether we can call Jesus the Son of God can't be answered with a simple yes or no. Jesus himself never uses the term "Son of God" to describe himself in the first three gospels.[28] He does speak of others being sons or daughters of God: "Blessed are the peacemakers, for they shall be called children of God" (Matthew 5:9). This was common phraseology in his day, as when the apostle Paul says, "All who are led by the Spirit of God are children of God."[29] Scholars generally agree that the exclusive use of the title "Son of God" would have been incomprehensible to Palestinian Jews of Jesus's time, although not to those who later taught or learned about the post-Easter Jesus in the non-Jewish, Hellenistic world outside of Palestine.[30]

Part of the answer might be found in making a seventh claim about Jesus. He can fairly be called a mystic. It's entirely appropriate for us to refer to the historical Jesus by the term "spirit person."[31] Jesus is reported in Luke 4:18 to have said, quoting Isaiah, in his first moment of public ministry: "The Spirit of the Lord is upon me."[32] Like the prophets of Israel before him, Jesus had intense mystical experiences in which he felt totally in the presence of what he would call God. These were ecstatic moments—nonordinary states of consciousness.

For example, when John baptized him, Jesus had a vision of the heavens opening up and "the Spirit descending like a dove on him."[33] Jesus also had a number of visions during the following forty days that he spent alone out in the desert on what a modern anthropologist would call a vision quest or wilderness ordeal, which is typical for mystics.[34] It is also clear that Jesus regularly engaged in spiritual exercises common for mystics, like fasting and long periods of extended prayer.

His mysticism helps to explain Jesus's power for others as a wisdom teacher, healer, and announcer of the kingdom of God. Mystics have historically found themselves in trouble with mainstream members of their own religious tradition and with political authorities, especially when they took actions that radically challenged the status quo.

Although Jesus during his lifetime on earth would never have recognized certain titles later applied to him—"coequal with God," "of one substance with God," "the second person of the Trinity"—the early church began developing these ideas about him soon after his death. There's no doubt that his followers after his death moved from considering him a spirit person or mystic to increasingly speaking of him as having qualities of God and then as being divine himself.[35]

Yet, many liberal Christians like me see Jesus as the Son of God only in the sense described by the apostle Paul in Romans 8:14: "All who are led by the Spirit of God are children of God." Jesus was surely led by the Spirit of God in a very special way—as a true avatar in the words of the Hindu priest, and as a mystic who also had extraordinary abilities as prophet, healer, and wisdom teacher. Yet, personally, I don't believe that Jesus was or is identical with God, nor do I think that's what he believed either, based on the biblical evidence.

But that has no impact on my decision joyfully to choose to try to walk in his footsteps. In fact, in makes him more accessible to me as a fellow human being to whom I can relate. He is as Spirit-filled as I can imagine, and I proudly call him my "lord and savior"—in the sense of being my spiritual master and bringing ultimate meaning and purpose into my life. As Emerson said, "He saw with open eye the mystery of the soul." We can too, if we follow him.

CHRISTIANITY CAN BE RATIONAL AND SCIENTIFIC

There are a number of hot-button issues that separate liberal and conservative Christians, including views on evolution, abortion, and marriage for same-sex couples. I'll take on these three directly in this first chapter in order to clear the air, or at least to put my cards on the table, in these controversial areas. Then, I believe I'll be freer to look at essential dimensions of Christianity from a liberal perspective, including love, God, Jesus, the church, the Bible, and faith.

So, what do we do with the biblical claim in Genesis that the universe as we know it—including the earth with vegetation, living creatures of every kind, and human beings—was all created in six days?[36] How does Christianity square with modern science? What would really have happened if Jesus had thrown himself off the temple, when he was tempted by the devil to defy the law of gravity early in his ministry? He wisely responded, "Do not put the Lord your God to the test."[37]

Questions about the relationship of religion and science were at a high pitch in 2008 at Stanford. We were treated to lectures on this subject by journalist Christopher Hitchens and scientists Richard Dawkins and Francis Collins. Hitchens is the author of a best seller entitled *God Is Not Great: How Religion Poisons Everything*. In the first chapter of that book he states one of his irreducible objections to religious faith: "It wholly misrepresents the origins of man and the cosmos."[38] He explains that he "distrust[s] anything that contradicts science or outrages reason."[39] One of the major problems for religion is that it "comes from the period of human prehistory where nobody...had the smallest idea of what was going on. It comes from the bawling and fearful infancy of our species, and is a babyish attempt to meet our inescapable need for knowledge...Today the least educated of my children knows much more about the natural order than any of the founders of religion...All attempts to reconcile faith with science and reason are consigned to failure and ridicule for precisely these reasons."[40]

By contrast, the late Rev. Jerry Falwell, founder of Liberty University in Lynchburg, Virginia—a university that now has more than 20,000 students[41]—wrote that "The Bible is the inerrant...word of the living God. It is absolutely infallible, without error in all matters pertaining to faith and practice, as well as in areas such as geography, science, history, etc."[42] In 2007 the *New York Times* published an article about a professor of earth sciences at Liberty University, Marcus Ross, who received his Ph.D. in geosciences from the University of Rhode Island. He believes that the Bible presents a literally true account of the creation of the universe and that the earth is at most 10,000 years old.[43]

Each year at the Stanford Memorial Church we celebrate Evolution Sunday. We're part of a growing national movement of more than 500 congregations across the country and around the world committed to affirming that timeless religious truths and the discoveries of modern science can comfortably coexist. I am among more than 10,000 Christian clergy who have signed an open letter that states, in part, that the majority of Christians don't read the Bible literally, as they would a science textbook, and that many of the beloved stories found in the Bible, such as the Genesis account of creation, convey truths of a different order than scientific truth. They touch hearts, as is the province of great literature, poetry, and art, but they are not intended to convey scientific information. Here's where I feel both Hitchens and Falwell are wrong. As we state in that open letter:

> We believe that the theory of evolution is a foundational scientific truth, one that has stood up to rigorous scrutiny and upon which much of human knowledge and achievement rests. To reject this truth or to treat it as "one theory among others" is to deliberately embrace scientific ignorance and transmit such ignorance to our children. We believe that among God's good gifts are human minds capable of critical thought ... We ask that science remain science and that religion remain religion, two very different, but complementary, forms of truth.[44]

In 2008 at Stanford we also had physician-geneticist Francis Collins, director of the National Human Genome Research Institute, on campus. He directs the multinational 2,400-scientist team that mapped the three billion letters of the human DNA blueprint. He's also a devout Christian who converted from atheism at the age of 27 and now advises evangelical scientists on how to reconcile their faith with their scientific careers.[45] He's a best-selling author himself, having written *The Language of God* (2006).

In his Stanford talk "God and the Genome" to an overflow audience in our largest auditorium, Collins asserted that science and religion tend to address different questions: how versus why. Science discovers natural laws that tell us how the universe operates. Religion asks big existential questions like, "Why is there something instead of nothing?" But there are also ways in which religion and science overlap, of necessity. Collins says that his faith must rest squarely upon what he knows through logic and reason and science. Skepticism and doubt, of the sort encouraged by the scientific method, are critical to the development and testing of faith. Evolution is a scientific theory like gravity, which has been proven beyond a shadow of a doubt. Biblical literalism is a major problem when it leads to results such as seeing the universe as we now know it as having been created in six days, or human beings as having been created just as we are now, out of the blue, rather than having evolved from other living organisms that first appeared on the earth billions of years ago. Our own species, homo sapiens, evolved from primate ancestors about 200,000 years ago.[46]

Collins calls himself a theistic evolutionist. For him, DNA is the way God spoke life into being, and evolution is the mechanism by which God's plan has been carried out. One might ask, though, why do you need God at all? Why aren't the scientific answers alone enough? Darwin himself, at the close of his revolutionary book *On the Origin of Species,* wrote of the Creator behind the natural laws of the universe:

> To my mind it accords better with what we know of the laws impressed on matter by the Creator, that…[we] view all beings not as special creations, but as the lineal descendants of some few beings which lived long before the first bed of the Silurian system was deposited…It is interesting to contemplate an entangled bank, clothed with many plants of many kinds, with birds singing on the bushes, with various insects flitting about, and with worms crawling through the damp earth, and to reflect that these elaborately constructed forms, so different from each other, and dependent on each other in so complex a manner, have all been produced by laws acting around us…There is grandeur in this view of life…having been originally breathed into a few forms or into one; and that, whilst this planet has gone cycling on according to the fixed law of gravity, from so simple a beginning, endless forms most beautiful and most wonderful have been, and are being, evolved.[47]

There's another way that Francis Collins references God. He talks about the improbability of life, and especially of human life, as having occurred just by chance. Several scientific constants were necessary. Gravitation was one of them, and if it had been off by just "one part in a hundred million million, then the expansion of the universe after the Big Bang would not have occurred in the fashion that was necessary for life to occur." A designer becomes "a rather plausible explanation for what is otherwise an exceedingly improbable event—namely, our existence." Collins recognizes that other scientific theories have been proposed, such as our universe being only one of a very large number of parallel universes, which increases the odds that a tiny minority of universes, like ours, will have just the right fine-tuning to support life somewhere within them. But Collins finds the explanation of a creator God to be more compelling in its simplicity and elegance than "the bubbling of all these multiverses."[48]

However, he disagrees with the modern proponents of so-called Intelligent Design, a theory that many claim was first propounded by a University of California–Berkeley law professor, Phillip Johnson, in 1991.[49] Advocates of Intelligent Design challenge the theory of evolution by claiming that there are cases of irreducible complexity, like the human eye or the blood-clotting mechanism, which could not have occurred stepwise through the long process of evolutionary natural selection. Instead, an intelligent designer must have stepped in and created these particular organs and functions, full-blown in all of their complexity, in one fell swoop. Collins retorts that these arguments have no scientific merit, and each of the claims that particular mechanisms could not have evolved through step-by-step natural selection have since been refuted.[50] There are also important theological objections to Intelligent Design theory since it reduces God to certain gaps in current scientific explanation. As in the past, God will be whittled away even more in the future as these gaps are filled in scientifically. Also, Intelligent Design theory ends up portraying God "as a clumsy Creator, having to intervene at regular intervals to fix the inadequacies of his own initial plan" that supposedly had included trustworthy, consistent natural laws.[51] In summary, Collins finds Intelligent Design to be simultaneously bad science and bad theology.

Evolutionary biologist Richard Dawkins was also on campus in 2008. A year earlier a cover story in *Time* magazine entitled "God vs. Science"[52] featured a debate between Dawkins and Collins. Collins suggests that atheists like Dawkins "sometimes come across as a bit arrogant...characterizing faith as something only an idiot would attach themselves to."[53] Dawkins suggests that Christians like Collins should realize from the discoveries of modern science that "If there is a God, it's going to be a whole lot bigger and a whole lot more incomprehensible than anything that any theologian of any religion has ever proposed."[54]

One area where the two of them seem to agree, however, is in resisting the attempts of the religious right and the federal government to denigrate or curtail modern science. Both scientists are in favor of opening new stem-cell lines to develop medical cures and save lives. They are both concerned about good science education in our schools, from kindergarten all the way through graduate and medical school. This is an area that the 10,000 signatories of the clergy letter for Evolution Sunday are also deeply concerned about: "We urge school board members to preserve the integrity of the science curriculum by affirming the teaching of the theory of evolution as a core component of human knowledge."[55]

It's astounding to note that in a 2004 Gallup poll, when asked which of three views on the origin and development of human beings came closest to their own, 45 percent of Americans chose this statement: "God created human beings pretty much in their present form at one time within the last 10,000 years or so."[56] Stanford professor of evolutionary biology Joan Roughgarden in a little book called *Evolution and Christian Faith,* in which she reconciles science and religion for herself, cites another 2004 poll that found 35 percent of Protestant doctors believe that "God created humans exactly as they appear now." These are American physicians who have made it all the way through college and medical school and are now practicing medicine! A larger percentage (65 percent) of all physicians approve of teaching biblical creationism alongside evolution in our public schools. Perhaps this wouldn't be utterly worrisome if polls didn't also show that 40 percent of Americans want to replace evolution with creationism in our public school science curriculum.[57]

There's too much that really matters in our world to allow conservative religion to trump science education about evolution. Without understanding evolution, medical cures based on the genome project and stem-cell research are impossible. There are implications for our economy as well—will we not train our children to be scientifically competitive in the global marketplace? There are also implications for understanding our environment and ultimately for saving the earth.

It's time now for a reconciliation between science and religion that allows both to flourish and to complement each other. Francis Collins at the end of his book calls for "a truce in the escalating war between science and spirit." He claims that "Like so many earthly wars, this one has been initiated and intensified by extremists on both sides, sounding alarms that predict imminent ruin unless the other side is vanquished...Abandon the battlements. Our hopes, joys, and the future of our world depend on it."[58]

A CHRISTIAN RATIONALE FOR ABORTION

I preached a sermon after the national elections in 2004 mentioning that exit polls showed 22 percent of Americans nationwide put "moral values" as their top issue. Commentators had explained that, "No doubt about it, abortion and gay marriage were the wedge issues that separated the [Republicans from the Democrats] in the voting booth."[59] Those "moral values" voters went for President George W. Bush by 79 percent, as compared to 18 percent for Senator John Kerry.[60] *I* am personally deeply concerned about moral values, and I didn't cast my ballot for Bush in 2004. I affirmed in a post-election sermon that "I'm a professing Christian among many, who on religious grounds, is pro-choice on abortion and in favor of gay marriage."[61]

At the talk-back after the sermon, a Stanford student asked me to explain my statement that I'm pro-choice on abortion on *religious* grounds. He could understand how I might be pro-choice on *pragmatic* grounds, or on the basis of a political philosophy that we shouldn't legislate what other people can do in their private sexual lives. But he'd certainly never heard anyone defend a pro-choice position on explicitly *religious* grounds. He thought the only genuine Christian position was, and ever could be, anti-abortion and therefore anti-choice. I gave him a brief answer in the talk-back, reminding him that most mainline Protestant Christian denominations, along with Reform and Conservative Jews, have issued pro-choice proclamations consistently over the last thirty years. I also admitted that I hadn't preached on this subject in my years at Stanford, and that I should probably say something about it from the pulpit.

So in December, in the midst of Advent—when the gospel reading in the lectionary was the Magnificat of Mary,[62] her hymn of praise to God for the promised birth of Jesus from her very womb—I preached my Christian rationale for abortion. Why in the midst of a period of expectation of the birth of the Christ child in the liturgical calendar would I speak about the religious justification for abortion? Precisely because Mary's position in the Advent story is similar to that of many women who choose to have an abortion and yet so very different. She's young and poor. She faces unexpected pregnancy—not something she has planned for or wants at this time in her life. She isn't married yet. She knows what this might mean to the man she wants to marry, Joseph. He'll realize that this can't be *his* baby she's carrying because they haven't had sexual relations yet. Even though she's formally engaged to him, this could mean the end of their marriage before it begins.

And sure enough, as it's reported in Matthew's gospel, once Joseph found out Mary was pregnant, "being a righteous man and unwilling to expose her to public disgrace, [he] planned to dismiss her quietly." The account in Matthew continues in this way: "But just when he had resolved to do this, an angel of the Lord appeared to him in a dream and said, 'Joseph, son of David, do not be afraid to take Mary as your wife, for the child conceived in her is from the Holy Spirit.'"[63] So Mary's situation is utterly unique. She is the most blessed among all women.[64] She is to be favored by becoming the mother of the Son of God.[65] After she questions the angel Gabriel when he first visits to tell her of her favor with God, and after some soul-searching, Mary makes a voluntary decision, as the Gospel of Luke puts it, to allow the Holy Spirit to come upon her, to have the power of the Most High overshadow her. Mary says: "Here am I, the servant of the Lord; let it be with me according to your word."[66]

Precisely because Mary's situation is utterly unique, it places in bold relief other girls and women who have *not* voluntarily chosen to become pregnant. How about an 11- or 12-year-old, or a teenager, who has been continually forced to undergo incest by her father or stepfather? What about a woman who is forcibly raped on her way home from work by someone she never met, or a Stanford student who is date-raped by a fellow student whom she thought she knew rather well but obviously didn't? What about the very young and the very ignorant who may have voluntarily engaged in sexual relations but lacked information about effective contraception because they did not receive sex education at school or at home? What about a mature woman—even one who's happily had other children—whose physical or mental health might be severely compromised by this pregnancy? What about a fetus that has been found through amniocentesis or ultrasound to be severely and irreversibly impaired? Of course, the cases go on and on, including those so often cited by anti-abortion activists—those women who are allegedly having "abortions of convenience" (which undeniably does happen).

I want to make it clear that I respect the views of religious people who are opposed to abortion because they truly consider it to be murder or simply to be wrong on other conscientiously considered grounds. There are many of them on the Stanford campus in the Catholic community, evangelical Protestant groups, and other religious organizations. My job as dean for religious life is to be sure that their voices are not squelched or censored and that they can flourish and thrive in religious communities. I personally would join them on this issue if I thought that an embryo or a fetus is fully a human being or a person. I don't think "a woman's right to choose" is a sufficient answer to the claim that "abortion is murder." If by abortion we're killing human beings or persons, then a woman does not have a right to choose to kill, except in the very limited circumstances of self-defense—where it's a matter of either she dies or the fetus dies (say in an ectopic pregnancy or with certain kinds of cancer).

Yet, fetus as "person" or "human being" has never been a settled question within Christianity or Judaism. There are large segments of the Judeo-Christian world that, historically and currently, see the embryo or fetus as *potential* human life, but not as fully human until birth or until some stage in fetal development well past conception. My personal religious understanding is that human life or personhood begins at birth, but I also think there are important protections that should be applied to *potential* human life at certain stages of fetal development. Let me trace some of that religious history now, especially since the Bible is appealed to by so many anti-abortion Christians. This discussion may seem a bit technical, but I believe the background is important to understand.

There's nothing explicitly said in the Bible about induced abortion. Zero. The Jewish position begins with Exodus 21:22: "When people who are fighting injure a pregnant woman so that there is a miscarriage, and yet no further harm follows, the one responsible shall be fined what the woman's husband demands, paying as much as the judges determine." So, only a fine; no punishment for homicide. On the basis of this passage, the rabbis argued in the Talmud that a fetus is not considered *adam* (human) and has no legal standing as a person. Killing a fetus is not murder and it is not treated that way.[67] The mainstream Jewish position historically and today is that human life or personhood begins at birth, when we take our first breath.[68] There are a number of biblical passages that have been cited by rabbis over the years as connecting the breath and human life, starting with the creation story in Genesis 2:7: "The Lord God formed man from the dust of the ground, and breathed into his nostrils the breath of life; and the man became a living being."[69]

This is not to say that Judaism doesn't take the value of potential life in the womb very seriously, before and after the heart starts beating and brain activity begins. Historically, as required in Exodus, there have been fines for killing a fetus, and, in the words of the Conservative rabbinate, "the decision to abort should not be taken lightly." Most Orthodox rabbis approve abortion only to protect the life or health of the mother. Conservatives sanction abortion under a wider range of circumstances, but always thoughtfully and prayerfully. The Reform rabbinate leaves the decision whether or not to terminate a pregnancy in the hands of a woman or her family, but recognizes how difficult that decision often is.[70]

For most of the history of the Catholic Church, one did not become a human being or a person until well after conception. Saint Augustine in the fourth century adopted the Aristotelian belief that the human soul didn't enter the fetus until 40 to 90 days after conception. In roughly the same era Saint Jerome emphasized human shape: "The seed gradually takes shape in the uterus, and it [abortion] does not count as killing until the individual elements have acquired their external appearance and their limbs."[71] The Apostolic Constitutions of the late fourth century allowed abortion if it was done both before the human soul entered and before the fetus was of human shape. St. Thomas Aquinas of the thirteenth century followed Augustine in not considering the abortion of a non-ensouled fetus to be murder. Pope Innocent III earlier in the same century as Aquinas emphasized that the soul enters the body at the time of quickening—when a prospective mother first feels movement of the fetus. When Pope Gregory XIV affirmed the quickening test for ensoulment in 1591, he set the time for it as 116 days into pregnancy, or the sixteenth week. The great reversal came with Pope Pius IX in 1869. He assumed ensoulment at conception and by 1917 church canon law had been revised, dropping the prior distinction it had upheld between "animated" and "inanimated" fetuses. Pius's position has been maintained by the Catholic Church ever since.[72]

Likewise, criminal abortion statutes generally didn't come into effect in the United States until the latter part of the nineteenth century. The common law had long held that an abortion performed prior to quickening was not an indictable offense. Even abortion of a quickened fetus was generally not considered a criminal act under the common law, or at most a mere misdemeanor.[73] The U.S. Supreme Court in its 1973 Roe v. Wade decision used religious references to explain, in part, why the word "person" as used in the U.S. Constitution does not include the unborn: "There has always been strong support for the view that [human] life does not begin until live birth. This was the belief of the Stoics. It appears to be the predominant...attitude of the Jewish faith. It may be taken to represent...a large segment of the Protestant community."[74]

I'm personally part of that large Protestant community that believes that human life and personhood begin at birth. Some of my feelings admittedly may stem from the connotations of the words "birth" and "conception" with which I have grown up within the church. We speak of Esau and others in the Bible having a birthright, not a conception-right. After a strong religious experience we might say we've been "born again," but not "conceived again." Various biblical characters speak of the land of their *birth*. We honor the *birth* of the nation of Israel. We celebrate birthdays, including Christmas as the birth of Christ. I have done a concordance check of the Bible and found 216 references to "birth" or "born" and only 43 to "conception" or "conceive," a 5-to-1 ratio. The majority of the uses of "conceived" were linked to being born in this way: "she conceived and bore a child."

I'm also personally compelled by the notion that it's the breath of life that makes us full human beings. I'll never forget the sight of each of my children emerging into the world blue and lifeless, being struck on the back by the doctor, taking their first breath, and becoming ruddy-colored as they began crying their way into life. *Now* they were tiny people. *Now* they had joined the human race, not before.

On the other hand, it seems religiously important to me to be very concerned about potential life, not just actual life. Christians celebrate Advent as a time of waiting in the darkness for the light that will come at Christmas. The nine months of pregnancy for an expectant mother is a very important time of preparation for the baby-to-come and, ideally, of careful monitoring of maternal and prenatal health. Fetal life is a magnificent continuum of development from the zygote at the time of conception, to the manifestation of the embryo at about fourteen days, to the formation of what we call the fetus at about three months. Of course, for those first two weeks it's not at all clear that the zygote will become a singular embryo, much less a human being. Two-thirds of the time, the zygote doesn't develop into anything at all. Sometimes it develops into a tumor. Or it could become an embryo or more than one if it splits into twins.[75] Once it's an embryo, it'll be a long time—another

22 weeks or so—before it reaches viability or the stage of development when it might survive outside the womb.

This is where I personally think the Supreme Court got it right in 1973 in terms of protection of potential life. During the first trimester—when abortion could occur with an IUD, a morning-after-pill, RU486, or minor surgical procedures—the decision to abort is entirely the woman's. In the second trimester, with quickening, human shaping, and the necessity of more complicated surgical procedures, the state has a right to regulate medical procedures to protect the health of the mother. (In fact, less than 10 percent of abortions now take place after the first trimester.)[76] By the third trimester, though, the potential life has become viable; since the fetus could now live outside the womb, the state has a right to protect that potential life by prohibiting abortion except to preserve the life or health of the mother.

Despite all of this discussion, I want to emphasize that I and many other religious people of all persuasions would like greatly to reduce the incidence of abortion. As the Lutheran Women's Caucus resolved in 1990, abortion should not be the stopgap for lack of contraception, for inadequate sex education, or for irresponsible sexuality—not to mention being resorted to because of insufficient social support for new human life, such as lack of health care, child care, or parental leave. I join in the call of the Lutheran Women's Caucus to work actively for social and cultural changes that will reduce the incidence of abortion and also stop the scapegoating of women who have abortions.[77] Nonetheless, there are strong religious grounds, historical and contemporary, to defend a woman's right to an abortion.

THE SANCTIFICATION OF
MARRIAGES FOR SAME-SEX COUPLES

I have been deeply moved by the decisions of the supreme courts of California, Connecticut, and Massachusetts to affirm the rights of same-sex couples to marry. It's about time, religiously as well as politically. There's a true story from an earlier time that makes this particularly poignant for me. It's the story of Davis and Perez, who fell in love and tried to get married, only to be turned away by a county clerk who refused to issue them a marriage license simply because of who they were as a condition of their birth. A courageous state court in California became the first in the nation, albeit by a very close 4 to 3 majority, to find that clerk's refusal unconstitutional. And that decision was made after more than 30 state legislatures had put laws on the books that said no such marriage would be recognized in their states.

"Marriage is something more than a civil contract, subject to regulation by the state. It is a fundamental right..." Those are the words of the California court. As the United States Supreme Court has also long held, marriage is one of the "basic civil rights of man."[78] From a religious perspective, marriage of course has long been held to be sacred, and it's often noted that, in the Gospel of John, Jesus's very first miracle was performed at a wedding at Cana of Galilee.[79] The California court made it clear that "there can be no prohibition of marriage except for an important social objective and by reasonable means." Moreover, that "Legislation infringing... [the fundamental right to marry] must be based on more than prejudice and must be free from oppressive discrimination to comply with the constitutional requirements of due process and equal protection of the law." The court then went on to consider and reject claims that the unions under consideration were unnatural and that they were not the ideal context within which to raise children. To the claim that children within such unions would experience stigma and suffer societally, the court responded: "If they do, the fault lies not with their parents, but with the prejudices in the community and the laws that perpetuate those prejudices by giving [them] legal force..."

The three-judge dissent argued that who should marry is a matter for legislatures, not for courts to decide "in order that the well being of society as a whole may be safeguarded or promoted." The dissenters stated, "It is not within the province of the courts to go behind the findings of the legislature," which "in the first instance" should decide "what is necessary for the public welfare. Earnest conflict of opinion makes it especially a question for the legislature and not for the courts." Bolstering their case, the dissenting judges also noted that laws prohibiting these unions "have been in effect since before our national independence and in this state since our first legislative session." The majority opinion, however, retorted that "certainly the fact alone that the discrimination has been sanctioned by the state for many years does not supply...justification." The majority made it clear that when it comes to constitutional law, statutes duly enacted by state legislatures or the U.S. Congress must be struck down if they fail to meet judicial standards of due process or equal protection of the law.

And so, in 1948, the year I was born, the California Supreme Court became the first in the nation to strike down an antimiscegenation law at a time when marriages between blacks and whites could not be performed in a majority of these United States.[80] The *Nation* magazine, touting itself as "America's Leading Liberal Weekly Since 1865," commended the religious organization that had represented Sylvester Davis, a Negro, and Andrea Perez, his white fiancée. As the *Nation* explained, at that time "Most of the civil rights organizations failed or refused to participate in the case on the assumption that miscegenation statutes could not be successfully challenged in the courts."[81]

It took almost another 20 years until the United States Supreme Court spoke on this subject in a 1967 case coincidentally named *Loving v. Virginia*.[82] By that time I was in college, and we were within a year of the end of Martin Luther King's life, but more than half of the states with antimiscegenation laws in 1948 would still not permit a black person to marry a white person. The state of Virginia had argued that there was a rational basis to treat interracial unions differently from same-race unions and to refuse them marital status. They argued that, at minimum, the scientific evidence about black-white differences and their implications was still in doubt. Virginia claimed that the courts should stay out of these matters, and instead, they should defer to the democratic wisdom of legislatures in the matter of who should be allowed to marry or not, and why. The U.S. Supreme Court responded that it had the duty to decide whether laws passed muster under the due process and equal protection clauses of the Constitution. It then explained that under our Constitution the freedom to decide whom to marry is a fundamental right that resides with the individual and cannot be infringed upon by any state legislature without compelling justification.

Religion had a central role to play in the public debate about black-white marriage. It explicitly worked its way into the *Loving v. Virginia* decision. When Richard Loving and Mildred Jeter were convicted of violating Virginia's ban on interracial marriages by establishing their marital abode in the state after having been lawfully married in the District of Columbia, the state trial court judge wrote in his opinion: "Almighty God created the races white, black, yellow, malay, and red, and he placed them on separate continents. And but for the interference with his arrangement, there would be no cause for such marriages. The fact that he separated the races shows that he did not intend for the races to mix."[83]

In the 1948 California decision, it was the Catholic Church, however, through its Interracial Council in Los Angeles, that made a religious argument on behalf of the partners in the case, both of whom were Catholic.[84] The claim was that Davis and Perez were being denied their right to participate fully in the sacraments of their church by being denied the right to marry. One of the concurring judges cited the Bible as a positive authority on intermarriage, using these words: "The Apostle Paul declared that 'God...hath made of one blood all nations of men for to dwell on all the face of the earth.'"[85] Ironically, this was probably the same biblical passage that the Virginia judge used in denying people the right to marry because of the color of their skin. For the apostle Paul's words continue by stating that along with God making of one blood all nations of men, God also "hath...determined the bounds of their habitation."

What can we learn from this chapter in American history for our nation's current debate about the boundaries of the fundamental, sacred right to marry? In particular, what does the Bible teach us about how to approach this question as religious people, especially when very different conclusions seem to be drawn from the same Bible passage?

First of all, it should be noted that there are only a few references to homosexuality in the Bible, compared to a huge corpus, for example, that assumes and defends slavery. The abolitionists had much more of an uphill battle eliminating slavery in the face of its biblical defenders than the proponents of marriage equality for homosexuals should have in eliminating this form of discrimination. Jesus never references homosexuality. It's not found in the Ten Commandments as adultery and covetousness are. The Old Testament Sodom and Gomorrah story refers not to consensual sex but to homosexual rape.[86] The two references in Leviticus[87] are in the context of setting Jews apart from their Gentile neighbors by avoiding so-called ritual impurities like eating pork, having tattoos, wearing clothes made of two different kinds of materials, and having sex when a woman is menstruating.[88] In the New Testament, homosexuality is referred to in three letters of the apostle Paul,[89] in which it's likely that he was referring to pagan practices of prostitution and sex with children.[90] In none of these cases was anything vaguely contemplated along the lines of a lifelong monogamous commitment between same-sex partners.

Secondly, it should be remembered that Jesus went out of his way to bless those who are hated, excluded, reviled, and defamed. He also blessed those who weep, who are hungry, who are impoverished.[91] It seems to me that there are two central messages that Jesus tries to convey again and again throughout the New Testament: first, a message of deep concern for those who are oppressed, and, second, a message of profound love that passes all understanding. The scandal of Jesus's ministry in its time, and today as well, is that he constantly stood with the outcast, those who were discriminated against, and those who suffered at the hands of the established principalities and powers of his day.[92] Upon the oppressed he pronounced God's blessing. Jesus also brought a lesson of love that turned the world on its ear. He went beyond the love represented between husband and wife at Cana of Galilee to ask us to love our neighbors as ourselves,[93] and then beyond that to ask us to love even our enemies.[94] The apostle Paul explains in a passage often read in marriage ceremonies that "If I speak in the tongues of mortals and of angels, but do not have love, I am a noisy gong or a clanging cymbal...Love is patient; love is kind...It does not insist on its own way; it is not irritable or resentful;...It endures all things."[95]

None of this helps us specifically to know what Jesus and his disciples would say about marriages between blacks and whites, and it's possible to find a proof text in the Bible for virtually any claim, but for me it's clear. Instead of the judge's proof-texting—"the fact that he [Almighty God] separated the races shows that he did not intend for the races to mix"—the New Testament record as a whole leads me to believe that Jesus had a generous view of lifelong, committed, monogamous, loving relationships between any two people who freely choose each other to marry.

Jesus also speaks of prophets and false prophets.[96] How can you or I know which tradition we're in? Jesus explains that often true prophets run against the social consensus, being hated, excluded, reviled, and defamed, while false prophets run with the crowd, with all speaking well of them. The 1948 California decision that allowed blacks to marry whites was so far outside of the social consensus that not even major civil rights organizations were willing to sign onto the court challenge. It was a closely divided

4–3 decision within the court, with the attorney for the county of Los Angeles arguing, "The amalgamation of the races is not only unnatural, but always productive of deplorable results."[97] Some twenty years later, though, a unanimous United States Supreme Court would strike down the remaining antimiscegenation laws across the country in a brief opinion, stating that the only basis for such racial classification could be to maintain white supremacy. Social consensus can shift dramatically in one generation.

On the other side of the question of social consensus lie those individuals who are deeply hurt and harmed by claims that they are inferior or sinful, that their marriage would be unnatural and productive of deplorable results. How horrible for them. Again, it seems to me that these are precisely the kinds of people whom Jesus always comforted and sanctified first: "Blessed are you who weep now, for you will laugh."[98] I read the New Testament record as a whole as placing a very generous conception of love at the very center of Jesus's teaching and actions. These are the criteria—standing with the oppressed and a generous conception of love—on which I believe we should try to distinguish true prophets from false prophets.

Yet, Jesus also manifested a kind of humility that we would all do well to remember. He said, "Do not judge and you will not be judged; do not condemn, and you will not be condemned."[99] In a panel discussion at Stanford during which I advocated for marriage between same-sex couples, an audience member asked me how I respond to the claim that such marriages undermine or harm traditional institutions. I responded by saying that "The harm that is done to someone when you say they can't marry the person of their choice is unconscionable."[100] Afterward I apologized for the use of the word "unconscionable" to my colleague on the panel from the Campus Crusade for Christ, who is opposed to same-sex marriages and thinks they might undermine the structure of the traditional family.[101] I know him well personally and respect how conscientiously he thinks about and struggles with this question. And, according to all the polls I read, the majority of Americans, religious and secular, agree with him and not with me. I need to have enough humility of the sort Jesus called for to state my own beliefs clearly and act upon them, while at the same time understanding and respecting how people of conscience can differ on important questions.

By way of conclusion, though, on the issue of conscience, I must say that I'm haunted by the fact that it took the largest Protestant denomination in the United States, the Southern Baptists (the religious tradition of two recent American presidents, Jimmy Carter and Bill Clinton), until 1995 to apologize for the role it played in the biblical justification of slavery in the nineteenth century and in the maintenance of a culture of racism in the twentieth century. In their efforts, the denomination had used biblical proof texts like the words of Paul I've cited or this one from the Letter to the Ephesians: "Slaves, obey your earthly masters with fear and trembling, in singleness of heart, as you obey Christ."[102] The social historian C. Eric Lincoln wrote in 1995, after the church's historic apology: "Just think of all the violence and bitterness we might have been spared if the Southern Baptists had repudiated racism earlier."[103] To that I can only say Amen.

TWO

THE ESSENCE OF LIBERAL CHRISTIANITY

I came that they may have life, and have it abundantly.

—*John 10:10*

Love bears all things, believes all things, hopes all things, endures all things.

—*1 Corinthians 13:7*

You shall love your neighbor as yourself.

—*Leviticus 19:18; Matthew 22:39*

There is no fear in love, but perfect love casts out fear.

—*1 John 4:18*

The essence of Christianity, as shared by conservatives and liberals alike, is love. Conservatives often argue that liberal Christians don't take truth seriously enough: biblical truth, the truth about how God rules, and the truth of Jesus Christ as the divine way, truth, and life. Yet, all Christians are clear about the fundamental proclamation that God is love. Jesus is the human incarnation of that divine love. Here's where we need to begin for any understanding of the Christian life.

The radical kind of love that Jesus embodied and taught—loving even one's enemies—also makes Christianity unique among the major faith traditions of the world. University of California (Berkeley) professor Huston Smith is the author of *The World's Religions,* a best-selling book that has chapters on Hinduism, Buddhism, Islam, Judaism, and Christianity, among others. As the author examines Christianity comparatively with other religions, he finds that its unique contribution, the essence of its good news, is a new and different kind of love as preached and practiced by Jesus, and ultimately by many of his followers. Smith writes, "Conventional love is evoked by lovable qualities in the beloved, but the love [that] people encountered from Christ embraced sinners and outcasts, Samaritans and enemies." Smith points out that this kind of love dramatically reduced Christians' fears, including their fear of death. It also released Christians from the crippling confines of ego. They were freed to find the joy of their full selves after letting go of their small, everyday selves.[1]

CHRISTIANITY IS JOYFUL

I can remember as a child in Sunday school thinking that the Christian life sounded pretty burdensome. "Take up your cross." "Give away all that you have." "Sacrifice." "Follow the straight and narrow way." Basically, it didn't seem like a lot of fun. Did Christians ever laugh and play? Did they ever just hang out? Did they ever do anything I'd now call frivolous or indulgent? A biblical commentary I use articulates my childhood feelings in this rather elegant way: "The Christian mode of life must be an intolerably dull and boring affair, a repressing of what everyone wants to do, a forcing of oneself to comply with what nobody could wish or choose, a shivering with chattering teeth in the gloom of a chilly monastic twilight."[2]

But that's not it at all! It took me a while, but later in life I stumbled upon these wonderful words of Jesus: "I came that they may have life, and have it abundantly."[3] Now you're talking! A breath of fresh air! The abundant life, not the life of renunciation. Out of the cold gloom into the warm sunlight. Maybe laughter and playfulness and fun have a role after all. So Christianity took on a completely different cast for me. I began seeing things in terms of the joy of unconditional love that Jesus represented. I started experiencing holy days as holidays or occasions for celebration, not just obligation. It became a kick to sing in church and to listen to the magnificence of the organ. I came to delight in the sense of friendship and community I could have in church.

Christmas was the holiday that epitomized celebration and warm human relations for me. In college I heard anew the biblical story of an angel announcing to shepherds out in the field: "I am bringing you good news of great joy for all the people."[4] As I came to understand, that means for all of *us:* for those of us rushing about desperately trying to get ready for the winter holidays, for those overwhelmed by the commercialism of the season, for those who can't find enough time for families and friends, for those who experience this as one of the most stressful times of the year, for those who have lost jobs in a sour economy, for those who despair of peace and justice ever coming in a world filled with terrorism and oppression.

I used to struggle with exactly what the "good news of great joy" was that the angel speaks about in the gospel story. Luke explained that it was news of the birth of the Savior, the Messiah, the Lord.[5] This earth-shattering announcement came first to common people, and the announced Messiah was not the crown prince whom most modern commentators say[6] was described by the Jewish prophet Isaiah more than seven hundred years before Jesus. Worldly authority was to rest upon that prince's shoulders, and he was to be named Wonderful Counselor, Mighty God, Everlasting Father, Prince of Peace.[7] Instead, Luke tells us, the Messiah was born to an unmarried couple staying with animals in a barn.[8] Instead of being dressed in royal garments and laid in an ornate crib, the long-expected Messiah was wrapped in mere bands of cloth and placed in a feeding trough.[9] A third of a century later, after less than three years of active ministry, this Messiah was ignominiously and painfully executed on a cross at the hands of the colonial rulers of Israel. He died being taunted by soldiers who had put a crown of thorns on his head and a plaque on the top of his cross titling him "The King of the Jews."[10]

So, again, what's the "good news of great joy" for Christians? Here's what I came to understand. First of all, it's the momentous news that, through Jesus, God is seen to have entered into the daily life of this workaday world and redeemed it. Everything is thrown into a new light with God represented in this particular human form. Exactly how God has redeemed or saved the world through Jesus, I learned, has been debated by theologians for millennia. For me, though, it primarily came to mean that, through a new kind of divine love, all of our evil deeds are ultimately forgivable, and we're given a vision of loving-kindness as our ultimate meaning and purpose in life. Progressively I came to appreciate some of the practices that Christians have historically used to exercise love and to demonstrate our gratitude for God's gift to the world: simplicity, loving-kindness, and prayer.

As a young adult, I learned an old American Shaker hymn, "'Tis a Gift to Be Simple," that praises simplicity as the source of the fullest freedom and delight. In the end, the hymn tells us, through simplicity we discover love; through simplicity we find ourselves in just the right place and we come out right in the end. Compare normal life in modern America. It's complex. It's sophisticated. It's technologically advanced. It's busy. Yet, it's still possible and critical to pursue a life of simplicity here, amidst complexity or on the far side of complexity. It turns out too that simplicity is valued in modern science and technology. Mathematicians search for the "more elegant solution," and engineers strive for simplicity of design.

In high school I read the work of the English poet William Wordsworth, who laments: "The world is too much with us; late and soon. Getting and spending we lay waste our powers. Little we see in Nature that is ours. We have given our hearts away, a sordid boon."[11] I came to recognize how we desperately need to stop regularly to smell the flowers, to remember that other people are ends in themselves and not means to our ends. We need to keep our eyes on what really matters in our lives—and what matters inevitably lies in relationships, not in material possessions. Good news of great joy appears to simple shepherds and loving parents as they gaze at a baby in a cold barn, not as they enjoy worldly riches in a sumptuous castle.

The King James translation of the angels' appearance to the shepherds ends with the words, "Glory to God in the highest, and on earth peace, good will toward men."[12] Jesus comes into the world with a message of peace and goodwill. How can we regularly exercise gratitude and goodwill, I wondered. The Reverend John Haynes Holmes, a minister who helped found both the NAACP and the American Civil Liberties Union,[13] described Christmas "as though a spell were cast upon us, to save us...from our cruelties...and make us ministers of love...This is our task—to seize and hold and perpetuate the Christmastide. To live a life, and not merely a single day or season, which is delivered of prejudice and pride, hostility and hate, and committed to understanding, compassion and goodwill!"[14] The way to exercise gratitude and good will is through regular acts of loving-kindness.

Reading more about Jesus in the gospel of Matthew, I learned that this sort of kindness is worked out in a practice that includes doing good to those who hate you, turning the other cheek, forgiving others their trespasses, feeding the hungry, and sheltering the homeless. These may seem like radical demands, but Jesus sums them up this way: "In everything do to others as you would have them do to you; for this is the law and the prophets."[15] So, our practice should have not only elements of social service but also commitment to social change for the poor, the oppressed, and the war-torn throughout the world.

Finally, along with simplicity and loving-kindness, I came to appreciate the practice of prayer. A Christmas service is filled with prayer, both spoken and sung. Many churches begin at the crèche with a prayer that we may enjoy forever the love of Christ, and worshipers sing "Joy to the World" that earth may receive her King. There are usually prayers of the people, prayers at the Eucharist or Communion, and a prayer of benediction. Would that we could live as if our whole lives were a prayer.

My way of praying changed as I grew older. It became less a matter of addressing God in praise or petition and incorporated varied forms of contemplation. Christian prayer has traditionally also had a listening dimension, which is called meditation. That can be done not only sitting but also walking and acting with an open, attentive attitude. A third form has been contemplative prayer, centered on the divine presence within us—perfected by mystics who report experiences of unity with God. A fourth way has been prayer in communion with other people, most obviously in a worship service but also in many smaller contexts in which we join with others for support and companionship to evoke the presence of God.[16] I learned how prayer, through a variety of forms, can help free us from our own ego, help us see the big picture rather than the petty and the transitory, and help us put everyday stress into context.

So, my prayer for each of us became that through the practice of simplicity we might slow down enough to see into the true heart of things, that through loving-kindness we might open ourselves to true relationships in a transformed world, and that through prayer we might transcend ourselves in true commitment to the life force itself, which for Christians goes by the name of Jesus the Savior, the Messiah. Then we can truly hear the good news of wondrous joy for all people that's announced on the wondrous Christian holiday of Christmas.

THE ROMANCE OF CHRISTIANITY

Now, what about romance and Christian love? As a teenager, I found that romantic feelings were my most powerful experience of love. Daydreaming in school, reading novels, going to movies, and talking to friends—it was this form of love that really hit home. Valentine's Day came to symbolize love far more potently than Christmas. Eventually I learned that Saint

Valentine's Day actually began in commemoration of a third-century Christian priest who was martyred in Rome. By the Middle Ages, Saint Valentine had become associated with the union of lovers under conditions of stress. By the twentieth century his holiday was being celebrated with the widespread exchange of romantic little messages called valentines.[17]

As a minister, I began to see the evolution of Saint Valentine's Day this way: It begins as a commemoration of *spiritual* love, later becomes a celebration of *committed interpersonal* love, and is now primarily a rather commercialized carnival of *romantic* love. I should make it clear that as a minister I have nothing against romantic love. When I officiate at weddings, I often describe romantic love as a great gift. But I then go on to explain that it's not a sufficient foundation for a strong, devoted partnership. I'm convinced there needs to be a thoroughgoing connection between romantic love, committed partnership, and spiritual love.

In terms of romantic love, the Song of Solomon in the Old Testament does a pretty good job of describing the feelings of two people who have fallen, hopelessly, head-over-heels, in love with each other: "You have ravished my heart, my sister, my bride; you have ravished my heart with a glance of your eyes, with one jewel of your necklace. How sweet is your love...how much better is your love than wine, and the fragrance of your oils than any spice! Your lips distill nectar, my bride; honey and milk are under your tongue." The recipient of these sentiments then exclaims: "My beloved is all radiant and ruddy, distinguished among ten thousand. His head is the finest gold; his locks are wavy, black as a raven...His lips are lilies, distilling liquid myrrh. His arms are rounded gold, set with jewels. His body is ivory work, encrusted with sapphires. His legs are alabaster columns, set upon bases of gold...He is altogether desirable." The narrator then adds: "Many waters cannot quench love, neither can floods drown it."[18]

Note the qualities of this romantic love. Very physical. All about arms and legs, lips and tongues, hair and eyes. All about bodies, and all about overwhelming desire. It's powerful; it's wonderful; there's nothing like it. I'll never forget *my* first romantic experiences, filling up every thinking and feeling moment of the day and night, as incredibly exciting, as blissful.

Yet, there are some major downsides to romantic love. There's the pain of not being able to be with a lover in an all-fulfilling way all of the time. That pain reaches its extreme expression in Shakespeare's *Romeo and Juliet,* in which the lovers take their lives when each thinks the other is dead.

Romantic love also tends to objectify the other—physically focusing on bodies and on the desire for sexual gratification. It also exists largely in fantasy land, either never being consummated or slipping away as real familiarity with the other person grows.

Many social scientists have described romantic love as essentially narcissism. What one loves is not the other, but one's *own image* of the other. One loves one's *own projection* of what an ideal lover should be, which ultimately bears little resemblance to the actual person to whom affections are directed. In Jungian psychological terms, one loves the image of one's *own* anima or animus that is projected onto the other person. Romantic lovers also tend to love the state of "being in love" as much or more than the actual object of love. One becomes lost in one's own daydreams, sexual fantasies, romantic feelings, and aspects of the chase, like making oneself as attractive as possible.

More mature, committed interpersonal love is described well by author and Stanford alumna bell hooks in her books *All About Love: New Visions*[19] and *Salvation*.[20] She cites mutuality as the heart of love: "The essence of true love is mutual recognition—two individuals seeing each other as they really are. We all know that the usual approach is to meet someone we like and put our best self forward, or even at times a false self, one we believe will be more appealing to the person we want to attract. When our real self appears in its entirety, when the good behavior becomes too much to maintain or the masks are taken away, disappointment comes."[21]

In true love, mutual love, "individuals usually feel in touch with each other's core identity. Embarking on such a relationship is frightening precisely because we feel there is no place to hide. We are known."[22] There is also a dynamic dimension to this kind of love, as each person gets to know herself or himself better, as well as coming to know the other more deeply. Honesty and openness are critical, as is the commitment to put mutuality of relationship ahead of power—ahead of any attempt to control the other.[23]

Mutual love is not something that we fall into, or that falls into our laps. After the giddiness and sliding on the slippery slope of romantic love, mutual love requires practice, discipline, devotion, and commitment. The compassionate, empathetic listening to the other that's required takes energy, especially when it triggers one's own feelings of powerlessness, helplessness, and vulnerability. Therefore, hooks counsels, make time for those conversations when we're not bone weary, irritable, or preoccupied, and practice making that time available.[24]

The rewards are great: the courage to face reality, to embrace our true self and that of our partner, and then to grow and change together through our mutual emotional vulnerability. As hooks puts it, "We can only move from perfect passion to perfect love when the illusions pass and we are able to use the energy and intensity generated by intense, overwhelming, erotic bonding to heighten self-discovery." When that self-discovery is linked with openness and empathetic listening to the other, partners grow and change together. In the best sense, in loving fully and deeply, we risk changing ourselves.[25] As Catholic monk Thomas Merton asserted: "Love affects more than our thinking and our behavior toward those we love. It transforms our entire life. Genuine love is a personal revolution. Love takes your ideas, your desires, and your actions and welds them together in one experience and one living reality which is a new you."[26]

This gets us close to the third dimension of love—spiritual love. In my career of more than thirty years in the ministry, there have been many, many times when couples have asked me to read from the thirteenth chapter of the apostle Paul's First Letter to the Corinthians as they are united for life: "Love is patient; love is kind; love is not envious or boastful or arrogant or rude. It does not insist on its own way; it is not irritable or resentful; it does not rejoice in wrongdoing." This kind of spiritual love at its core is giving and forgiving. Giving generously to one's partner means recognizing and responding when the other person needs our attention. It means freely sharing time, skills, and resources, to find that by giving in this way we receive many times over. Perhaps the greatest gift we can give, though, at the spiritual level is forgiveness: "Love is kind...it is not irritable or resentful."

Almost fifty years ago a Harvard classics professor named Erich Segal wrote a sentimental little novel called *Love Story*. It became a best seller and was turned into a high-grossing Paramount film starring Ali McGraw and Ryan O'Neal. It begins with the line, "What can you say about a 25-year-old girl who died?" Perhaps its most famous line, however, is "Love means never having to say you're sorry." I've always felt Erich Segal got it half-right but then profoundly wrong. I'd say instead: "Spiritual love means always being able to forgive the other when he or she genuinely says, 'I'm sorry.'" In the movie, preppy Oliver Barrett IV marries a woman from the other side of the tracks, Jennifer Cavalari, soon after they graduate from Harvard and Radcliffe respectively. Oliver's successful, wealthy, and distant father doesn't approve of the marriage, and he cuts Oliver off financially as he is beginning to attend Harvard Law School. Jennifer works hard to put Oliver through law school. Near the end of the three years, his father tries to initiate a reconciliation by sending his son and daughter-in-law an invitation to his sixtieth birthday. Oliver refuses to go and makes Jenny do the dirty work of calling his father to say no. He becomes enraged at Jenny when she adds this comment to Oliver's father over the phone: "You know, in his own way your son loves you very much." When Oliver later apologizes to Jenny for his hard-heartedness, she speaks that famous line, "Love means never having to say you're sorry."

By the end of the movie, though, it becomes clear that Oliver hasn't gotten the spiritual point of Jennifer's capacity to forgive. Jenny dies of cancer and Oliver's father drives to the hospital, finds Oliver, and again tries to effect a reconciliation by telling Oliver how sorry he is. Oliver uses the famous line like a bludgeon, walks away from his father, and the movie ends. In Oliver's hands, the line becomes a condemnation of his father for supposedly never having loved him, otherwise, why would his father have to say he was sorry? And Oliver's *resentment* triumphs over the *spiritual* capacity for loving forgiveness that he should have learned from his wife, Jenny.

Ultimately we're all imperfect beings. The Christian message is one of *divine* forgiveness and reconciliation to God through the kind of love Jesus modeled. Spiritual love between partners, from the perspective of the Christian tradition, is one that has repentance and forgiveness at its core. Beyond that lies the willingness to give totally of oneself to the other, even unto death. The highest level of spiritual love may then be saintly love, exemplified in Saint Valentine's martyrdom for his unstinting love of Christ. My valentine love message, though, is pitched a bit lower than saintly love: Give a valentine joyfully to one you love, but don't stop at romantic love. If you have a partner, try to practice mutual love, which involves a discipline of openness and honesty, empathetic listening, personal vulnerability, and willingness to change. Work on developing spiritual love—love which is freely giving and forgiving. Then perhaps Saint Valentine's Day can again be what it once was meant to be.

WHAT'S SPECIAL ABOUT CHRISTIAN LOVE?

Christians seem to claim they have a corner on what others would call a human universal—love. A so-called new commandment is given by Jesus to his disciples at the Last Supper, according to the gospel of John: "You should love one another."[27] Yet, in the third book of the Old Testament, Leviticus, which dates back in written form to the sixth century before Christ,[28] it's stated "You shall love your neighbor as yourself."[29] Jesus himself cites Leviticus, along with a verse from another Old Testament book, Deuteronomy, when asked by his religious enemies which commandment is the greatest. He responds, "You shall love the Lord your God with all your heart, and with all your soul, and with all your mind. This is the greatest and first commandment. And a second is like it: You shall love your neighbor as yourself. On these two commandments hang all the law and the prophets."[30]

In addition, much of Jesus's ministry of love seems derived from specific injunctions in Leviticus that lead up to the commandment to love one's neighbor as oneself. For example, the poor and the alien are to be provided for; the deaf and blind are to be protected; judgments are to be just, without deferring to the great; slander is proscribed along with theft and fraud; no one is to hate another in his or her heart, take vengeance, or even bear a grudge.[31]

Perhaps what's new about Jesus's commandment to his disciples to love one another is the context in which it's given. He's to be betrayed by one of his disciples very soon. Most of the rest of them will run away as soldiers take Jesus to be tried, flogged, and crucified. And the apostle Peter—upon whom Jesus says he will build his church[32]—will deny him three times. It seems like a sorry and spineless group of so-called friends whom Jesus calls upon to love him and to love each other. Yet, the important point, I think, is that Jesus is calling upon them for a new kind of love beyond that requested in Leviticus. He's calling for a kind of love for which one is willing to die, and at first his disciples don't seem to be up to it. Most of us can probably identify with their sentiments!

In the gospel of John, Jesus puts the point more explicitly: "This is my commandment, that you love one another as I have loved you. No one has greater love than this, to lay down one's life for one's friends."[33] Jesus has so loved his friends, and so radically acted out his love in the world, that he's about to be crucified as a threat to the Roman empire, not to mention to the religious establishment of his day. This is the man who, just days before his Last Supper, rode into Jerusalem to the enchantment of crowds waving palms and shouting "Hosanna! Blessed is the one who comes in the name of the Lord—the King of Israel."[34] Jesus overturned the moneychangers' tables in the temple, saying that they had made the most sacred place in Israel a den of robbers.[35] He cured the blind and the lame.[36] He preached against the scribes and Pharisees, calling them hypocrites, claiming they lock people out of the kingdom of heaven, and on earth neglect the weightier matters of the law: justice, mercy, and good faith.[37] He said that the mighty will be brought low, while the lowly hungry should be fed, the thirsty given drink, the stranger welcomed, the naked clothed, the sick cared for, and the prisoners visited.[38] Brave and powerful words and actions then. Brave and powerful in today's war-torn world as well, as when we think, for example, of how the mighty treated those incarcerated in the prisons of Iraq before and after the fall of Saddam Hussein. Jesus saw all that he said and did as an expression of true love. That's what he expected of his disciples, even though it put them at risk of their lives. And that's what he expects of us as well.

Perhaps one of the best modern exemplars of this commandment of a new type of love was Martin Luther King Jr. He lived and died trying to manifest the radical form of love to which Jesus has called us. Remember how he put it in the sermon he delivered the very night before he was assassinated: "Now we're going to march again...For when people get caught up with that which is right, and they are willing to sacrifice for it, there is no stopping point short of victory...We need all of you...Let us develop a kind of dangerous unselfishness...The question is not, 'If I stop to help this man in need, what will happen to me?' [The question is] 'If I do not stop to help the sanitation workers, what will happen to them?'...[When] I got into Memphis...some began to...talk about the threats that were out. What would happen to me from some of our white brothers?...Like anybody, I would like to live a long life. Longevity has its place. But I'm not concerned about that now. I just want to do God's will...I'm not fearing any man. Mine eyes have seen the glory of the coming of the Lord."[39]

King said more than once that we're not fully alive until we've found something for which we're willing to die. In his book *The Strength to Love,* he explains that "The kind of love which led Christ to a cross and kept Paul unembittered amid the angry torrents of persecution is not soft, anemic, and sentimental. Such love confronts evil without flinching..." Looking at the arms race of his day, though, designed to ease fear through strength, he wrote that "Not arms, but [only] love, understanding and organized goodwill can cast out fear."[40]

Now, the reality is that most of us are not Martin Luther Kings. How can we, realistically, in our own daily lives, understand and practice the love that Jesus spoke of? To start with, for each of us there's our mother's love. Most mothers I know say that they love their children so deeply and fully that in an instant they would unquestioningly give up their own lives to save one of their children's lives. Many fathers might say that too. So, there's a multitude of parents whose love is so strong that they are willing to die for another. They meet King's test of being fully alive.

I've conducted weddings for which the bride and groom asked me to read the aforementioned passage from John's gospel. I've found myself saying to these couples that "Your joy as husband and wife will be complete only when you can call each other true friends and when you are ready to lay down your lives for each other." I really believe that's true. Being fully alive, fully committed, and fully fulfilled in a marriage entails the willingness to give up one's life instantaneously and unquestioningly to save your spouse's life. Children and spouses are a group of people for whom many of us ordinary folk would be willing to give up our lives. So, it would seem as if we have exceeded the threshold for Jesus's commandment of love.

But what about friends who are not family members? When I was a child, I was told the story of Damon and Pythias, two friends in the Sicilian city-state of Syracuse in the fourth century B.C. Pythias spoke out against the king, who ordered him executed for treason. Pythias asked permission to go home long enough to say goodbye to his wife and children and put his household in order. His friend Damon instantly volunteered to be imprisoned until Pythias returned and to be killed himself if Pythias didn't show up on the execution date. As the fatal day approached without Pythias returning, the king came to the prison to sneer at Damon and to see if he was sorry for having made such an arrangement. "You were a fool to rely on your friend's promise," scoffed the king. "Did you really think he would sacrifice his life for you or anyone else?" Damon simply replied, "He is my friend. I trust him." As Damon was being led out to be executed on the crucial day, Pythias suddenly appeared, breathlessly exclaiming, "You are safe, praise the gods. My ship was wrecked in a storm, and then bandits attacked me on the road. But I refused to give up hope, and at last I've made it back in time. I am ready to receive my sentence of death." The king was so astonished and moved that he revoked the death sentence out of respect for their friendship.[41]

If we have friendships of this level of devotion, our group of people to fulfill Jesus's commandment of love may now include children, spouses, and close friends. Our challenge, then, is to keep expanding the circle to take in increasing numbers of people. Jesus's commandment becomes both aspirational and inspirational. Will we be ready to follow a new Martin Luther King who calls us to love even our enemies unto death? Will we be ready to put our lives nonviolently on the line, without fear, to promote peace and justice for all?

I assume many of us recognize how wide and deep mother love can be. I hope many of us have or will have some life experience with a partner to whom we're committed unto death. I hope each of our lives has or will include at least one friendship at the level of Damon's and Pythias's. The next step for Christians is to follow fully in Jesus's footsteps, building an expanding circle of self-sacrificing love that includes the hungry and the thirsty, the alien, the homeless, the sick, and the imprisoned. And ultimately, the Christian message is that it's only by being willing to lose our lives in service to others that we will ever truly find our lives.[42]

LOVE CONQUERS ALL, EVEN FEAR

Christian love has another important dimension that needs to be described explicitly: Love conquers fear. Soon after the terrorist attacks of September 11, 2001, I preached a sermon in the Stanford Memorial Church entitled "Nothing to Fear but Fear Itself." Osama bin Laden had spoken these words: "There is America, full of fear from its north to its south, from its west to its east. Thank God for that."[43] In response, I quoted Franklin D. Roosevelt's famous words from his first inaugural address in 1933 in the midst of the Great Depression: "The only thing we have to fear is fear itself."[44] Those are words that many also needed to remember as the worldwide financial crisis struck in late 2008. Yet, years after September

11, 2001, fear about terrorism is still very much in the air. Thousands of American men and woman have died on the soils of Iraq and Afghanistan, and many more civilians have been killed in those countries. Threats of violence against innocents still loom large, abroad and at home. Much of the world long ago moved from a sympathetic solidarity with Americans—"We are all Americans"—to a deep hatred for America. We have gone through profoundly divisive election seasons. Instead of being united as Americans, we have been torn asunder into blue states and red states, liberals and conservatives—although president Barack Obama gives us hope that we can now find new bipartisan consensus as one United States of America. I have known many liberal Christians during the period since 9/11 who have been genuinely fearful to speak out, to organize, to act politically or even religiously. They have felt a new McCarthyism in the air, an atmosphere in which they can be labeled a terrorist sympathizer, a socialist, a communist—all labels that were bandied about in the 2008 election season. On the other hand, I know conservative Christians who are genuinely fearful of where our culture is headed in terms of what they consider its abandonment of fundamental values and national security.

Martin Luther King wrote at some length about fear in his 1963 book *The Strength to Love*. He wondered: "In these days of catastrophic change and calamitous uncertainty, is there anyone who does not experience the depression and bewilderment of crippling fear, which, like a nagging hound of hell, pursues our every footstep?"[45] He invoked courage, one of the four classic virtues, as a critical antidote against fear. Quoting Saint Thomas Aquinas, King described courage as "the strength of mind capable of conquering whatever threatens attainment of the highest good."[46]

King also writes about many historical figures' ideas about fear and courage. He reminds us that Roosevelt's quote was derived from Henry David Thoreau, who wrote in his *Journal* in 1851 that "Nothing is so much to be feared as fear." A century before Christ, the Stoic philosopher Epictetus, once himself a slave, exclaimed, "It is not death or hardship that is a fearful thing, but the fear of hardship and death." King's own theology was deeply influenced by the contemporary liberal Christian theologian Paul Tillich, who explained that "Courage is self-affirmation 'in spite of' that which tends to hinder the self from affirming itself." King agrees. He makes sure that this isn't confused with selfishness, though, "for self-affirmation includes both a proper self-love and a properly positioned love of others." Citing psychoanalyst Erich Fromm, King reminds us that self-love and love of others, properly understood, are interdependent.[47]

King's understanding of courage was by no means facile, either. He insisted that courage is not the absence of fear, it is the ability to act in spite of it. As he put it, "Many of our fears are not mere snakes under the carpet. Trouble is a reality in this strange medley of life, dangers lurk within the circumference of every action...and death is a stark, grim, and inevitable fact of human experience."[48] With hindsight, we see that King's own fears were often realized: His home was bombed, he was stabbed with a knife, just shy of his aorta, and ultimately he was assassinated by a racist's bullet. Meanwhile, he constantly put himself in harm's way and reaped the consequences of his nonviolent direct action as he defied unjust laws, marched through mean streets, and was carried off to inhospitable jails.

King does not counsel trying to eliminate fear from our lives. Indeed, he even calls fear "a powerfully creative force" when it is linked with the virtue of courage. Fear is part of the animal fight-or-flight instinct, and without it human beings could not have survived in either the primitive or modern worlds. "Every great invention and intellectual advance represents a desire to escape from some dreaded circumstance or condition...If people were to lose their capacity to fear, they would be deprived of their capacity to grow, invent, and create. So, in a sense, fear is normal, necessary, and creative."[49]

Yet, King is well aware that fear can poison and distort our inner lives as surely as it can motivate us to improve our individual and collective welfare. Therefore, the problem is not how to be rid of fear, but how to harness it. The main way to do this is through love. The particular kind of love he's talking about is one that leads to disciplined nonviolent action, in the face of all blows and beatings, even unto death. The kind of love that becomes organized goodwill. The kind of love that seeks justice for both blacks and whites, for both the oppressed and the oppressors. Internationally, King claimed that war is not at root a consequence of hate. "Close scrutiny reveals this sequence: first fear, then hate, then war, and finally deeper hatred." In terms of personal anxieties, fear generates a feeling of insecurity, lack of self-confidence, and concern about failure, which can then harden into hatred. Hatred then paralyzes life; only love can release it. Hatred darkens life; only love can illuminate it.[50]

Where does this kind of courage-engendering love come from? King believed that deep, effective love is linked with faith in God. God for King is a "benign Intelligence whose infinite love embraces all of humankind." When fears inevitably come, faith "assures us that the universe is trustworthy and that God is concerned . . . Irreligion, on the other hand, would have us believe that we are orphans cast into the terrifying immensities of space in a universe that is without purpose or intelligence." [51] It's understandable why the latter view would drain courage and exhaust our energies. By contrast, "Religion endows us with the conviction that we are not alone in this vast, uncertain universe . . . This universe is not a tragic expression of meaningless chaos, but a marvelous display of orderly cosmos . . . Beneath and above the . . . uncertainties that darken our days and the vicissitudes that cloud our nights is a wise and loving God."[52]

This may all be a bit abstract and hard to fathom, leading our scientific minds to begin debating and questioning chaos versus order. Don't go there right now; there will be time for that in the next chapter. For now the point is that Christians have an actual manifestation of divine love in the person of Jesus, and Jesus concretizes it all in the human sphere. Jesus models a life of turning the other cheek and loving his enemies. Jesus is the one who talks about love in relation to the hated Samaritans, outsiders and foreigners, one of whom stops and cares for the beaten man on the dangerous road to Jericho when the Jewish exemplars of priest and Levite have passed by on the other side. Jesus, both in his own life and in his teachings, demonstrates the capacity, as King puts it, "to project the 'I' into the 'thou,' and to be concerned about one's brother."[53]

Near his death, Jesus affirms that for all human beings his kind of love is the ultimate law of the universe. He tells his disciples: "In the world you face persecution. But take courage; I have conquered the world!"[54] Christian hope, grounded in Jesus's life, death, and resurrection, is that one's present and future belong to God, and that, as a result, all things are possible.[55] Take courage, for fear is never the last word. Ultimately, "There is no fear in love, but perfect love casts out fear."[56]

A Southern white preacher and his wife, who both supported Martin Luther King and the civil rights movement in the 1950s, wrote openly in a published memoir that the fear they experienced because of angry racists was overwhelming until they turned to Psalm 27, which begins "The Lord is my light and my salvation; whom shall I fear? The Lord is the strength of my life; of whom shall I be afraid?" As they put it, "Our enemies were everywhere. They hated us and did not slacken their determination to harm us. But God's circle of love, made up of our white and Negro friends who stood by us [even as our house was bombed], never allowed us to feel alone. Our entire outlook changed. We became bolder than ever."[57]

So, for those of us who fear terrorism, who fear how we Americans are seen in the world, who fear our divided country, who fear being silenced or having our fundamental values betrayed, let us learn the lesson of the church-based civil rights movement. Let's roll up our sleeves and go to work in God's circle of love, under the example of Jesus and in the activist tradition of Rev. King. Maybe we too can then say that we've been to the mountaintop. That we just want to do God's will. That we're happy and not worried about anything. That we're not fearing anybody. That we can truly sing, for our eyes have seen the glory of the coming of the Lord.[58]

THREE

GOD

I am the Alpha and the Omega, the first and the last, the beginning and the end.

—Revelation 22:13

God gives the sun for light by day and the fixed order of the moon and the stars for light by night.

—Jeremiah 31:35

God is not far from each one of us. For "In him we live and move and have our being."

—Acts 17:28

No one has ever seen God; if we love one another, God lives in us, and his love is perfected in us.

—1 John 4:12

I grew up in the heartland of America as a Presbyterian Christian, duly baptized and confirmed. Yet, by the time I finished high school I was an atheist. Both intellectually and emotionally I couldn't fathom the notion that there could be a God. For how could an omniscient, omnipotent, and loving creator and sustainer of the universe allow all of the horrific and gratuitous suffering that occurs in this world? Some of the worst instances, from torture of individuals to the genocide of entire races of people, could be explained, perhaps, by the inhumanity of humans to other humans. (Yet, even there, I thought God should miraculously intervene to save the oppressed from their oppressors, as he had so often in biblical history.) But how about the painful death of innocent babies and children, due to birth defects, disease, or "acts of God" like hurricanes, earthquakes, and tsunamis? How about plagues and droughts and floods? There was no way I could imagine that all of the agony and misery of blameless people and their loved ones might somehow be part of "God's plan."

Searching the Bible diligently for answers didn't help. In fact, it made things worse. For then I realized that it was God himself who "hardened the heart" of the pharaoh to make him oppress the Israelites in ancient Egypt.[1] Later, when the Israelites conquered the "promised land" of Canaan in a series of bloody battles, God demanded not only that all enemy soldiers be put to the sword at the conclusion of fighting, but also that all innocent civilians—including women, children, and the elderly—should be slaughtered, along with all of their livestock.[2] God had earlier caused a flood that killed every human and every animal on earth except for those lucky enough to be on Noah's ark. It was God who ordered Abraham to kill his own beloved son Isaac, only at the last minute substituting a ram caught in a thicket, after Abraham had already bound Isaac and laid him on a pile of wood to be burned.[3] The Jesus story in the New Testament began to look much worse to me, because it appeared that God was now purposefully giving up his own son to be cruelly tortured and excruciatingly executed, without substituting any kind of animal offering this time. I came to be viscerally repulsed by belief in God if this is what it meant. The religious slate had been wiped clean for me—I thought once and for all.

What follows is my story of how, in college, a new faith in God was rewritten for me on my atheist clean slate. These four convictions emerged: God is the infinite and the eternal; God is the law and order of the universe; God is the spirit that infuses all of life; and God is love. I didn't arrive easily at those four insights. Ultimately, though, they came to lie at the base of my liberal understanding of Jesus. Let's see if they have any resonance for you as reader.

GOD IS THE INFINITE AND THE ETERNAL

When I arrived at Yale as an undergraduate in the fall of 1966, I was confronted by a new perspective on the infinite, one that had nothing to do with a personlike God who intervened in history. In the first semester I took "Human Evolution" with a geneticist and evolutionary biologist named Theodosius Dobzhansky. He had an enormously synthetic mind, stretching from the primary genetic research he had long been doing on fruit flies to a deep understanding of human culture, including religion. Not only did he teach about the human being's place in the much larger web of life, and life's place in the much larger nonliving universe, he also made connections between human biological development and the evolution of human culture and its symbol systems. We used his 1962 book *Mankind Evolving* as the text for the course. On the very first page of the book he talked about the infinite: "Infinity is a notion that most people find hard to conceive of. Creation myths were accordingly constructed to show that man and the universe did have a beginning."[4] He had grown up in Russia, and he knew and loved the works of the great novelist Fyodor Dostoevsky.[5] Dobzhansky explained in a 1967 book what he'd told us in class the year before: "There is no more succinct, and at the same time accurate, statement of the distinctive quality of human nature than that of Dostoevsky: 'Man needs the unfathomable and the infinite just as much as he does the small planet which he inhabits.'"[6]

(Reader alert: Math theory coming! If you're part of the majority of people who don't get a charge out of higher mathematics, feel free to skip to the next section on the law and order of the universe and pick up the story there.)

At the same time, I was taking a course in symbolic logic with a philosopher named Frederic Fitch. There I learned about the elegant proof by German mathematician Kurt Gödel that in 1931 demonstrated that no formal system of logic, however powerful, could ever be both consistent and complete with regard to mathematics. This crushed the dream of renowned philosophers Bertrand Russell and Alfred North Whitehead, who thought they had constructed just such a logical system in their *Principia Mathematica* of 1910–1913.[7] Yet, Professor Fitch claimed that Gödel's proof posed no problem for him in achieving both completeness and consistency. Russell and Whitehead's finite formal systems just hadn't been powerful enough. Fitch allowed for "infinite proofs." With them, one could build into the body of a proof the statement, for example, that all integers have a certain property (even though not all steps in the proof could be written down, since the set of integers is infinite). That allowed him to get around the logical paradoxes that Gödel had used to challenge *Principia Mathematica*.[8] I know this is sounding a bit technical. But for the second time in my first semester of college, in two different courses, I'd found that infinity played a special and critical role in human affairs. By assuming it, and using it conceptually, people seemed to be able to make progress that they couldn't without it.

So, I became fascinated by infinity and wanted to learn everything I could about it, starting with its role in mathematics. I pursued this quest throughout college, culminating in a senior thesis on "Computers and Infinity" in which I questioned whether computers would ever be able to symbolize and utilize mathematical infinity the way humans do (and how that might matter). Along the way, I realized that simply in doing calculus—and building bridges and skyscrapers and airplanes—we routinely assume notions of the infinitely large and infinitely small.[9] I also learned that mathematics generally accepts ideas of transcendental numbers and transfinite numbers, and that they are enormously useful beyond pure mathematical theory. Let me explain just a few points that particularly captivated me.[10]

Infinity was behind the first major crisis in the history of mathematics, which occurred at the end of the sixth century B.C. The problem arose in trying to apply arithmetic to two relatively simple problems: the determination of the length of the diagonal of a square and the determination of the circumference of a circle.[11] With a square that has one-unit sides, we know the diagonal is the square root of two, but it turns out that can be expressed arithmetically only by an infinite series. Babylonian mathematicians had been convinced that if only they laboriously carried out their calculations to enough decimal places,[12] somewhere along the line they would reach that last digit where there would be no remainder and the square root of two would be expressed exactly.[13] Unfortunately, as was later proved, that could only happen at infinity. As for the circumference of a circle, it equals the diameter times the number pi. Pi also cannot be exactly described without running the decimals to infinity. It came to be called a "transcendental number," along with e, the base of the natural logarithms. By the end of the nineteenth century, mathematician Georg Cantor had demonstrated that the transcendentals are actually the most common of all numbers.[14]

Now this idea of infinity was not just pie-in-the-sky, so to speak. Mathematical infinity turns out to be very practical, allowing us to do much and explain much that we couldn't without it. The physicist Jean Baptiste Joseph Fourier (1768–1830) claimed that mathematics is only justified inasmuch as it can help solve physical problems. Then, in attempting to solve the problems of heat conduction, Fourier originated and explained for the modern world the idea of convergence of infinite series.[15]

His use of such a conception was made necessary by the demands of physical problems related to heat conduction. The twentieth-century Russian mathematician Tobias Dantzig explained in his book *Number: The Language of Science* that "the importance of infinite processes for the practical exigencies of technical life can hardly be overemphasized. Practically all applications of arithmetic to geometry, mechanics, physics, and even statistics involve these processes directly and indirectly."[16]

From the time of the Greeks until the end of the nineteenth century, though, the mainstream of mathematical thought regarded infinity as only "potential," not "actual." Infinity didn't really exist. It was always in the process of becoming, or being produced, but it could not be spoken of as a completed entity or totality.[17] Georg Cantor broke explosively with the past with his theory of transfinite numbers, in which all the integers, for example, might be viewed as a whole, rather than as a progressively growing body.[18] Cantor's use of transfinite numbers attracted vicious critics, perhaps the most outspoken of them being the German mathematician Leopold Kronecker. He regarded Cantor's "positive theory of infinity" as a dangerous type of mathematical insanity that was leading the entire discipline to the madhouse.[19] That was because Cantor assumed that infinity actually exists.[20] This was mystical fantasy to Kronecker. His position was that unless mathematicians can provide a definite means of *constructing* the mathematical entities they're talking about, they're speaking utter nonsense. In fact, when confronted by the proof that pi is a transcendental number and cannot therefore be finitely constructed, Kronecker replied that pi does not exist.[21] My college mathematics professor Abraham Robinson tried to strike a middle ground between Cantor and Kronecker by saying that even if you think infinite totalities don't exist and any mention of them is meaningless, we should continue the business of mathematics as usual, and at least continue to act as if infinite totalities really exist because they're so useful.[22]

Cantor's positive theory of infinity has been well accepted now, and many high school students understand that you can write a number as big as you want, but it will still be no closer to infinity than the number 1. Although adding 1 to a finite number will change that number, adding 1 to infinity will not—nor will infinity be affected by trying to double it or halve it. And an infinite set is equal to any part of itself, so that the set of all integers is equal to the set of just the even integers. The simple mathematical dictum emerges that we should not apply finite standards to infinity.[23]

What does this all have to do with God? Cantor spoke of an Absolute Infinite beyond his transfinite numbers and called it God.[24] God is the highest possible degree of totality or completeness. In terms of finite, rational thinking there is no way fully to construct, reach, or encompass God, just as finite standards do not apply to transfinite numbers. But there may still be some partially meaningful ways to talk about God, just as we can talk about mathematical infinity.[25] Of course, none of this proves that God, the Infinite in space and time (the Eternal) actually exists, but I came to find the story of the infinite in mathematics highly suggestive of something greater going on in the cosmos.

The sociologist of religion Peter Berger asks in his book *A Rumor of Angels* whether God has any reality outside of being a product of the human mind. The answer, he suggests, may be simply a matter of one's frame of reference. What appears as a human projection in one case may appear as a reflection of transcendent reality in another. Still, it's perfectly possible for both perspectives to coexist; the logic of the first does not preclude the potential reality of the second. Tellingly, he turns to mathematics to make his point, for "If there is any intellectual enterprise that appears to be a pure projection of human consciousness, it is mathematics." Berger explains that mathematicians can be totally isolated from any contact with nature, going about their business of constructing mathematical worlds that spring from their minds as pure creations of human intellect. "Yet the most astounding result of modern natural science is the reiterated discovery (quite apart from this or that mathematical formulation of natural processes) that nature, too, is in its essence a fabric of mathematical relations. Put crudely, the mathematics that man projects out of his own consciousness somehow corresponds to a mathematical reality that is external to him, and which indeed his consciousness appears to reflect."[26]

Berger also introduced an idea in this book that suggested what might have happened to my atheist blank slate. He spoke of "signals of transcendence" that people can experience even if they don't have a religious worldview. My encounter with mathematical infinity was exactly this kind of intimation of transcendence. I had begun saying to myself, "There may be something real beyond the finite world of experience, Scotty, which could be called the Infinite, the Eternal, the Absolute. Now, pay attention to the hints you're getting, not only in your studies of mathematics, but also of other subjects like human evolution."

GOD IS THE LAW AND ORDER OF THE UNIVERSE

I remember how struck I was in my "Human Evolution" course when I read the conclusion of Charles Darwin's revolutionary book *On the Origin of Species.* In the next to last paragraph he declared (as cited in the first chapter of this book):

> Authors of the highest eminence seem to be fully satisfied with the view that each species has been independently created. To my mind it accords better with what we know of the laws impressed on matter by the Creator, that...[we] view all beings not as special creations, but as the lineal descendants of some few beings which lived long before the first bed of the Silurian system was deposited.[27]

How clearly this scientist expressed his understanding that there are universal laws not only like the fixed law of gravity throughout the universe but also like the laws of biological evolution that tie all of life on this planet earth together as a whole. I was personally dubious about a creator God setting up these laws. Yet, the order of nature itself was indeed staggering.

It was amazing to me, when I thought about it, that the universe coheres at all. Why are there established laws that apply everywhere and always, rather than having one thing happen here but then another there (gravity in America, but not in China), or something occur at this time but something else occur at another (genetic transmission now but not in the past)? The universe turns out not to be awry or askew in this way, though, but instead is ordered and trustworthy in some basic way. We humans can establish a scientific method by which we can consistently test hypotheses against the evidence of the real world. Then when we establish scientific truths, the findings underlying them must be replicable again and again, no matter who's running the experiment. If there's one convincing demonstration that the hypothesis doesn't hold, then this can't be the truth; we have to throw out the hypothesis and start all over again.

The universe could have been such that there were no such universal, trustworthy laws to be discovered by science. Then we'd have to develop another method to deal with the truths of our world and our life. But science assumes there's a natural order and natural laws, and it's been able to produce solid and glorious results on the basis of that assumption. Professor Dobzhansky had quoted Albert Einstein to this effect in our human evolution text: "The most incomprehensible thing about the world is that it is comprehensible."[28]

Over my college years I became more and more entranced by Einstein's views on what Darwin had called the fixed laws of life and the universe. So, this became my second "signal of transcendence" after infinity. My blank slate of atheism was beginning to have some writing on it: "Well, there's no personal God, but there seems to be infinity and eternity. There's no Creator, but there seems to be a natural order of the universe with fixed laws."

In 1929 Einstein sent a now-famous telegram to a New York rabbi who asked if he believed in God. Einstein replied: "I believe in Spinoza's God who reveals himself in the orderly harmony of what exists, not in a God who concerns himself with the fates and actions of human beings."[29] In the same year he wrote philosopher Eduard Busching of Stuttgart, "We followers of Spinoza see our God in the wonderful order and lawfulness of all that exists."[30] Baruch Spinoza was a seventeenth-century philosopher who rejected the idea of God as person, describing God instead as the structure of the impersonal cosmic order.[31] In his "Credo" of 1932 Einstein spoke more poetically: "To sense that behind anything that can be experienced there is a something that our mind cannot grasp and whose beauty and sublimity reaches us only indirectly and as a feeble reflection, this is religiousness. In this sense I am religious. To me it suffices to wonder at these secrets and to attempt humbly to grasp with my mind a mere image of the lofty structure of all that there is."[32]

As might be expected, Einstein was roundly criticized by religious conservatives for his refusal to accept that there's a personal God who intervenes in the world with miracles. He was often called an atheist, but this charge upset him most when it came from atheists: "In view of such harmony in the cosmos, which I, with my limited human mind, am able to recognize, there are yet people who say there is no God. But what really makes me angry is that they quote me for support of such views."[33]

Presumably, then, Einstein would be quite angry with modern philosopher Daniel Dennett. Dennett, author of *Breaking the Spell,* says "You're an atheist in my book" if "what you hold sacred is not any kind of Person you could pray to."[34] He speaks contemptuously of those who would "turn an atheist into a theist by just fooling around with the words." Such "fooling around" occurs if someone uses the term "God" for "just the name of *whatever it is* that produced all creatures great and small." As Dennett puts it, "Then God might turn out to *be* the process of evolution by natural selection."[35] Exactly! That does seem to be what Einstein is saying, if we extend his views from physics into biology. Einstein's response became increasingly acerbic as atheists kept insisting that he wasn't really religious but was instead one of them:

> Then there are the fanatical atheists whose intolerance is of the same kind as the intolerance of the religious fanatics and comes from the same source. They are like slaves who are still feeling the weight of their chains which they have thrown off after hard struggle. They are creatures who—in their grudge against the traditional "opium for the people"—cannot bear the music of the spheres. The Wonder of nature does not become smaller because one cannot measure it by the standards of human moral[s] and human aims.[36]

Scientist Richard Dawkins takes another tack in *The God Delusion.* He asks that we distinguish what could be called "Einsteinian religion" from "supernatural religion," and then wants physicists like Einstein to refrain from using the word "God" at all. Dawkins would have that term properly applied only to a personal God who miraculously intervenes in human life, not to the order and natural law of the universe: "Deliberately to confuse the two is, in my opinion, an act of intellectual high treason."[37] Yet, Einstein defended his own intellectual integrity zealously, insisting that he believed in God. That cannot be taken from him either by conservative religionists or by atheists.

GOD IS THE SPIRIT THAT INFUSES ALL OF LIFE

Einstein seemed at times to go beyond the notion of God as natural law to God as some kind of spirit that infuses all of life and extends to the inanimate universe. The first prime minister of Israel, David Ben-Gurion, remembered discussing religion when he visited Einstein at Princeton in 1951. He reported that "even he, with his great formula about energy and mass, agreed that there must be something behind the energy."[38] As noted, Einstein wrote about it in his "Credo" as the sense that "behind anything that can be experienced there is something...whose beauty and sublimity reaches us only indirectly."[39] He regularly used terms like "cosmic religious feeling" or "awe" or "sense of the mysterious" to describe his response to it. He explained that it "is very difficult to elucidate to...anyone who is entirely without it."[40] Is this a kind of mystical awareness?

In his comprehensive text on mysticism, which he sees to be at the root of all religions, F. C. Happold explains that a true mystic apprehends "the temporal in the eternal and the eternal in the temporal," which occurs both in feeling and in thought. Mysticism involves an understanding that there's a "Divine Ground in which all partial realities have their being." Happold also speaks of a spiritual dimension within each of us, or spark of the Divine, that can be consciously reunited with the Divine Ground of being through mystical awareness. That can take place in a variety of ways, often through contemplation or meditation.[41] In fact, atheist Sam Harris in *The End of Faith* writes generously of mystical experience as revealing "a far deeper connection between ourselves and the rest of the universe than is suggested by the ordinary confines of our subjectivity."[42]

Yet, Einstein made clear that he personally didn't want to be identified with mysticism: "What I see in nature is a magnificent structure that we can comprehend only very imperfectly, and that must fill a thinking person with a feeling of 'humility.' This is a genuinely religious feeling that has nothing to do with mysticism." As one of his biographers explains as he cites this quotation, "if mysticism denotes immediate intuition of, or insight into, a spiritual truth in a way different from ordinary sense perception or the use of logical thinking, Einstein was never a mystic."[43]

But by the second semester of my freshman year, I'd become interested in the human phenomenon of mysticism. Having already experienced two hints or intimations of transcendence in my studies that were affecting my atheism—infinity and cosmic order—I was about to add a third: God as some kind of spirit that infuses all of life and the inanimate universe. I'd come upon a book by Aldous Huxley called *The Doors of Perception*. First published in 1954, the book discusses Huxley's claim that identifiable biochemical changes in the brain produce the state of mind which has long been called mystical awareness. This state is not only central to religion but also to much of the aesthetic sensibility behind great art. He frequently quotes William Wordsworth, a poet who I'd come to love from a high school course on the English romantic poets. There's one part of his "Tintern Abbey" that particularly resonated with me, as I had spent a lot of my childhood outside in nature:

> ...I have felt
> A presence that disturbs me with the joy
> Of elevated thoughts; a sense sublime
> Of something far more deeply interfused,
> Whose dwelling is the light of setting suns,
> And the round ocean and the living air,
> And the blue sky, and in the mind of man:
> A motion and a spirit, that impels
> All thinking things, all objects of all thought,
> And rolls through all things.[44]

I'd also had two personal experiences that might be called "mystical." One occurred the summer before my freshman year in college when I almost fell a couple of hundred feet to my death in the Grand Teton mountains of Wyoming. The other happened one night on a beach in Florida during a freshman-year vacation.[45] In the first case, I became hyperalert, and all of my sense perceptions were heightened well beyond anything I had ever experienced—feeling my heart beating, every breath in and out, each muscle tightening and loosening. I tasted the incredibly bitter saltiness of my sweat, sailed through a huge range of emotions, and saw more brilliant colors than I'd ever imagined. In the second case, I felt I'd merged with the wind and waves and light of the moon. Everything, including me, throbbed with connection and pulsated with the same rhythm.

Aldous Huxley explained for me that this probably all had to do with certain altered brain chemistry related to an adrenaline rush in the first case and either physical exhaustion or too much alcohol in the second. Huxley had become interested in the systematic, scientific study of a cactus named peyote, whose active chemical ingredient is the hallucinogen mescaline, and which is used in religious ceremonies by certain Native American peoples of the American Southwest. Huxley then described in detail his own participation in a scientifically monitored experimental use of mescaline in 1953. For example, he related what he experienced under the influence of mescaline when he looked at a small glass vase containing three flowers:

> [I]n their living light I seemed to detect the qualitative equivalent of breathing—but of a breathing without returns to a starting point, with no recurrent ebbs but only a repeated flow from beauty to heightened beauty, from deeper to ever deeper meaning. Words like Grace and Transfiguration came to my mind, and this of course was what, among other things, they stood for.[46]

As he researched the drug's effect on other people, Huxley began sounding to me like the mathematician Georg Cantor reflecting upon the Absolute Infinite:

> Other persons discover a world of visionary beauty. To others again is revealed the glory, the infinite value and meaningfulness of naked existence, of the given, unconceptualized event. In the final stage of egolessness there is an "obscure knowledge" that All is in all—that All is actually each. This is as near, I take it, as a finite mind can ever come to "perceiving everything that is happening everywhere in the universe."[47]

He then linked this kind of perception to that of religious mystics like Meister Eckhart and St. John of the Cross. Huxley's book title is taken from these lines by the English visionary artist and poet William Blake in his *Marriage of Heaven and Hell:* "If the doors of perception were cleansed every thing would appear to man as it is, infinite. For man has closed himself up, till he sees all things through narrow chinks of his cavern." Huxley surmised that religious mystics had long used other methods, besides ingesting mind-altering drugs, to alter their brain chemistry and thereby cleanse the doors of perception: fasting, sensory deprivation, yogic breathing exercises, prolonged chanting, shouting or singing, and even self-flagellation. He predicted that it would not be long until mystical experiences could be stimulated simply "by touching certain areas of the brain with a very fine electrode."[48]

Wait a minute. So isn't this proof that mysticism, which Happold tells us lies at the root of all religions, is merely a matter of biochemistry operating in specific locations of the human brain? We're not talking about a transcendent God here but about altered states of the human mind, aren't we? Or maybe that's all this so-called transcendent God is anyway—a hallucination (or, as Richard Dawkins would put it, a delusion). And wouldn't we all be better off without hallucinogenic drugs, sensory deprivation, and fasting anyway, not to mention self-flagellation and lots of shouting?

Huxley's answer was that all of our experiences are chemically conditioned: "[I]f we imagine that some of them are purely 'spiritual,' purely 'intellectual,' purely 'aesthetic,' it is merely because we have never troubled to investigate the internal chemical environment at the moment of their occurrence."[49] Therefore, the logical, rational thinking of scientists and philosophers is just as chemically conditioned as the mystical experiences of religious people. And to rule out mysticism is not only to rule out the insights of great religious figures but also those of eminent artists and poets throughout history:

> Systematic reasoning is something we could not, as a species or as individuals, possibly do without. But neither, if we are to remain sane, can we possibly do without direct perception, the more unsystematic the better, of the inner and outer worlds into which we have been born. This given reality is an infinite which passes all understanding and yet admits of being directly and in some sort totally apprehended. It is a transcendence belonging to another order than the human, and yet it may be present to us as a felt immanence, an experienced participation. To be enlightened is to be aware, always, of total reality in its immanent otherness—to be aware of it and yet to remain in a condition to survive as an animal, to think and feel as a human being, to resort whenever expedient to systematic reasoning.[50]

So, Huxley suggests, rationalists and scientists, if they aspire to be complete human beings, "should turn out of their respective pigeon-holes, to the artist, the sibyl, the visionary, the mystic—all those, in a word, who have had experience of the Other World and who know, in their different ways, what to do with that experience."[51]

I sensed through my reading, and was told by a number of people in college, that Hindus had developed mystical awareness more acutely than any other culture. So, I managed to get myself into a program that placed me in the home of a Hindu Brahmin priest in northeastern India for the summer after my freshman year, as I mentioned in the first chapter. He taught me how to meditate, and he spoke to me for hours about his mystically based understanding of God: There is one Ultimate Reality, infinite and eternal, and it includes all animate beings and all inanimate objects in the universe. It connects *Brahman,* the transcendent order and law of the universe, with *Atman,* the infinite soul or self deep within each of us. As finite beings, though, we're usually not able to align ourselves well with the Ultimate Reality, externally or internally. That's because of *maya* or the worldly illusion that's part of our finitude. It's only during moments of mystical awareness, most often achieved in meditation, that we're able to see clearly through the *maya* to the infinite consciousness behind it. Yet, in daily life, to ignore or work against either the transcendent law or internal wisdom of the soul is to develop bad *karma* or moral erosion which will continue to affect us in the long run.

GOD IS LOVE

This Hindu view of God seemed to bring together so much of what I'd learned academically in that first year of college, from Cantor's infinity to Darwin's and Einstein's natural order, to Wordsworth's and Huxley's awareness of a spirit that's deeply interfused in all that is. Yet, this Hindu priest was as pragmatic as he was otherworldly. He'd also been trained as an engineer, and he ran a heavy-machine manufacturing plant nearby. He'd been active in Mohandas Gandhi's successful nonviolent campaign to free India from the British during the 1940s. He had lots of Gandhi's books in the house and often used to read to me from them. The primary lesson was that God is most clearly recognized in human life as the law of love:

Scientists tell us that without the presence of the cohesive force amongst the atoms that comprise this globe of ours, it would crumble to pieces and we would cease to exist; and even as there is cohesive force in blind matter, so must there be in all things animate, and the name for that cohesive force among animate things is Love. We notice it between father and son, between brother and sister, friend and friend. But we have to learn to use that force among all that lives, and in the use of it consists our knowledge of God.[52]

Gandhi's perspective was that just as there is the law of nature operating both in the universe at large and within human psychology and culture, there is the law of love aligning humans in relations with each other; we deny or defy it at our peril. It's realized most concretely in nonviolent action: "All well-ordered societies are based on the law of nonviolence... Whenever... you are confronted by an opponent, conquer him with love... In India we have had an ocular demonstration of the operation of this law on the widest scale possible."[53]

For Gandhi, following the law of love was important not just as a practical matter. It was also critical as part of his spiritual practice leading to mystical union with God:

> What I want to achieve—what I have been striving and pining to achieve these thirty years [since his mid-twenties]—is self-realization, to see God face to face, to attain *moksha*. I live and move and have my being in pursuit of this goal. All that I do by way of speaking and writings, and all my ventures in the political field, are directed to this same end.[54]

My Hindu priest also noted that Martin Luther King Jr., another religious figure whom Gandhi had deeply influenced, directly connected God with love. He cited King quotations like this one:

> I still believe that love is the most durable power in the world. Over the centuries men have sought to discover the highest good... What is the *summum bonum* of life? I think I have discovered the highest good. It is love. This principle stands at the center of the cosmos. As John says, "God is love." He who loves is a participant in the being of God. He who hates does not know God.[55]

By the end of my summer with the Hindu priest, I'd come to see clearly the inadequacy of the purely impersonal understanding of God that I'd built up through the several signals or hints of transcendence I'd experienced over the prior year. One can speak of a law of love along with the law of gravity, but love after all is relational in a way that gravity is not. It refers to persons and not just to objects or particles. God must include the personal and must have a human dimension if God is the eternal totality of all that is, the order of the universe, and the spirit that infuses all of life. Put a bit differently, when we people try to fathom infinite reality with our finite, human brains, it makes sense for us (at least sometimes) to use metaphorical language that is anthropomorphic—language that ascribes human characteristics to God.

One of the greatest Christian theologians of the twentieth century, Paul Tillich, explained that since we can't directly express our relation with the infinite, we have to use symbols. One of those symbols is that of God as person. He warned that if "He" (or "She," I would add) is left out, then describing God only in the language of "It" reduces the suprapersonal to the subpersonal. In addition, a neutral, objectifying term like "It" for God cannot grasp the center of our personality as human beings. Although "It" might be intellectually correct, the word doesn't include the fullness of faith as a response of one's whole personality: "[I]t cannot overcome our loneliness, anxiety, and despair," and "this is the reason that the symbol of the personal God is indispensable for living religion."[56]

Seeds of this perspective had been sown for me during my freshman year when I took a noncredit class with the university chaplain that was called "A Seminar for Friendly Disbelievers."[57] The Reverend William Sloane Coffin Jr. was by then a nationally famous civil rights and antiwar activist. I was certainly a disbeliever, but I wasn't unfriendly to one who had repeatedly put his body on the line for what seemed to me to be the great social causes of the day. To the contrary, I was deeply impressed by Coffin's moral depth, and I wanted to be in his presence in order to learn as much as I could from him.

Coffin repeatedly said that Descartes was mistaken when he said, *"cognito ergo sum"* ("I think therefore I am"). Instead, he should have said, *"amo ergo sum"* ("I love therefore I am"). Coffin had nothing against thinking per se;[58] he was a graduate of Yale College and the Yale Divinity School.[59] He explained that the Christian preachers he most admired were those who sought to inform minds as much as to engage hearts: "They have tried to link learning with love, intellect with piety, knowing that aroused but uninformed Christians are as dangerous as quack physicians,"[60] as he later put it in a 1982 book. Nonetheless, he insisted that the essence of faith is being grasped by the power of love.[61] He made clear why he was a dedicated practitioner of nonviolent social change: "I believe God dwells with those who make love their aim. And there is no sentimentality in this love; it is not endlessly pliable, always yielding. Prophets from Amos and Isaiah to Gandhi and King have shown how frequently compassion demands confrontation."[62] Coffin ended the last book he wrote before his death in 2006 with these words from Emily Dickinson: "That Love is all there is, Is all we know of Love."[63]

By the time I left India to begin my sophomore year in college, I had a tentative grasp of the four insights about God with which I began this chapter: God is the infinite and the eternal. God is the order and the law of the universe. God is the spirit that infuses all of life. And God is love. I've spent the rest of my life trying to discern more deeply and live out those dimensions of awareness.

But what had happened to my high school repulsion for an omniscient, omnipotent, and loving creator and sustainer of the universe who could allow such horrific and gratuitous suffering as occurs in this world? What about all of those "acts of God" that kill innocent babies and children? How could the agony and misery of so many blameless people and their loved ones somehow be part of "God's plan?"

Part of what had happened was simply a matter of personal spiritual development. I no longer experienced God as an all-powerful supernatural being who miraculously intervenes in history at certain times and doesn't at others. I certainly didn't take Bible stories literally anymore. Anything I believed in had to be integrated with what I knew to be true scientifically, logically, rationally, and emotionally. I couldn't imagine praying to some man in the sky, expecting that he would then somehow influence events here on earth. In other words, I was very far from what atheist Richard Dawkins claims to be "the interventionist, miracle-wreaking, thought-reading, sin-punishing, prayer-answering God of the Bible, of priests, mullahs and rabbis."[64]

As I came to see it, God doesn't have "a plan" for anyone or anything beyond the magnificent natural order of the universe, including all of its natural laws. As we humans gain more scientific knowledge, we're able better to understand our world—from the movement of tectonic plates that creates both majestic mountain ranges and tragic earthquakes, to the evolution of humans that has led to both the nurturing institution of the family and the history of warfare. There are no "acts of God" that are intentionally designed by a divine agent to drown particular people, animals, and plants in floodwaters while saving others from a long drought. Diseases like AIDS are no more the punishment of a wrathful father figure than medicinal plants are the gifts of the goddess Mother Earth.

As humans, it behooves us to align ourselves as much as possible with those laws of nature (in other cultures sometimes referred to by names such as Tao and Dharma) instead of ignoring or violating them. We need to recognize our own finitude as part of an infinite totality—to have the humility to realize that none of us can conceive, articulate, or encompass all of it (and to listen carefully for the truth in others' perceptions and perspectives). We need to be open, at least aesthetically if not mystically, to that "sense sublime of something far more deeply interfused." And our flourishing as human beings is dependent upon aligning ourselves with the law of love, which stretches from mother love to a social manifestation in nonviolent action for justice.

When I was in college, four fellow students died one winter night skidding off the icy interstate near Yale. Reverend Coffin spoke passionately against the claim that somehow this must have been the will of God. No, we live in a universe where water freezes at 32 degrees Fahrenheit and where the metal boxes we create to hurl us along stone ribbons on the earth's surface do not always protect our lives when they leave those roadways at a speed of more than a mile a minute. We can add to that various kinds of human error and imperfect skills. Deadly accidents will happen at a statistically predictable rate. Our response must be one of lovingly coming together in community to lay our friends to rest, of tender compassion for their parents and siblings and lovers and friends who grieve most personally. It must not be to tell them or anyone else that some kind of puppeteer God meant this to be.

Fifteen years later, Coffin's twenty-four-year-old son Alex died when his car plunged into the Boston Harbor. He'd been driving home at midnight from a bar during a bad storm.[65] His father preached a now-famous sermon a week later from his pulpit at the Riverside Church in New York.[66] Coffin began with thanks for his parishioners' outpouring of condolences: "[I]f in the last week I have relearned one lesson, it is that love not only begets love, it transmits strength." He then went on to describe how the night after Alex died, a woman who brought some food over for the Coffin family had said to him "I just don't understand the will of God." He was furious and immediately responded with these words: "Do you think it was the will of God that Alex never fixed that lousy windshield wiper of his, that he was probably driving too fast in such a storm, that he probably had a couple of 'frosties' too many? Do you think it is God's will that there are no streetlights along that stretch of road, and no guard rail separating the road and Boston Harbor?"

Coffin exclaimed to his congregation, "For some reason, nothing so infuriates me as the incapacity of seemingly intelligent people to get it through their heads that God doesn't go around this world with his finger on triggers, his fist around knives, his hands on steering wheels." He also noted that beyond human involvement there are also deaths simply caused by nature. But Coffin's way of personifying the law of love was to say, "When the waves closed over the sinking car, God's heart was the first of all our hearts to break." He explained that the reality of grief is the solitude of pain, and "That's why immediately after such a tragedy people must come to your rescue, people who only want to hold your hand, not to quote anybody or even say anything." He told his congregants that hundreds of them had understood this beautifully: "You gave me what God gives us all—minimum protection, maximum support. I wouldn't be standing here were I not upheld." He ended the sermon with these words: "So I shall—so let us all—seek consolation in that love which never dies, and find peace in the dazzling grace that always is."

Christians have a central focus for personifying the law of love—in the person of Jesus of Nazareth, whom we have come to call the Christ or the anointed one. In Jesus we're made concretely aware of what the fullness of love looks like here on earth. As Coffin put it, "When we see Jesus scorning the powerful, empowering the weak, healing the hurt, always returning good for evil, we are seeing transparently the power of God at work."[67] Jesus also suffered like any other human—in fact much worse than most of us will ever know—so it's possible to feel an empathy and companionship with him that's virtually impossible with the infinite God of the natural order. So, it's Jesus to whom we turn again in the next chapter.

FOUR

JESUS AND THE CHURCH

We, who are many, are one body in Christ, and individually we are members one of another...love one another with mutual affection... extend hospitality to strangers...live in harmony with one another.

—*Romans 12:5,10,13,16*

WHEN JESUS BECAME IDENTIFIED WITH GOD

A number of early Christians had mystical experiences in which they had personal visions of Jesus after his death. There are biblical reports of resurrection appearances of Jesus to his immediate disciples and followers.[1] Paul never knew the historical Jesus; yet, on the road to Damascus, he heard Jesus speak to him and instruct him.[2] The gospel of John (which was written as late as seventy years after Jesus's death and is more theological and less historical than the first three gospels) expresses a new postresurrection understanding in its most poetic form.[3] John describes Jesus with such terms as "the way, and the truth, and the life" (14:6), "the light of the world" (8:12), and the eternal *Logos* or Word which has existed as one with God since the beginning of creation (1:1–3).

It took some three hundred years of debate within the church, however, to come to the consensus that Jesus was the Son of God in the sense of being fully divine. For example, Arius (250–336), an Alexandrian priest, saw Jesus as the most perfect person in the world—with unquestioned moral integrity, but as a created being unlike the eternal Father and certainly subordinate to him. The Arian view was popular, and debate swirled in clergy circles of Egypt, Syria, and Palestine.

Constantine I, the first Christian Roman emperor, became concerned about the controversy's effect on peace and unity within the church after his emissaries failed to mediate the conflict. So, he summoned the first general church council in Nicaea in 325 to address the issue of Jesus's status, even though Constantine considered the whole matter to be "a fight over trifling and foolish verbal differences."[4] The council ultimately decided that absolute unity existed between Jesus, as Son of God, and God the Father. Without wholehearted support of all council participants, the nonscriptural word *homoousios* ("of the exact same substance") was then introduced into the Nicene Creed. Arius's view was condemned as heretical, and he was exiled by Emperor Constantine.[5] However, his understanding of Jesus has continued to surface in various forms throughout the history of the church, as with certain Anabaptists, Anglicans, Baptists, Congregationalists, Presbyterians, Unitarians, and Universalists, dating back to the beginning of the Protestant Reformation.[6]

Through the centuries, the church has at one time or another condemned some of its members as heretics, exiled them using the power of the state, and initiated inquisitions in which Christians and others were burned alive at the stake. I believe that's the dark, shadow side of the church, which we need to work hard to confront. The church at its best is the institution that has created a world of meaning for its followers— through whose rites of passage people are received lovingly into the world, come of age, marry, and ultimately are buried. It's committed to being a caring association of people, what Martin Luther King Jr. called the beloved community.[7]

Saint Paul, writing twenty years after Jesus's death, explained that all Christians are part of the one body of Christ. Each member has a different function, but each is reliant on all others: "If one member suffers, all suffer together with it; if one member is honored, all rejoice together with it."[8] Everyone should be honored and respected, so "that there may be no dissension within the body, but the members may have the same care for one other."[9] In the 1990s, the Catholic priest, teacher, and writer Henri Nouwen spoke of the church as a mosaic of Christ: "Together in the one mosaic, each little stone is indispensable and makes a unique contribution to the glory of God. That's community, a fellowship of little people who together make God visible in the world."[10]

This notion of the church as the body of Christ leads Paul to appeal to its members in this way: "Love one another with mutual affection...extend hospitality to strangers...live in harmony with one another; do not be haughty, but associate with the lowly...do not repay anyone evil for evil, but take thought for what is noble in the sight of all...live peaceably with all."[11]

I take this exhortation to apply to liberal Christians as much as to conservatives, to the nondoctrinal as much as the doctrinal, to the metaphorical-minded as much as to the literal-minded, to the rational as much as to the emotional. To be a Christian, regardless of background, is to live in the same master story of the life, death, and resurrection of Jesus—just as Jews live in the same master story of liberation from slavery in Egypt and exodus to the Promised Land of Israel. Each Christian may have a somewhat different interpretation of our common story—one that's worth continuing to discuss among us—but we still act out of the same story and are bound together by it. Even when we disagree, as Paul taught, we should treat each other with respect, care for each other, and live peaceably with one another.

THE CHRISTIAN MASTER STORY

What exactly does it mean to speak of the Christian master story? Michael Goldberg, in his 1982 book *Theology and Narrative,* explains that the master stories of the great religious traditions like Christianity, Judaism, Islam, Hinduism, and Buddhism "reflect the primary structure of existence, make basic claims about the truth of that existence, and display the ways whereby such existence may be fundamentally affected and transformed."[12] Christianity was born and developed in relation to a particular master story about Jesus, and Christians have continued to live within that story—finding their sense of identity, their inspiration, and their moral compass through this particular narrative. A story, of course, can be read in a variety of ways, and a single narrative can have many interpretations. This has certainly been true of the story of Jesus and his developing community.

Jaroslav Pelikan, an eminent modern historian of Christianity, wrote a fascinating study entitled *Jesus Through the Centuries.* "For each age," he says, "the life and teachings of Jesus represented an answer (or, more often, *the* answer) to the most fundamental questions of human existence and of human destiny [of that era]."[13] He cites eighteen different images of Jesus, including "rabbi" in the first century, "light of the gentiles" (starting especially with Constantine's conversion to Christianity in the fourth century), "perfect monk" of the Middle Ages, "universal man" of the Renaissance, and "prince of peace" following the Thirty Years War of the seventeenth century. Similarly, Albert Schweitzer wrote early in the twentieth century that "Each successive epoch found its own thoughts in Jesus, which was, indeed, the only way in which it could make him live."[14]

This is how the church develops and flourishes over time: by maintaining a master story about Jesus that is wide enough and deep enough to unite a disparate community of many types of members, including liberals, into Paul's "one body of Christ." As our ideas about Jesus have developed and changed over the centuries, so has the church evolved. Here are some examples in greater detail.

Jesus as the Mind of the Cosmos. Christian philosophers of the fourth and fifth centuries "made intellectual, philosophical and scientific history" as they applied the *Logos* title to Jesus, seeing him as "the divine clue to the structure of reality…and…to the riddle of being."[15] Jesus, in essence, was seen as the Reason or Mind of the cosmos, as ancient Greek philosophy had seen the *Logos* as the controlling principle in the universe.[16]

Alfred North Whitehead described Western science as having developed from the medieval Christian insistence on the rationality of God, a God who has both "the personal energy of Jehovah" and "the rationality of a Greek philosopher." This had been epitomized in the Christian doctrine of Jesus as the incarnate *Logos,* or Word, described early in the gospel of John.[17]

Seeing Jesus as the Mind of the Cosmos countered anti-intellectual tendencies in the Christian community. By assuring that there is indeed a rational order in the universe, this understanding of Jesus allowed both philosophical thought and scientific investigation to move forward and thrive. It also challenged the dominance of astrology, which had relied since antiquity on ideas of irrational arbitrariness and chance in the universe.[18] The church became a community that incubated modern philosophy and science, even as it often resisted some of their conclusions.

Jesus the Rationalist. The Enlightenment of the eighteenth century reaffirmed respect for rationalism by many within Christianity. Much was made, for example, of a comparison between the Greek teacher, Socrates, and the Hebrew teacher, Jesus. Although neither wrote anything, their followers remembered and preserved their great lessons. Both practiced simplicity of life and urged it upon others. Both challenged the orthodoxy of their community. And execution at the hands of the state ended both their lives.

The eighteenth-century scientist and scholar Joseph Priestley wrote an analysis of Jesus and Socrates that profoundly influenced Thomas Jefferson. Jefferson studied the Bible carefully, attempting to discover the true historical Jesus within the gospel accounts. The result for him was Jesus as teacher of common sense: "the greatest of all the Reformers of the depraved religion of his own country." Jefferson ultimately saw Jesus's basic message to be a morality based in commonly understood ideas of absolute love and service.[19] The church that inspired many of the founders of the American nation was a cradle of rationality, simplicity, and common sense.

The Poetic Jesus. By the nineteenth century, the Romantic movement was challenging the ideas of the Enlightenment: "By reducing mystery to reason and...flattening transcendence into common sense, the rationalism of the Enlightenment had dethroned superstition only to enthrone banality."[20] Although Jesus had been an inspiration to poets, musicians, and artists since the earliest days of Christianity, the nineteenth-century romantics tried to make their poetic understanding of him trump any philosophical or even moral view of Jesus.[21]

A major result of this view was the rise of personal religious experience as a primary marker of faith within the church that became more fully developed in twentieth-century evangelicalism. Both modern evangelicals and liberals can trace some of their heritage to English romantics like William Wordsworth and American transcendentalists like the Reverend Ralph Waldo Emerson.[22]

In his 1838 Harvard Divinity School address, Emerson reaffirmed reason and the natural law of the universe, including moral rules. But he then pushed his young ministerial audience far beyond these to the "infinite Beauty which heaven and earth reflect to you in all lovely forms." He complained of "the injustice of the vulgar tone of preaching" which profanes both Jesus and people in church pews by its "vaunting, overpowering, excluding sanctity." Instead, he called for "the reception of beautiful sentiments...I vibrate to the melody and fancy of a poem...music of the bards that have sung of the true God of all ages." When it comes to Jesus, he said, "Do not degrade the life and dialogues of Christ out of the circle of this charm, by insulation and peculiarity. Let them lie as they befell, alive and warm, part of human life, and of the landscape, and of the cheerful day."

Emerson also stressed the living Christ who can be experienced here and now, rather than "the revelation as somewhat long ago given and done, as if God were dead." Churches must help remind each person sitting in a pew that "the earth and heavens are passing into his mind; that he is drinking forever the soul of God." When this is done well, "The faith should blend with the light of rising and setting suns, with the flying cloud, the singing bird, and the breath of flowers."[23]

Jesus the Liberator. In the twentieth century, Jesus was cast as liberator for many involved in a variety of social revolutions. Paul made the great statement of Christian liberty asserted in his letter to the Galatians: "There is no longer Jew or Greek, there is no longer slave or free, there is no longer male and female; for all of you are one in Christ Jesus...For freedom Christ has set us free. Stand firm, therefore, and do not submit again to a yoke of slavery."[24] This became the Magna Carta for Christian abolitionists working to eradicate slavery in the nineteenth century,[25] and the rallying cry for the American civil rights movement in the twentieth century. For many of its parishioners, the black church became a church of liberation, and slowly some of the rest of the church joined in solidarity.

Jesus as liberator was also the centerpiece of the liberation theology movement in Latin America[26] that began after the Second Vatican Council of the Catholic Church in the 1960s. The seminal work describing it is Gustavo Gutierrez's 1971 book, *A Theology of Liberation.*[27] This movement challenged capitalist development that left the poor behind, as well as the military dictatorships and political repression that often accompanied that development. Clergy and lay people in the liberation theology movement developed "base Christian communities" throughout Latin America that combined Bible study, mutual support, and practical work to improve living conditions.[28] As Jesus was reported by Luke[29] to have said, "Blessed are you who are poor...but woe to you who are rich," the movement criticized local ruling oligarchies for taking advantage of peasant peoples and the developed world for profiting from the developing world's poverty and oppression.[30]

LIBERATING THE CHURCH FOR WOMEN (AND MEN)

The women's movement is now the most far-reaching demonstration of Jesus the liberator in the U.S. church. I still remember well a seminal event for me when I was a second-year divinity school student at Harvard in the early 1970s. For the first time, a woman was invited to preach at the Harvard Memorial Church in the center of campus. Philosopher and theologian Mary Daly arrived one fall Sunday from a Jesuit institution, Boston College, less than five miles away. After delivering a sermon entitled "Beyond God the Father," she led a walkout from what she called a hopelessly patriarchal church. Two years later in 1973 she published a book by the same name.[31]

The assistant minister at the time, Rev. Peter Gomes, who later became the minister, has written of her presence and action in Harvard's church as "truly revolutionary."[32] Many other women like Mary Daly, with some male allies, have been responsible for stimulating countless changes in the church over the last half century. Together those transformations have resulted in what Gomes has called a paradigm shift, the likes of which hadn't been seen since the Protestant Reformation in the sixteenth century.

Among the changes has been the development of a whole new field of feminist theology and Bible studies.[33] Biblical scholar Marcus Borg has described this change as "the single most important development of theology in my lifetime."[34] Innovative academic programs and centers have been created in seminaries and university-based divinity schools nationwide. Feminist theology has also deeply affected life in the pews of churches, providing a new lens through which to view the entire Christian tradition, a lens that has liberated men as well as women from the male monarch view of God with all of its political and social implications.[35] In terms of religious leadership, women have become ordained ministers, priests, and bishops in denominations that never previously allowed it. Inclusive language has become assumed in many church hymnals, liturgies, and Bible translations.

A major result has been a tectonic shift in notions of hierarchy in the church. Power has shifted away from patriarchy and, at the same time, from clergy to laity. For example, what Latin American Roman Catholic churches experienced with the development of "base Christian communities"—in which the center of gravity in a number of religious communities moved from priests to the people—has been paralleled in North American Catholic churches with significant shifts in leadership and decision-making to nonordained people, including increased roles for women within the church as lectors, sacristans, Eucharistic ministers, and chaplains.[36] Biblical scholar Phyllis Trible describes how this relates to the study of scripture:

> Born and bred in a land of patriarchy, the Bible abounds in male imagery and language. For centuries interpreters have explored and exploited this male language to articulate theology: to shape the contours and content of the Church, synagogue and academy; and to instruct human beings—female and male—in who they are, what roles they should play, and how they should behave. So harmonious has seemed this association of Scripture with sexism, of faith with culture, that only a few have even questioned it.[37]

Now we have entered the new millennium with a dramatically different biblical perspective, at least within liberal Christianity.

The new biblical scholarship has highlighted Jesus's relationships with women, showing how radically different his approach was from that of the culture and religion of his day. Since the Bible—Old and New Testament alike—was formed and recorded in a thoroughly patriarchal context, women's roles were primarily domestic and maternal. Women were their father's property, until marriage gave their ownership to their husbands. Fathers were to be obeyed by their daughters, and husbands were to be obeyed by their wives.[38] The community that Jesus built around him, however, was egalitarian and inclusive,[39] encompassing women in strikingly new ways.

For example, Luke records in his gospel that Jesus "went on through cities and villages [of the Galilee region], proclaiming and bringing the good news of the kingdom of God. The twelve [male apostles] were with him, as well as some women who had been cured of evil spirits and infirmities:

Mary, called Magdalene, from whom seven demons had gone out, and Joanna, the wife of Herod's steward Chuza, and Susanna, and many others, who provided for them [other ancient authorities read *him*] out of their resources."[40]

Women follow Jesus from Galilee to Jerusalem in the final days of his life. His female followers don't desert him at the time of his arrest, as do the twelve male apostles. They don't betray him or claim not to be disciples as he is tortured and crucified. Women are present at the cross, according to all four gospels. But their faithfulness doesn't end there. It is women who go to his tomb on Easter morning and find it empty. Then all four gospels record that it's Mary Magdalene, either alone or with other women, who reports the good news of Jesus's resurrection to his male followers.[41] Augustine calls her the "apostle to the apostles."[42]

For centuries, church tradition has denigrated Mary Magdalene as a prostitute or whore, although the new scholarship has established that there is no biblical evidence for this whatsoever. Instead, we have a conflation of other biblical texts that have nothing to do with her, starting as early as the second or third centuries. Legends about Mary Magdalene proliferated, and she was portrayed as partially or completely nude in many drawings, paintings, and sculptures. Ultimately, she became the patron saint of prostitutes, who were titled Magdalenes. Modern music presents her as the repentant whore, from a song in Whoopie Goldberg's *Sister Act* to one in Andrew Lloyd Weber's and Tim Rice's *Jesus Christ Superstar*.[43] But the new biblical scholarship sees her widespread and long-lived mischaracterization as a "male fantasy" and "a reaction against her power and authority as the major Christian witness, which they [the legends] obscure."[44]

The apostle Paul, largely responsible for the spread of Christianity from its Jewish roots in Israel to gentiles in the Greek and Roman world, as well as being the most authoritative interpreter of the gospel message in the early church,[45] described just how egalitarian and inclusive Jesus's church is meant to be in his letter to the Galatians, as mentioned above: "As many of you as were baptized into Christ have clothed yourself with Christ. There is no longer Jew or Greek, there is no longer slave or free, there is no longer male or female; for all of you are one in Christ Jesus."[46]

When people are initiated into the Christian community through baptism, the good news of Jesus's love is that persons who might be regarded as inferior or unimportant or unworthy of inclusion, like slaves and women, are in fact wholly incorporated into full communion. The waters of baptism bring with them a new vision for a new way to be human that is completely egalitarian and inclusive.[47] As biblical scholar Elisabeth Schussler Fiorenza has put it, "Jesus and his first followers were not well adjusted members of their society, but were in opposition to many cultural and religious values of their time. Jesus did not call into his fellowship the righteous, pious, and powerful, but all those who 'did not belong': tax collectors, sinners, prostitutes, poor people, and women."[48]

A careful reading of Paul's letters makes it clear that women were among the most eminent leaders in the early Christian church. They were missionaries, teachers, worship leaders, preachers, and prophets. Their power and influence were not restricted merely to providing service to other women or to providing traditionally feminine functions. Titles that Paul applies to them include co-worker (for Prisca or Priscilla), sister (for Apphia), deacon (for Phoebe), and apostle (Junia). The Greek verb "to labor" that Paul uses to describe his own missionary and teaching activities is also used in reference to women. For example, in Romans 16:6,12 he commends Mary, Tryphaena, Tryphosa, and Persis for having "worked hard" in the Lord. Philippians 4:2 explains that Euodia and Syntyche have struggled beside Paul in the work of the gospel.

Traditionally, however, the church has not recognized these women's contributions as equal to men's. Take the word *diakonos,* for example, which is applied to Phoebe. When used to refer to Paul or another male leader, Bible translators and scholars have tended to employ words like minister or missionary, but when applied to Phoebe it has been translated as deaconess, implying that she just fulfills a function for the women of the church at Cenchreae, the seaport of Corinth, rather than being a minister or missionary for the whole church.[49] The fact is that Phoebe is no different in recommendation than is Timothy in 1 Corinthians (16:10–11). She was recognized as a charismatic preacher and leader of the community of Cenchreae. It's also clear that she traveled to represent her community and served as a communication link with other Christian groups.[50]

A major problem for modern feminist biblical scholarship arises, though, with Paul's admonition in his first letter to the Corinthians that "women should be silent in the churches." Paul goes on to state: "For they are not permitted to speak, but should be subordinate, as the law also says. If there is anything they desire to know, let them ask their husbands at home. For it is shameful for a woman to speak in the church."[51] Prisca and Phoebe have been commended by Paul not only as members of the Corinth church but also as co-workers and ministers. How can he now be saying that it's shameful for them to speak in church?

Elisabeth Schussler Fiorenza claims that Paul makes a compromise here between his theology and his practical concern for social propriety. In the Greco-Roman culture of the time, men commonly expressed gratitude that they were born human and not animal, Greek and not Barbarian, and men and not women. The attitude seemed to have been adopted in the Jewish synagogue liturgy as well; three times a day Jewish men thanked God for not being created as a Gentile, slave, or woman.[52] During a time of Christian persecution, when martyrdom was a serious threat, Paul may have wanted to maintain a positive reputation among non-Christian neighbors in the broader society, rather than pushing social deviance too far. The result, however, was cognitive dissonance between the vision of Jesus's new community on the one hand and societally defined gender roles on the other. It seems that patriarchal patterns of the general society were vying strongly with the discipleship of equals that Jesus had instituted and Paul had affirmed.[53]

Almost two millennia later, these Pauline passages were still being used to counter women's demand for equality in the Christian church. Antifeminist preachers and theologians claimed that women's subordinate roles in their families, churches, and society were ordained and revealed through these words of Paul.[54] Elizabeth Cady Stanton (1815–1902) was active in the women's suffrage movement as an organizer of the first Women's Rights Convention in 1848 and as president of the National Woman Suffrage Association from 1869 to 1890. She initiated *The Women's Bible* project that led to the best-selling volumes published between 1895 and 1898 that challenged male interpretations of the Bible, especially those used to sanction the oppression of women.[55] She explained the methodology for her writers as follows: "Each person purchased two Bibles, ran through them from Genesis to Revelation, marking all texts that concerned women. The passages were cut out and pasted in a blank book, and the commentaries then written underneath."[56]

Stanton was a major forerunner of today's feminist theology. To celebrate the centenary of her efforts, feminist biblical scholars published two major works in her honor during the 1990s. *The Women's Bible Commentary*[57] was authored by North American women from the Catholic, Protestant, and Jewish traditions. *Searching the Scriptures,*[58] edited by Elisabeth Schussler Fiorenza, became a two-volume collection of biblical scholarship written by women from different parts of the world.[59] No doubt there had been considerable satisfaction when Schussler Fiorenza, now a professor at the Harvard University from which Mary Daly had led a walkout in 1971, became the first woman president of the prestigious Society of Biblical Literature in the late 1980s.[60]

There have also been dramatic changes in female leadership of the church in recent years. Antoinette Brown Blackwell was the first American woman ordained a minister (Congregational) in 1853, although without full denominational support; she resigned her pastorate within a year and became a Unitarian.[61] The first woman to be ordained to the ministry of an established denomination was Olympia Brown in 1863.[62] Her Universalist denomination merged with the Unitarians in 1961; by 1999 the Unitarian Universalist Association became the first major denomination to have women outnumber men in the ministry.[63] However, most Protestant denominations didn't begin officially ordaining any women and giving them full ecclesiastical equality with men until the second half of the twentieth century: for example, the United Presbyterian Church (later to become part of the Presbyterian Church in the U.S.A.) in 1956; the United Methodist Church in 1968; predecessor associations of the Evangelical Lutheran Church in America in 1970; the Episcopal Church in the United States in 1977.[64]

There are still a number of Protestant denominations that don't ordain women to this day, though, like the Missouri Synod Lutherans. The largest Protestant denomination, the Southern Baptist Convention, decided to restrict the office of pastor to men in 2000, even though by that time more than 1,600 women served individual Southern Baptist congregations as ordained ministers.[65] The other two major subdivisions of Christianity—Roman Catholicism and Eastern Orthodoxy—do not ordain women to the priesthood.[66] So, although the number of ordained women grows daily, the church still has a long way to go to achieve full gender equality in its leadership.

THE CHURCH AT ITS BEST

It should be clear by now that the church, the body of Christ, is a community of people—but they are disparate people who continually re-envision Jesus and the Christian story through the lens of their own time. The actions of the church in the world are always influenced both by Jesus's words and deeds, and by our ideas of who Jesus was and in what ways he wants us to act. There is a central master story of a community that formed around a particular historical figure, Jesus, and has tried to be true to his life and teachings, as well as to his continuing presence in our lives.

So, what good is the church? And, in particular, what good is the church in the twenty-first century? The church at its best creates a joyful sense of belonging, support, and strength for each of its members, all in the service of the highest and the best of which we are capable. William Sloane Coffin was known to quip, "It is often said that the Church is a crutch. Of course it's a crutch. What makes you think you don't limp?"[67]

The church is a unique kind of community. Henri Nouwen explained that it creates a sense of estrangement as much as a sense of belonging, because it's a community waiting for the fullness of the kingdom of God which has not yet come in all its glory.[68] When it gathers, it calls itself the body of Christ, but its work is far from fulfilled in this world. On the one hand, it represents Jesus on earth: "Without Jesus there can be no church; and without the church we cannot stay united with Jesus. I've yet to meet anyone who has come closer to Jesus by forsaking the church."[69] On the other hand, as Martin Luther King Jr. repeatedly reminded American Christians, it's a church divided into hundreds of denominations, many warring against each other with a claim to absolute truth.[70]

Yet, King rejoiced that, "One of the glories of the Montgomery [bus boycott] movement was that Baptists, Methodists, Lutherans, Presbyterians, Episcopalians, and others all came together with a willingness to transcend denominational lines . . . All joined hands in the bond of Christian love. Thus the mass meetings accomplished on Monday and Thursday nights what the Christian Church had failed to accomplish on Sunday mornings."[71]

As Coffin explains the contradictions, the church is conservative because it rightly has much to conserve. Yet, it's called to conserve a vision of the world's destiny as represented by Jesus, rather than structures of the world's past. It's not always easy for us to affirm that the church is, in Coffin's words,

> conserving the most uprooting, the most revolutionary force in all human history. For it was Christ who crossed every boundary, broke down every barrier. He crossed the boundaries of class by eating with the outcasts. He crossed the boundary of nations by pointing to a Samaritan as the agent of God's will. He transgressed religious boundaries by claiming the Sabbath was made for man and not man for the Sabbath. Everywhere he manifested his freedom and called others to theirs, calling them forth from family, national and religious loyalties to loyalty to the world at large.[72]

Coffin asked Christians not to argue about who was more committed to the true Christ—conservatives or liberals or others—but to work together to realize his vision: "In Christ's sight, there are no insiders and outsiders, for we are finally of one nature and one flesh and one grief and one hope. And in Christ's sight, if we fail in love we fail in all things else."[73]

But of course, we Christians will keep failing as much as we succeed. And this is where the uniqueness of the church as a societal institution helps again. Because no matter how much we distort and pervert Jesus's message, the church can't help but keep Jesus's name in circulation, "and where the name is remembered there is hope."[74] For, "in spite of its best efforts to domesticate that Jesus, the Church knows and frequently fears that his message will be rediscovered."[75]

Biblical scholar John Dominic Crossan concludes that the church will continue to discern divergent understandings of the historical Jesus as scientific research progresses. And, building upon that historical understanding, it will also continue to generate divergent images of the living Christ that can speak to the present day: "Christianity must repeatedly, generation after generation, make its best historical judgment about who *Jesus* was *then* and, on that basis, decide what that reconstruction means as *Christ now*."[76] This is what the church has always done and always will do, and this is how we live faithfully in community as Christians.

Just as Jesus instructed on the day before he died, the central ritual for Christians has been coming to the same table together in communion. The church brings separate individuals together to form the evolving mosaic of Christ. This mosaic, the church, is a conduit for God's love. The church provides basic moral teachings and a vision of the good life for its members. The church provides strength and hope in times of crisis, reminds people of their fundamental connection to each other, and provides regular opportunities for gathering together for celebration as well as mourning. The great holidays that we Christians commemorate—Christmas and Easter, and all the time leading up to them during Advent and Lent—help us to think well beyond ourselves and our own material desires and needs. The church preserves and develops spiritual resources such as prayer and meditation. It is responsible for the creation of great art, music, drama, and literature. The church at its best promotes peace on earth, a vision of justice, and personal and societal rebirth.

FIVE

UNDERSTANDING THE BIBLE

The use of books is endless, and much study is wearisome.

—Ecclesiastes 12:12

I have uttered what I did not understand, things too wonderful for me, which I did not know.

—Job 42:3

Then he opened their minds to understand the scriptures.

—Luke 24:44–45

THE BIBLICAL CONTROVERSY

The Bible has been central to Jews and Christians throughout history—to their spiritual lives, their understanding of morality, and their way of being in the world. This is especially true for Protestant Christians. In addition to the Bible, Jews have turned significantly to the Talmud (authoritative rabbinic commentary),[1] and Roman Catholics have been deeply influenced by the teaching tradition of their church, from priests and bishops up to the pope. Eastern Orthodox Christians have a strong teaching authority as well, although somewhat less hierarchical than Roman Catholics.[2] The great Protestant rallying cry, however, has been *sola scriptura* (only scripture, or scripture alone), to emphasize the centrality of the Bible in the Christian life.[3]

There's no doubt that for theological liberals and conservatives alike in all branches of Christianity, the Bible is absolutely fundamental. Every Sunday in many Christian churches around the world, we read from the same lectionary that presents Bible passages from throughout the canon of the Old and New Testaments on a three-year cycle.[4] Then we preach on those passages. As a Bible scholar at the Virginia Theological Seminary wrote,

"Reading the Bible in corporate worship is the most universal and probably the least contested of Christian liturgical customs."[5]

Liberal scholar Marcus Borg put it this way: "Christianity is centered in the Bible...the foundation upon which Christianity is built, without which the structure will fall into ruins."[6] Conservative scholar N. T. Wright likewise explained that, "The Bible is nonnegotiable. It's a vital, central element in Christian faith and life. You can't do without it, even though too many Christians have forgotten what to do *with* it."[7]

What indeed should we do with it? Gallup Polls over the last decade have found three very different views of the Bible among Americans as a whole. Around 30 percent of adults say that "the Bible is the actual word of God and is to be taken literally, word for word." On the other end of the spectrum, around 20 percent of Americans agree with the statement that "the Bible is an ancient book of fables, legends, history, and moral precepts recorded by men." In the middle are 50 percent who say "the Bible is the inspired word of God, but not everything in it should be taken literally, word for word."[8]

For a book published by the conservative InterVarsity Press entitled *The Divided Church: Moving Liberals and Conservatives from Diatribe to Dialogue,* the coauthors interviewed church leaders across the theological spectrum and found that it was their views of scripture that most essentially divided them. One prominent evangelical college president stated that "This is our most basic polarization." After trying to engage in dialogue, a liberal denominational executive agreed, "I felt the thing that divided us most basically...was our view of the Bible." Trying to elucidate the difference as clearly as possible, an evangelical pastor pointed out that "The distinction would be between those who see the Bible as divinely initiated revelation and those who see the Bible as a reflection of humankind's quest after God through the years."[9]

Marcus Borg writes that seeing the Bible as a divine product coming from God leads to claims either of biblical infallibility or inerrancy or, in a softer form, that the Spirit of God guided writers of scripture to prevent them from making any serious errors in matters relating to our salvation, although premodern science and archaic laws may be mixed in. The conservative view of the Bible emphasizes a literal-factual interpretation of what's written in the Bible, although softer views grant that not all biblical stories are to be understood in a literal-factual way.[10] "For example, the six days of creation might be understood metaphorically, perhaps as geological epochs; and the story of Jonah spending three days in the belly of a big fish may be a parable rather than factual history," but the really important events related to salvation, like the virgin birth of Jesus and his resurrection after death, happened more or less as they are described in the Bible. Also, since this literal-factual approach "tells us what God wants us to believe and how God wants us to live...considering the teachings of the Bible as anything other than absolute [conservatives feel] leads to a 'cafeteria' way of being Christian, in which we 'pick and choose' the beliefs and ethical teachings we like."[11]

By contrast, liberals take a historical and metaphorical approach. Historically speaking, the Bible was not written for us living in the twenty-first century, but for two communities of people who lived two thousand years ago and well before: ancient Israel (the Old Testament) and the early Christian community (the New Testament). Liberals, though, are more concerned with the metaphorical meaning of Bible stories than with their historical factuality. For example, we don't assume that the stories of Jesus's birth and resurrection are reporting on a scientifically provable virgin birth and a physical resuscitation of a dead body. Instead of asking whether these events actually happened this way, we ask, "What do these stories say to us? What meanings do they have for us?"[12] The metaphorical meaning of the virgin birth—that is, Jesus being conceived by the Spirit of God rather than having a human male involved—could simply be that Jesus should be seen as particularly close to God. He's a trustworthy person in that sense to follow as one's spiritual master. Likewise, the metaphorical meaning of the resurrection could be that "Jesus is a figure of the present and not just of the past. He continued to be experienced by his first followers after his death and continues to be experienced to this day...In short, Jesus lives."[13]

Borg reports that once when he was involved in a public dialogue with a conservative scholar about whether the resurrection was a physical resuscitation of a dead body, the conservative closed his case for the literal and factual truth of the Easter Day stories by saying: "In addition to all these historical arguments for being confident that Jesus rose physically and bodily from the dead, there is one more reason I know these stories are true—and that's because I walk with Jesus every day." Borg responded: "I accept completely the truth of your statement that you walk with Jesus every day. Now, if I were to follow you around with a camera, would there be a time during the day when I could get a picture of the two of you?" Borg continued, "Of course, that's silly. But my point is, I think your statement is really true, even though I don't for a moment imagine that it's literally true."[14]

There's no denying that a lot in the Bible is historically factual. But usually when a text preserves history, it's the metaphorical meaning of the events that matter most. The exile of many Jews from Jerusalem to Babylon after 586 B.C. really happened, but the story is told primarily for its metaphorical power of exile and return, which happens rather regularly in the Old Testament. There are other stories, though, like the creation account in Genesis, the Garden of Eden, and the expulsion of Adam and Eve, that are purely metaphorical. That doesn't mean they aren't true, though, in the sense of giving us powerful imagery for thinking about the spiritual side of humans since we're said to be created in God's image, for thinking about our sinful side since we eat of many forbidden apples, and for thinking about our suffering because of our sinfulness.

A Catholic priest once said, "The Bible is true, and some of it happened." A Native American storyteller made a similar point when relating his tribe's story of creation: "Now I don't know if it happened this way or not, but I know this story is true." Marcus Borg's audiences get this point immediately when he asks them how many listen to "The News from Lake Wobegon" on Garrison Keillor's radio show, *A Prairie Home Companion*. Usually about half have heard the show. Then Borg asks them, "Are these true stories?" As Borg explains: "They get the point immediately. We all know that Keillor is making them up, and yet we hear truth in these stories. We find them not only entertaining, humorous, and often moving, but often recognize ourselves and people we know in them."[15]

Unfortunately, conservatives and liberals can become very suspicious of each other over Biblical interpretation, even hostile. Conservatives think liberals are radically reducing Christianity. For if the Bible isn't a product of God, how can it be authoritative? If the virgin birth and the bodily resurrection aren't historical facts, how can Jesus be divine? From a liberal perspective, though, the conservative view of the Bible seems anti-intellectual, nonscientific, and illogical.[16]

It's always been my hope, though, to find ways to build bridges between conservatives and liberals so that the church can become the one body of

Christ that the apostle Paul said it was meant to be.[17] One possibility is to ask what conservatives and liberals might be able to teach each other about the Bible. The coauthors of *The Divided Church* have some suggestions. Peggy Shriver notes that her fellow liberals often lack a true passion for the beauty and power of the Bible. She says that "The approach of the liberal has a complexity that makes reading the Word less a comfort than an effort to grasp its meaning. The evangelical, who is by no means 'simple' in reading scripture, leaps more readily to quoting the Bible, savoring its message, and making unequivocal application. Perhaps we liberals sometimes make it too difficult!" Richard Hutcheson proposes that his fellow conservatives listen carefully to the "liberal insistence that Scripture is always interpreted by human beings and that God alone has absolute truth...The most treasured contribution of that [liberal] tradition is its openness to and respect for differing viewpoints, including differing interpretations of Scripture." Hutcheson also thanks liberals for their emphasis "on human rationality and on the necessity for religious scholarship," pointing out that "a wide-ranging evangelical scholarship is a relatively recent development."[18]

The conservative biblical scholar N. T. Wright points out that a lot of confusion can arise over the claim that the Bible is "inspired." For example, liberals might say that a sunset seems inspired in the sense that it looks a lot more glorious than the rest of the day. But can't liberals see that the Bible carries a special quality that sets it apart from mundane writings, just as they might say a particular piece of music or dance might be called inspired? On the other hand, Wright is concerned about claims at the other end of the theological spectrum in which some people seem to assume that the Bible was inspired as "an act of pure 'supernatural' intervention, bypassing the minds of the [biblical] writers altogether." This would suggest that God either dictated the Bible word by word or was "'zapping' the writers with some kind of long-range linguistic thunderbolt."[19] Many who don't want to call the Bible "inspired" are reacting to this kind of understanding. "Who can blame them?" Wright remarks. It would be better, he thinks, to see the writers, compilers, and editors of scripture, with all their individuality and foibles, as somehow caught up in their relation to God, and presumably to their religious community, so that they can effectively produce spirit-filled writing that touches other people.[20]

Wright also points out that the word "literal"—as in "the literal word of God"—is often, ironically, used metaphorically. When somebody with a bad sunburn says, "My arms were literally on fire after sitting there all afternoon," or someone at work says "My boss is literally an Adolf Hitler" or "The phone has literally not stopped ringing all day," that person really means their arms are metaphorically on fire, their boss is kind of like a dictator, and it seems as if the phone hasn't stopped ringing, though of course it has.[21] So, what do we mean when we read our Bibles to say Jesus "literally" rose from the dead? Even Wright, a conservative who thinks the resurrection means that Jesus's body was "transformed into a new mode of physicality" agrees that there are also metaphorical elements at work here, and he doesn't think the Bible is speaking of a resuscitated corpse.[22]

This conservative scholar also asserts that both literalists and the metaphorically minded can agree that there are some parts of the Bible that are meant to be interpreted literally. When the Book of Daniel tells us that the Babylonians besieged and captured Jerusalem, it means, quite literally, that they besieged and captured Jerusalem.[23] But when Egypt is described in Second Kings as a "broken reed of a staff, which will pierce the hand of anyone who leans on it,"[24] surely all readers, conservatives and liberals alike, must know this is to be taken metaphorically.

Perhaps the place that liberals and conservatives should most easily come together in our understanding of the Bible is in seeing it as a presentation of the master story that we need to live as Christians: following in the footsteps of a spiritual leader, Christ, who brought a radical new message of how to live lovingly in this world as harbingers of the coming kingdom of God. We are to be the people who will judge not, lest we be judged;[25] who will love even our enemies;[26] who will turn the other cheek when attacked;[27] who will care for strangers, the hungry, the sick, the imprisoned, as if they are Christ himself in need.[28] We are the people who will join together around the same table of communion, sharing bread and wine, whether we are saints or sinners.[29] As Wright puts it, the Bible is best understood not as a list of dos and don'ts, but as "a *story*—a grand, epic narrative." To speak of the "authority of the Bible" is to refer to "the authority of a love story in which we are invited to take part." As he explains rather elegantly, the authority of the Bible is like the authority of "a novel in which, though the scene is set, the plot well developed, and the ending planned and in sight, there is still some way to go, and we are invited to become living, participating, intelligent, and decision-making characters within the story as it moves toward its destination."[30]

LIBERAL INTERPRETATION OF THE BIBLE

How would Jesus and his immediate disciples have us read the Bible? In the gospel of Luke he is reported to have said to his disciples that "Everything written about me in the law of Moses, the prophets, and the psalms must be fulfilled." Then, according to the gospel writer Luke, Jesus "opened their minds to understand the scriptures."[31] What does it mean to "understand the scriptures?" This passage implies first of all that the message of the scriptures is not self-evident. Secondly, understanding it requires an opening of the mind. Thirdly, the Jewish scriptures—including the Torah, the prophets, and the psalms—are now rightly to be understood, according to Jesus, in the light of his own story.[32]

Luke was likely a gentile, writing about 50 years after Jesus's death, when it had become clear that few Jews had been attracted to the gospel, that is, the good news of Jesus's life, death, and resurrection. The future of the gospel now seemed to lie with the gentiles.[33] Many early Christians therefore had some major problems in terms of understanding the Jewish Bible. They needed to interpret the Jewish scriptures in relation to the death and resurrection of their leader, Jesus. Most Jews, meanwhile, saw these Jesus-followers, these "Christ-ians," as discontinuous with scripture at best; more likely, they saw them as blasphemers and heretics. So, the Christians had their work cut out for them in terms of going back through all of the Jewish scriptures and showing how they pointed to Jesus as their fulfillment, defying the claim that Jesus's resurrection was an event well outside of, and impossible to reconcile with, Jewish scripture.

In the short run, then, this act of interpretation was what Luke meant by saying that Jesus was "opening their minds to understand the scriptures." Jesus is portrayed as commissioning his disciples to show that he was the successor to Moses and all the prophets, who he claimed had referred to him. Jesus also became the fulfillment of the Psalms, which according to tradition were written by King David.[34] In the long run, as modern Christians opening our minds to understand the scriptures, we're now required to examine and interpret the whole Bible—the New Testament record of Jesus and the early church as well as the Old Testament record of the Jewish people's relationship to God.

However, the literal approach to biblical interpretation has, unfortunately, made the Bible implausible and ultimately irrelevant for vast numbers of people.[35] Peter Gomes, long the university chaplain at Harvard, wrote a best seller some years ago entitled *The Good Book: Reading the Bible with Mind and Heart.* He tells the story of a fundamentalist preacher describing a place in the outer darkness, referred to in Matthew 8:12, where the wicked will be thrown, "weeping and gnashing their teeth." An old toothless parishioner asks what will happen to those who have no teeth to gnash. The preacher immediately replies: "Teeth will be provided."[36] Gomes also cites a story by Robert McAfee Brown, former Stanford University professor and dean of the chapel, about those whose method of understanding scripture is simply to open the Bible and let one's finger fall upon a passage to read, supposedly guided by the Holy Spirit. A devout practitioner of this method found his finger pointing to Matthew 27:5: "And Judas went and hanged himself." Trying again, his finger happened upon Luke 10:37: "Go and do likewise."[37]

I haven't met a pure Biblical literalist yet during my years at Stanford, even among the fifteen or so Protestant evangelical groups on campus. Today the historical method of interpretation is taken for granted by most conservative as well as liberal scholars, even if the conservatives claim that scripture is inerrant or infallible. The historical method has long been taken for granted by Catholic scholars as well. This approach began in the nineteenth century with German Protestant biblical study that emphasized close analysis of the text, including its composition, its use of earlier sources and traditions, and its ideas in relation to comparable ones in the surrounding cultures.[38] Today we know more than ever about the cultural, social, linguistic, and archaeological background of the Bible. As a Protestant Bible commentary explains: "Cities long gone have been excavated. Lost languages have been recovered and have given us greater understanding of biblical Hebrew [and Greek]. Layers of composition in the text allow us to understand its significance at various points in its development."[39]

There's really no way to approach the Bible literally without engaging in interpretation. The original texts disappeared centuries ago, and current manuscripts have certain copyist's errors and attempted corrections.[40]

The Hebrew texts of the Jewish scriptures and Greek texts of the New Testament were translated first into Latin and then back again, and only then into the Elizabethan English from which our contemporary translations derive.[41] Any translation is by definition an interpretation, as anyone who's read a novel in its original language and then in English translation will attest.[42]

Furthermore, there are parts of the Bible that demand interpretation by their nature, like the parables of Jesus. There are other parts of the Bible that are obviously metaphorical and invite interpretation, as when describing Jesus as light of the world,[43] vine,[44] cornerstone,[45] bread of life,[46] shepherd,[47] bridegroom,[48] lamb,[49] alpha and omega,[50] word,[51] and way,[52] among many other names. God is regularly described as having hands and feet and ears and eyes, but of course both the biblical authors and we know that's not a literally accurate way of describing God.[53]

There's another problem, though, in understanding the scriptures that may be much more relevant to readers. Peter Gomes describes a woman who had heard Biblical readings in a liberal, mainline church every Sunday for years and years. She explained to him that "listening to the lessons in church is like eavesdropping on a conversation in a restaurant where the parties on whom you are listening in are speaking fluent French, and you are trying to make sense of what they are saying with your badly remembered French 101. You catch a few words and are intrigued, trying to follow, but after a while you lose interest, for the effort is too great and the reward too small." As Gomes puts it, "Because it is unlike any other book, reading the Bible is an intimidating enterprise for the average person. To remind the reader that the Bible is not a book but a library of books, written by many people in many forms over many years for many purposes, is to further complicate the ambition and add to the frustration."[54]

This kind of frustration must have been what President Grover Cleveland was feeling when he said: "The Bible is good enough for me, just the old book under which I was brought up. I do not want notes or criticisms or explanations about authorship or origins or even cross-references. I do not need them or understand them, and they confuse me."[55] Reading the Bible can indeed be confusing and daunting. Here are a few suggestions I passed on to the community that gathers at the Stanford Memorial Church.

First, get a copy of Peter Gomes's *Good Book*. It will get you fascinated in the Bible while entertaining you, stimulating you, and painlessly educating you. The first part generally explains what the Bible as a whole is all about, how to think about its interpretation, and how the Bible has been used in America. The second part takes on hard issues that the Bible seems to address from both sides: slavery, anti-Semitism, drinking, homosexuality, and the role of women. The last part examines the biblical perspective on a series of more general topics like wealth, joy, temptation, and the good life. By the time you're through, you'll feel much more confident about studying the Bible and understanding what it's saying in both ancient and modern contexts.

My second suggestion is to get a hold of biblical scholar Marcus Borg's book *Reading the Bible Again for the First Time*. He starts out by giving you new liberal lenses for seeing the Bible, recognizing twenty-first century realities: We know people now from other world religions, and we know something about their traditions; this makes exclusivist claims of Christianity to being the only way to God impossible to accept. We also know now that the way people think and act is pervasively shaped by the time and place in which they live, as well as by their race, gender, and social and economic class. Furthermore, we're modern people with an Enlightenment mindset who accept scientific ways of knowing and also insist on historically reliable information. But we're also living on the boundary of a postmodern worldview that looks beyond the limits of our current scientific and historical perspectives to appreciate art, narrative, and spirituality in new ways that help us supplement our scientific and historical understanding of reality.[56]

Looking through this twenty-first-century lens, the Bible becomes seen as the product of two historical communities, ancient Israel and the early Christian movement. The Bible is a human product—not "God's revealed truth" but a response of these two ancient communities to God that describes what they think is required of them ethically by God, how God has entered and influenced their lives, what kinds of prayers, praises, and practices are the most appropriate way to honor and worship God, and their hopes and dreams as a people of God. As a human product, the Bible is not "absolute truth" but a relative and culturally conditioned truth. It sprang from a particular time and place and not others, particular peoples and not others, particular languages and worldviews and not others.[57]

This is not to deny the reality of God, certainly, nor to deny that the Bible was written and compiled by people who felt inspired by God. But the Bible does not have "plenary inspiration" in the sense that every word was directly inspired by God and therefore is a divine product rather than a human one. Instead, the Bible is a product of people moved by their experience of the Spirit of God, in their own specific times and circumstances.[58]

Borg then spends most of his book providing an overview of the contents of the entire Bible, divided into seven major areas: creation stories; the Torah or Pentateuch, or first five books of the Hebrew Bible; the Prophets of Israel; the wisdom tradition of Proverbs, Psalms, Ecclesiastes, Job, and more; the four gospels; the letters of Paul; and the book of Revelation. By this time Gomes's parishioner would have moved from French 101 to intermediate French and really be enjoying the conversation. President Cleveland would be mesmerized by explanations about authorship and origins and doing his own cross-referencing.

Now you, along with him and our French speaker, should be chomping at the bit for a good study Bible, if you don't already have one, but one that doesn't give you more than you really need. Here I'd suggest the *HarperCollins Study Bible*.[59] It has a small set of color maps at the back with an index, a brief introduction to the Bible as a whole with time lines from 3000 B.C. to 150 A.D., brief introductions to all the books of the Bible, and enormously helpful notes to the entire text that consume up to half of each page at the bottom (all of which you can ignore if you want). You can also ignore, or find quite useful, various tools scattered about the study Bible, like a chronology of the kings of Israel and Judah and tables of parallel passages in the four gospels.

So, is there anything missing now in understanding the scriptures, or at least getting a running start at it? Peter Gomes, when he was being trained for the ministry at the Harvard Divinity School, was asked to write this on the flyleaf of his Bible: "Apply yourself closely to the text; [then] apply the text closely to yourself."[60] Marcus Borg speaks of the sacramental use of the Bible: using it for personal and communal devotional practice as "a mediator of the sacred, a means whereby the sacred becomes present to us."[61] Jeremiah, Ezekiel, and the author of Revelation even speak about "eating" God's words. Analogously to the sacrament of the Eucharist, where we eat bread and wine as a way to have Jesus become concretely present to us, we are asked by these authors to inwardly digest the words of the Bible, making them a kind of nourishment or morsels of bread themselves.[62]

I've personally found two traditional Christian spiritual practices to be very helpful in applying the text of the Bible closely to myself in this sacramental way, after doing the intellectual work of applying myself closely to the text. One is the method of prayer designed by the founder of the Jesuits, Saint Ignatius of Loyola. It involves meditating on biblical passages by trying to put oneself fully into the characters and settings of the text. Ultimately, when this is done fully, Ignatius teaches that one becomes aware of the presence of the Holy Spirit in and through the prayer exercise and of a deep kind of scriptural understanding that manifests itself in personal transformation. The other practice is *lectio divina*. One sits in a contemplative state and listens while a passage of scripture is read aloud a number of times, with interspersed periods of silence. Again, the purpose is to listen for the Spirit of God speaking through the words of the biblical text.[63]

The experience of the Christian community in general is that Jesus has continued to appear through the Holy Spirit generation after generation up to the present time. The scriptures are a primary mediator of his presence with us. Yet, the message of the scriptures is not self-evident. It requires a process of opening the mind, both intellectually and spiritually. For Christians, the Jewish scriptures become part of a long story that culminates in the life, death, and resurrection of Jesus the Christ. Then, in the words of Samuel Longfellow's hymn "Light of Ages and of Nations," Jesus becomes directly identified with the light of ages and of nations that has inspired every race and every time. The Word that is God abides forever and revelation is not sealed. It is written deep in all of our souls and continues to shine today, forever new.[64]

PREACHING THE BIBLE

Now that may be all well and good. But why would we want preachers up in pulpits interpreting the Bible for us on a weekly basis? One reason is that reading it by ourselves—even with the aids I've suggested—simply isn't very easy. It's a long, complex book, written by a lot of different people over a period of a thousand years, ending almost two thousand years ago. It's repetitive. It often seems internally contradictory. But most important, it's often hard to relate this ancient document to our daily lives in the twenty-first century. That's an important job of preachers: application and inspiration, after explication and interpretation. What can we take away from this text on Sunday that will improve our lives Monday through Saturday? And it's often simpler to listen than to read, and to learn in community rather than alone, especially if you know there might be discussion with others to follow based on what you've all heard.

So, let me give you an example of my own biblical preaching at the Stanford Memorial Church (even though you're reading now, not listening). My hope is that in this way the Bible might become a bit more accessible and inviting and that you might avail yourself of local preaching as one approach to scripture in your own spiritual life. I'll use Job, a "wisdom book" from the Hebrew Bible or Old Testament, since my emphasis so far has been on the New Testament.

"God sends rain on the righteous and on the unrighteous." So Jesus told his disciples in the Sermon on the Mount.[65] Why do bad things happen to good people? Why be good if it doesn't seem to make any difference? Why throw down your fishing nets to follow this great teacher and miracle-worker named Jesus, only to die in a raging storm in the lake with him on board? What's the point? In the biblical story of Jesus on the Sea of Galilee with his disciples, it seems Jesus is able to effect a miracle; he calms the wind and the seas, and they live.[66] But later he's not able to save himself from crucifixion at the hands of the Romans. He cries out on the cross, "My God, my God, why hast thou forsaken me?"[67] And later most of the apostles from that boat trip on the Sea of Galilee are martyred themselves by crucifixion.

How are we to face stormy weather in our lives? How do we find the strength to do so? What can sustain us, especially when we actually seem to be suffering at the very hands of God, or at least with God seeming to look the other way? ("Why have you forsaken me?" beseeches Jesus, and "Teacher, do you not care that we are perishing?" ask Jesus's disciples during the storm on the Sea of Galilee.)

Here's where I've consistently found the book of Job to be the most powerful and the most helpful resource in the Bible. Let's go back over Job's story, which culminates in God himself appearing in a powerful windstorm.[68] It's a fascinating and very enlightening tale, but not at all like the one I learned in Sunday school.

The background of Job's suffering is really quite outrageous, even shocking. The book begins with these words: "There once was a man in the land of Uz whose name was Job. That man was blameless and upright, one who feared God and turned away from evil."[69] So, it's made crystal clear to us from the start that this is a just man, a good man, a holy man. No hidden flaws, Achilles' heel, or normal mix of virtue and vice here. He also happens to have a wife and ten children, all of whom he appears to love very much.[70] And he's very rich—"He had seven thousand sheep, three thousand camels, five hundred yoke of oxen, five hundred donkeys, and very many servants; so that this man was the greatest of all the people of the east"[71]—a Bill Gates and a Saudi prince all rolled into one.

Now it happens that Satan and God are having one of their periodic conversations up in Heaven,[72] and God says to Satan: "Where have you come from [now]?" Satan answers, "From going to and fro on the earth, and from walking up and down on it." God then boasts, "Have you considered my servant Job? There is no one like him on the earth, a blameless and upright man who fears God and turns away from evil." Satan cleverly responds, "Does Job fear God for nothing? Haven't you put a fence around him and his house and all that he has, on every side? You've blessed the work of his hands, and his possessions have increased in the land. But stretch out your hand now, and touch all that he has, and he'll curse you to your face." So God, astoundingly, takes the bait and sends Satan off to do evil, "Very well, all that he has is in your power; only do not stretch out your hand against him!"

Job soon learns that all of his children have died, along with all of his servants and all of his animals. Only he and his wife remain. How does Job respond? Just as they taught me in Sunday school: "Job...fell on the ground and worshipped. He said, 'Naked I came from my mother's womb, and naked shall I return there; the Lord gave, and the Lord has taken away; blessed be the name of the Lord.' In all this Job did not sin or charge God with wrong-doing."

The next time God and Satan are having a heavenly conversation,[73] God boasts a second time: "Job still persists in his integrity, although you incited me against him, to destroy him for no reason." Yet Satan responds, "Skin for skin! All that people have they will give to save their lives. But stretch out your hand now and touch his bone and his flesh, and he will curse you to your face." God agrees to the next test. (Can you believe it? What is he doing wagering with Satan?) "Very well, [God says,] he is in your power; only spare his life." This time Satan inflicts "loathsome sores on Job from the sole of his foot to the crown of his head." Job then takes a piece of broken pottery with which to scrape himself and sits among the ashes. His wife comes and says to him, "Do you still persist in your integrity? Curse God, and die." But Job responds, in good Sunday school style, "Shall we receive the good at the hand of God and not receive the bad?" And as the Bible explains, "In all this Job did not sin with his lips."

Job has three friends who come to console and comfort him, Eliphaz, Bildad, and Zophar. They weep, and as the text puts it, "They sat with him on the ground seven days and seven nights, and no one spoke a word to him, for they saw that his suffering was very great."

Well, that's as far as we ever read in Sunday school—to the end of chapter 2. The moral was that the long-suffering Job didn't complain or criticize God in any way. It was presented as a lesson of ultimate faith in God, even though we, the readers, know that God is 100 percent to blame for his suffering, for the astounding reason of making a destructive and inhumane bet with Satan. Actually, I stand corrected on only reading through chapter 2. In Sunday school we also read the account at the very end of the book, chapter 42, in which God restores the fortunes of Job, giving him twice as much wealth as he had before. His sores are cured too, and he gets ten new children. The book ends this way: "After this Job lived one hundred and forty years, and he saw his children, and his children's children, four generations. And Job died, old and full of days."

But there are 39 remarkably provocative chapters in between that my Sunday school teachers never told me about. Structurally, it turns out that those chapters are in poetic form—in fact, the longest ancient Hebrew poem that has survived and perhaps that was ever written. Chapters 1 and 2 and 42 are in prose form and are probably a later addition, by a different author, to the original Hebrew poem.[74]

Here's the rather different way the poetic section begins in chapter 3: "After this Job opened his mouth and cursed the day of his birth. Job said, 'Let the day perish in which I was born, and the night that said, A man-child is conceived. Let that day be darkness! May God above not seek it, or light shine on it … Why did I not die at birth, come forth from the womb and expire? Why were there knees to receive me, or breasts for me to suck?'"[75] Before too long Job begins directly criticizing God: "Why is light given to one who cannot see the way, whom God has fenced in?"[76]

His friends can't stand being quiet any longer, and they begin giving him traditional reasons why someone could suffer like this. First, since God surely couldn't be responsible for his suffering, Job must have done something wrong to deserve all this. Second, Job is certainly condemned out of his own mouth for speaking out against God, and he must make humble supplication to God now if he ever expects any relief. Third, suffering will do him good and make him a better person in the end. Fourth, God's ways are mysterious, but it's likely that it will all be cleared up and make sense someday.[77] And there's even more in this vein from the so-called comforters.

But Job will have none of it, and he becomes increasingly angry with his friends and shrill and confrontational with God: "The arrows of the Almighty are in me; my spirit drinks their poison; the terrors of God are arrayed against me .... My companions are treacherous ... I will not restrain my mouth; I will speak in the anguish of my spirit; I will complain in the bitterness of my soul ... Will you not look away from me [O God] for a while, let me alone until I swallow my spittle?..."[78]

Then Job begins framing his situation as a matter of justice and asking for his day in court. "Though I am innocent ... if I summoned God and he answered me, I don't believe that he would listen to my voice ... He's not a mortal, as I am, that I might answer him, that we should come to trial together. There is no umpire between us, who might lay his hand on us both ... [O God,] You know that I'm not guilty, and there is no one to deliver me out of your hand."[79]

Job's cursing and criticizing and complaining, his legal defense of himself, his challenge to God's justice, and his angry exchange with his pious friends goes on and on and on for 35 chapters—powerfully and poetically, beautifully and bravely. And then finally God answers him in the thirty-eighth chapter. But deeply disappointingly, God doesn't directly respond to any of the questions that Job has posed. Instead, God simply demonstrates awesome power: "Then the Lord answered Job out of the whirlwind: 'Who is this that darkens counsel by words without knowledge? Gird up your loins like a man. I will question you, and you shall declare to me. Where were you when I laid the foundation of the earth? Tell me, if you have understanding ... Or who shut in the sea with doors when it burst out from the womb—when I made the clouds its garment, and thick darkness its swaddling band, and prescribed bounds for it...?" "[80]

God goes on for two chapters along these lines, and then concludes with these words: "Shall a faultfinder contend with the Almighty? Anyone who argues with God must respond."[81] So Job does respond. How would you respond in the face of the power of a divine whirlwind? Job simply says, "See, I am of small account; what shall I answer you? I lay my hand on my mouth. I have spoken once, and I will not answer; twice, but will proceed no longer."[82] Shouldn't that be enough for the Almighty and Everlasting, looking down upon a puny, finite human being? No. God winds up again and bellows from the whirlwind: "Gird up your loins like a man; I will question you, and you declare to me. Will you even put me in the wrong? Will you condemn me, that you may be justified? Have you an arm like God, and can you thunder with a voice like his?"[83]

Two more chapters go on this way. Now what's Job to say? What would you say? Here's Job's response: "I know that you can do all things, and that no purpose of yours can be thwarted ... Therefore I have uttered what I did not understand, things too wonderful for me, which I did not know... I had heard of you by the hearing of the ear, but now my eye sees you; therefore I despise myself, and repent in dust and ashes."[84]

So, how satisfactory is all this? Does it help in any way with my initial concerns about why bad things happen to good people and why we should be good if it doesn't seem to make any difference? Many commentators down through the centuries, including relatively recently Carl Jung in his *Answer to Job* and Archibald McLeish in his *J.B.*, have tried to make sense out of this story. Let it be said that my Sunday school teachers, lauding the long-suffering, never-complaining Job, really missed the mark.

Here's my current take on the book of Job. First of all, the poetic section is a fantastic expression of everything all of us have ever felt when we've been mistreated by life, unjustly punished by the forces-that-be, or hurt by a so-called act of God, such as an earthquake or a hurricane. Job's words are gutsy, in your face, and no-holds-barred. It's comforting having something like that in the Bible for me, because it expresses deep human feelings so eloquently. Second, I take very seriously what God says to Eliphaz in the last chapter: "My wrath is kindled against you and against your two friends; for you have not spoken of me what is right, as my servant Job has."[85] I hear that as God saying, "Of course Job was right to engage me so personally, so emotionally, so humanly, in real relationship. You and your friends have been throwing around pious platitudes that were in no way comforting or helpful to Job and were outright lies about me. I *was* in fact responsible for his suffering. Suffering is an inherent part of life, of being human, in case you hadn't noticed. He's not condemned out of his own mouth by challenging me; I expect it in situations like this, and I can take it. Suffering doesn't always do people good and make them better in the end; imagine saying that to survivors of the Holocaust. And yes, my ways are mysterious, but it's not likely that it will all be cleared up some day. In fact, it's impossible to understand the ways of the Almighty and the Everlasting from the perspective of the partial and the transitory of human existence."

God then tells Eliphaz: "Now take seven bulls and seven rams, and go to my servant Job, and offer up for yourselves a burnt offering; and my servant Job shall pray for you, for I will accept his prayer not to deal with you according to your folly; for you have not spoken of me what is right, as my servant Job has done."[86] For me the bottom-line lesson of Job lies in the importance of honest, genuine, engaged relationships both with God and with one's friends. The best thing Job's friends ever did for him was to cry with him and to sit with him in silence for seven days, understanding that his suffering was very great. Once they opened their mouths with their traditional explanations and became defensive when Job disagreed, they lost their usefulness as friends and simply began furthering their own egos and transposing their own fears. And God seems to be saying, by the end, that it's all right to have real dialogue with God, especially when one is suffering deeply. In fact, that's when the dialogue should be the most profound.

It's an unequal relationship, to be sure, between the eternal life force of the universe and the finite human animal. Yet, it can be a deep and sustaining relationship, which through Jesus is clearly framed in terms of love. Jesus loves his disciples, even as they're afraid in the face of the storms of life, even as they doubt his steadfastness, even as they temporarily abandon him in his own times of need. Ultimately God, as the *Logos* of the universe, becomes a mighty fortress, who through the law of love stands by our side and suffers with us amid the flood of mortal ills. Ultimately it's our job both to appreciate the infinite power and mystery of God, and also to strive to remain in faithful relationship with the most complex and complete friend we could ever have.

CONCLUSION

So that's what the Bible can look like in the hands of a liberal Christian preacher. It's not a dry old tome or a dogmatic harangue. It needs to be studied and interpreted. It has to be understood in its own historical context before it can usefully be applied to issues today. It's full of fantastic stories and pithy words of wisdom, as well as powerful lessons of history. We can engage it not only with our intellects and emotions, but also with our imaginations and rambunctiousness. Ultimately, it should touch us deep in our being, inspire us, and transform our lives.

SIX

FAITH

Fools say in their hearts, "There is no God."

—Psalms 14:1 and 53:1

The apostles said to the Lord, "Increase our faith!"

—Luke 17:5

The biblical story of Job puts the question of faith in sharp focus. But what does it really mean to have faith? Best-selling atheist Sam Harris defines "faith" as "unjustified belief in matters of ultimate concern." He explains that "Faith is what credulity becomes when it finally achieves escape velocity from the constraints of terrestrial discourse—constraints like reasonableness, internal coherence, civility, and candor." In his opinion, "Ignorance is the true coinage of this realm" of faith. We are asked to "disregard the facts of this world" out of deference to God—who's only a figment of our imaginations in the first place.[1] On the other hand, in the view of the Old Testament Psalmist, those who say there is no God are themselves fools. Instead, God "looks down from heaven on humankind to see if there are any who are wise, who seek after God." God asks of those who don't call upon the divine, "Have they no knowledge?"[2] So what's faith really all about: ignorance or knowledge, foolishness or wisdom?

FAITH AS A UNIVERSAL HUMAN QUALITY

One of my favorite professors in divinity school was a scholar of the history of religion named Wilfred Cantwell Smith. He began his career as a Presbyterian missionary to India, but over his four years there he began to count Hindu, Muslim, and Sikh intellectuals among his closest friends. Ultimately he became a professor of comparative religion at Harvard and ran its Center for the Study of World Religions.[3] Among his many books is one called *Faith and Belief,*[4] which I've found very helpful in thinking about the nature of faith.

Faith, Smith explains, is a universal quality of human life like love. That's not to say that everyone has experienced it, just as not everyone has experienced love, but most people throughout history have, sooner or later. Faith is the ability to live at more than a mundane level: to see, to feel, and to act in terms of a transcendent dimension that integrates all that is. Though it's an orientation of the individual personality, it's been nurtured and shaped by religious traditions and therefore comes in different forms: Christian, Muslim, Buddhist, etc. It enables one to feel at home in the universe—to find meaning and purpose in the world and in one's own life. That meaning is profound and ultimate, relating us as finite beings to an infinite reality far beyond us, as well as to a sense of centeredness deep within us. That sense of ultimate purpose is stable regardless of what happens to each of us personally in the buffeting of life events. In fact, a great strength of faith is how it allows us to look beyond ourselves and beyond material realities to the ideal and the absolute.

The opposite of faith, as Smith describes it, is nihilism. Other terms might be despair, alienation, ego disintegration, or anomie. Nihilists are unable to find any significance in the universe or their own lives. They feel lost in the world, not to mention in the cosmos. Without faith, we become almost totally dependent on immediate, everyday events, and yet we don't feel that those events can really be depended on for very long. Without faith, we can't commit to anything, and we find it hard to get far enough outside of the self to love anyone else. We become largely victims of our own whims internally and social pressures externally. In essence, without faith, we grow to be organisms simply reacting to the environment.[5]

What does this look like in concrete lived reality? The quintessence of someone without faith is the main character, Meursault, in Albert Camus' novel *The Stranger.* He lives at a completely mundane, day-to-day level, having no awareness of anything transcending his own feelings. For example, he spends a lot of time describing how he feels very hot in his Algerian setting or how he's being burned or blinded by the sun. He even explains that the reason he murdered another man was the feeling of the burning sun on his forehead when he pulled the trigger. Meursault can't commit himself to anything or anyone. When he's with his girlfriend, all that seems to matter is the sensual experience. He rarely visited his mother late in her life when she was in a rest home and he seems to be indifferent at her funeral. He's continually saying, "It doesn't matter" about a wide variety of things.[6] He sees no significance in his own life or in the world generally. As he sits in prison awaiting his execution for the murder, he comforts himself with this thought: "But everybody knows life isn't worth living. Deep down I knew perfectly well that it doesn't much matter whether you die at thirty or at seventy."[7]

So nihilism is the opposite of faith. But why does faith matter? Specifically, why would faith matter for a person like Meursault? Well, first of all, he might feel less alone in the universe; indeed, he might experience love and compassion rather than the hate he imagines facing at the end of the book. Perhaps he'd escape his enslavement to a sensate daily routine, the humdrum and the ordinary. He might find some sustaining hope in his future or that of the world, and even discover that something beyond himself matters. Life could be worth living for others, or for something even more transcendent, rather than just for himself.

STAGES OF FAITH

Faith is not a steady state, though. All of us naturally go through different stages of faith development in our lives, as has been documented by the work of psychologists James Fowler, Sharon Parks, George Scarlett, Fritz Oser and Paul Gmunder.[8] This isn't surprising to religious education teachers in all traditions, who use different curricula and techniques to teach children, adolescents, and adults, since their views and experience of the universe, other human beings, and God change, often dramatically, as they mature. My own counseling experience in over thirty years of ministry has confirmed the usefulness of stage theory.[9] I use descriptive names for six stages of faith development that I adapted from several different theorists. Research continues in this area, and stage theory itself has been variously criticized in the psychological literature, but it remains indispensable in current developmental psychology.[10] What follows here is an abbreviated summary of the six stages: Magic and Reality arising during childhood,

Dependence and Independence during adolescence and early adulthood, and Interdependence and Unity during late adulthood. Very few of us ever reach Unity—the realm of the mystics—and many of us stay happily at an earlier stage like Dependence throughout our lives. No judgment should be implied of what's better or worse.

Children between the ages of two and twelve generally move from a magical perception of the world (stage one) to a reality-based view (stage two). That is, a fairy-tale world full of imaginary friends and demons, superheroes, and villains gives way to one where the child's primary question becomes, "Is it real?" The Bible and other scriptures start to be read concretely and literally now, rather than as mere tales. One's experience of God also tends to shift from a mysterious all-powerful God who directs everything to a more tangible cause-and-effect God—often imaged in Western culture as an old man with a long white beard—who can be influenced by one's good deeds and prayerful promises and vows.

Entering adolescence, one becomes deeply affected by peer pressure and can be easily influenced by the leadership of respected older people beyond one's parents. At the Dependence stage (stage three), the individual is susceptible not only to cult involvement and brainwashing, but also to the development of a meaningful outlook on life through following religious doctrine and moral rules. At this time in the life cycle, God is usually imaged as an idealized parental figure, unconditionally loving, although sometimes deeply judgmental. At Independence (stage four), which for many occurs during the college years or later in the twenties and thirties, one begins to find spiritual authority within, instead of relying on peers, social conventions, and respected elders. At this time it's very common, natural, and understandable for the individual to say, "I'm spiritual, but not religious," not wanting to be part of any institution or under anyone's control. If one doesn't become an atheist or agnostic at this stage, God usually becomes distant or impersonal, and is described as Spirit or Natural Law or Life Force or Energy in the universe, but not as a person who answers prayers or intervenes directly in human affairs.

In the Interdependence stage (stage five)—reached by some, but not too many of us, starting in our mid-thirties or forties—there's an expressed need for community again, within which to place one's more fully evolved sense of self. God or Ultimate Reality is experienced paradoxically, so that many people at this stage, during crisis or celebration, can pray to God the person, even though they intellectually understand the divine to be an impersonal force in the universe. One can live with ambiguity and paradox at the Interdependence stage, while also looking for religious community, seeing the shortcomings of trying to go it completely alone. Stage six, reached only by the very few of us who are mystics, is that of Unity. Mystics tend to see God in all things and all things in God. They speak of having a direct experience of God, or of becoming fully enlightened, and ironically they can usually talk more easily with mystics of other religious traditions than with nonmystics within their own tradition. Relatively recent examples may be the Catholic monk Thomas Merton, Hindu saint Mohandas Gandhi, or the current (Buddhist) Dalai Lama, Tenzin Gyatso. Historically, we might think of people such as the Christian contemplatives Teresa of Avila and Julian of Norwich, Muslim Sufi poets Rumi and Al-Ghazali, and Jewish Kabbalist rabbis Isaac Luria and Israel ben Eliezer.

Most college students find themselves either in the Dependence or Independence stage of faith development. The tension between these two stages can cause considerable stress and strain, I've discovered, not only internally for individuals but also among people. For example, I knew a Protestant Christian student, who I believed was at the Independence stage, who explained that he no longer felt comfortable or welcome at most Christian worship services. He saw Jesus as a great historical teacher and exemplar, but not as identical with God and not as his personal Lord and Savior. When he expressed these thoughts, he got into arguments and felt excluded by many other Christians. Institutional religion generally seemed rigid and judgmental, pietistic and moralistic to him. Rejecting dogma and doctrine, he said, "There's a river of spirit deep within each of us that can't be named, that's completely non-denominational, and that doesn't require any labels like 'God' and 'Jesus.' There's no one right way to find that river and get into its flow."

I wouldn't be surprised if this same Christian, years from now, might open up to his institutional religion and newly accept much of the dogma and doctrine of his once-rejected faith. That doesn't necessarily mean that he'll have reentered the Dependence stage. The Interdependence stage has been called a "second naïveté,"[11] because religious symbols become sacred once again and are found to have new power. Like the onion-peeling effect of discovering symbolic depth in great literature, adults at the Interdependence stage are able to read scripture, for example, appropriately at the literal, allegorical, historical, conceptual, poetic, and inspirational levels. Religiously, people at the Interdependence stage are also open to dialogue between different religious traditions because they understand that truth is multidimensional. Any particular religious symbol, myth, or ritual is necessarily limited and incomplete, bound by the follower's personal and cultural experiences.[12]

ATHEIST STRAW MEN?

The authors of the current atheist books write as if they're unaware of the fact that all people naturally go through different stages of faith during their lifetimes. They cite none of the developmental psychologists who are doing work in this area, and their own definitions of religion and of God are limited to the stages that arise primarily during childhood and early adolescence, even as these atheists appear to be at stage four (Independence) themselves. It almost seems as if they're deliberately setting up straw men whom they can easily destroy, without taking religion seriously at the level of respect that they demand for science and philosophy.

Richard Dawkins declares, "Though the details differ across the world, no known culture lacks some version of the time-consuming, wealth-consuming, hostility-provoking rituals, the anti-factual, counter-productive fantasies of religion."[13] He sets up his "God Hypothesis" in order to make the case that "God, in the sense defined, is a ... pernicious delusion."[14] The God Hypothesis states that there is "a supernatural agent who designed the universe and—at least in many versions of the hypothesis—maintains it and even intervenes in it with miracles, which are temporary violations of his own otherwise grandly immutable laws ... miracles, by definition, violate the principles of science."[15] This concept of God corresponds best to one of the first two stages of faith—those arising from approximately age two through twelve years old: "God" here combines elements of magic with an immediate cause-and-effect relationship to everyday events. This God is a powerful agent or actor intervening in history. Biblical stories of miracles are read literally.

Dawkins goes on to suggest that as a matter of evolution the "imaginary-friend" phenomenon of childhood "may be a good model for understanding theistic belief in adults."[16] He reminds us that as children many of us had imaginary friends. As an example, he reminds us of Binker, Christopher Robin's imaginary friend from the Winnie the Pooh series.[17]

When we're very young, imaginary friends provide us with companionship, consolation, and even counseling, Dawkins explains. Then, when we grow up, God takes on that role for us as companion and confidant.[18] Dawkins also notes that God, exactly like an imaginary friend, has the time and patience to devote to us when we are suffering in life, and does it in a way that is "much cheaper than psychiatrists or professional counselors."[19] So, from the perspective of developmental psychology, this notion of God is planted firmly in the first stage of faith development, Magic, which usually ends by about age seven!

Dawkins does briefly mention what I'd call a stage-four (Independence) religious understanding of God: the deist conception held by American founding fathers and mothers such as Thomas Jefferson, Benjamin Franklin, and John and Abigail Adams. As Dawkins puts it, "Compared with the Old Testament's psychotic delinquent, the deist God of the eighteenth-century Enlightenment is an altogether grander being...a physicist to end all physics, the alpha and omega of mathematicians, the apotheosis of designers; a hyper-engineer who set up the laws and constants of the universe, fine-tuned them with exquisite precision and foreknowledge, detonated what we would now call the hot big bang, retired and was never heard from again."[20] This understanding is not of God as a person who intervenes directly and immediately in human affairs but as the distant creator of what becomes Natural Law. In that sense, the deist God is still tangentially part of the God Hypothesis to be disproved, since it assumes a supreme intelligence that created the universe. Dawkins is not particularly interested in this conception of God, though, since it currently has so few adherents.

There's another stage-four perception of God that both interests and troubles him. He does feel this view deserves respect. It's "the God of Einstein" and certain "other enlightened scientists," primarily physicists, as I mentioned in chapter 3. This is not a supernatural being but God in Nature. God is perceived as the order and harmony in all that exists. Dawkins, however, wants physicists and other scientists to stop using the word "God" in this sense. He claims it becomes confusing, because for so many people God is a supernatural being. As I described in chapter 3, he makes crystal clear what he means by the God that he has set up to disprove: "the interventionist, miracle-wreaking, thought-reading, sin-punishing, prayer-answering, God of the Bible, of priests, mullahs and rabbis and of ordinary language."[21] This God surely doesn't touch the "river of spirit deep within each of us that can't be named" that inspired the stage-four Christian college student I've described. So, stage-four awareness of God is ruled out by Dawkins (not to mention stages five and six), and we are back to understandings grounded in the earlier stages of faith development.

Daniel Dennett puts another spin on this and rules out all understandings of God in the later stages of faith development entirely. Rather self-servingly, it seems, he labels everyone beyond stage three as atheists! As I mentioned in chapter 3, he claims that "If what you hold sacred is not any kind of Person you could pray to, or consider to be an appropriate recipient of gratitude (or anger, when a loved one is senselessly killed), you're an atheist in my book."[22] He goes the next step and claims that we're not even talking about religion anymore: "If what they call God is really *not* an agent in their eyes, a being that can *answer* prayers, *approve* and *disapprove, receive* sacrifices, and *mete out* punishment or forgiveness, then, although they may call this being God, and stand in awe of it (not *Him*), their creed, whatever it is, is not really a religion according to my definition."[23] So much for those founding fathers and mothers of America whom I've mentioned. Before he's done, Dennett has called an Episcopal bishop and a priest he knows "atheists" and implied that they are cowards for not admitting it from the pulpit: "It would never do to upset the fragile fiction that 'we are not atheists' (heaven forbid!)."[24]

BELIEF VERSUS FAITH

Part of the problem with these atheists' understanding of religion may also be a confusion of "faith" and "belief." Sam Harris writes that "A man's faith is just a subset of his beliefs about the world."[25] He also defines "faith" as "nothing more than the license religious people give one another to keep believing when reasons fail."[26] Similarly, Richard Dawkins sees religious faith as "a persistent false belief held in the face of strong contradictory evidence."[27] A history lesson is in order here on the terms "faith" and "belief."

Wilfred Cantwell Smith produced a careful study of these two terms in his *Faith and Belief*. He explained in detail how it's a fundamental error to confuse faith with mere belief. He documents that when John Wycliffe translated the Bible into English for the first time, in the fourteenth century, "faith" and "belief" had the same meaning and were often used interchangeably. However, by the seventeenth century, when the King James Bible was published, "belief" had come to refer to a merely intellectual process or state. It had to do only with certain propositions held in the mind. It lacked the fullness of the term "faith" that referred to a total response of the whole person to the transcendent, including how one feels, how one acts, and how one celebrates. "Belief" was therefore used only once in the entire King James translation.[28]

With the eighteenth-century Enlightenment, rational conceptualization became the major mode of understanding and insight, and this was applied to religion as much as it was to the natural world through science and to the human community through political liberalism. People began to privilege the mind over the rest of our being. "I think therefore I am," Descartes had said. Christian discussion too began to be centered not as much on the experience of the transcendent beyond us or of our soul deep within us, but instead on certain propositions about God that could be debated and organized into systematic statements or theologies.[29]

By the nineteenth century, "belief" was not just an important religious and secular category; it was understood that "believing" is primarily what Christians do.[30] For secular rationalists, this had the effect of reducing faith to manageability in their own terms. Instead of understanding faith as a complete response of the human personality, faith could be limited to the optional mental processes and conceptual frameworks of religious people. In essence, faith became reduced to this in the secular mind: "Given the uncertainty of God, as a fact of modern life, so-and-so reports that the idea of God is part of the furniture of his mind."[31]

Unlike an earlier form of knowing, "believing" also lost its connection to reality. People could "believe" that which was untrue, and that is how those who were skeptical of religious people came to see them.[32] As Smith puts it, for secularizing culture, "The concept [of belief] served as an inherently irreligious interpretation of a phenomenon that it could not authentically appreciate. To imagine that religious people "believe" this or that is a way of dominating intellectually, and comfortably, what in fact one does not truly discern."[33] Ironically, the Christian church became a willing accomplice in this development, partly because of how much it had been influenced by the larger culture for more than a century, but also because the question "what do they believe?" allowed Western Christians to disparage other religious traditions as untrue—other traditions that these Christians were learning more about in the ongoing age of colonization.[34]

By the twentieth and twenty-first centuries, this whole development had become largely unconscious. For example, one can now pick up a Random House dictionary and find that the first entry for the word "belief" is "an opinion or conviction" and the example given is "the belief that the earth is flat." So a dictionary reader learns right off the bat that "belief" connotes something that is false or wrong.[35] The emphasis on "belief" in religion has also created a barrier to faith for many who might otherwise be religious, especially with waning intellectual intelligibility in much of the church. Like the schoolboy who quipped that "Faith is believing what you know ain't so," many sensitive, thoughtful people have been needlessly turned away from Christianity.[36] That has not been true in the same way for Judaism, though, because for Jews faith is defined much more by practice than by belief—Are you living an ethical life? Keeping the great commandments of the Torah? Gathering together in community and telling the stories of the Jewish people? Keeping kosher or lighting candles at home on Friday night or having a Passover seder or going to high holiday services every year, if not to synagogue every Sabbath? That's how faith is experienced and expressed: through *orthopraxy* (right action) much more than *orthodoxy* (right belief).[37]

Meanwhile, through the emphasis on "belief" in Christianity, attention to faith as the primary religious category has suffered deeply. For religion is not just a set of propositions in one's mind. It's something you sing and dance and eat and pray. It's enmeshed in art and literature and architecture and drama—in symbols and myths and rites and liturgy. It has to do with vocation and morality and character. It's experienced through taste and smell and sight and touch and hearing, not just thinking. It's a matter of heart as much as head. As Smith proclaims, faith includes recognizing "the goodness of a cup of cold water given in love or the horrendous evil of Auschwitz, the glory of a sunset or a cherry blossom."[38] It's an utter travesty to reduce faith to a "subset of beliefs about the world."[39]

It needs to be clearly affirmed that faith as a quality of the whole person also has an intellectual dimension. It requires valid insights into the nature of the universe and it requires personal intellectual integrity and sincerity. The Dalai Lama represented that kind of intellectual honesty, for example, when he said publicly in a visit to Stanford in 2005 that if scientific evidence clearly refutes any tenets of Buddhism, then those Buddhist tenets will have to be rejected and Buddhism will have to change.[40] For academics like me who teach in a university, faith of course includes an attitude toward truth and the will to know and understand. It's not enough to sing and preside over liturgy and have my own heart touched. I must also conceptualize my faith and communicate it to others, as well as listen openly and attentively to their religious ideas, applying my mind to all they say. For, as Wilfred Cantwell Smith has insisted, religious conceptualizing must, "if it is to be *faithful,* be *the closest approximation to the truth of which one's mind is capable.*"[41]

WORLD THEOLOGY

"Theology" is the term that has been used historically for intellectual conceptualizing of faith. Huge tomes have been produced in the Christian world by the likes of Augustine (*De Doctrina Christiana* in the fourth century), Thomas Aquinas (*Summa Theologica* in the thirteenth century), and Paul Tillich (*Systematic Theology* in the twentieth century), along with parallel efforts in other religious traditions. Smith, however, speaks of humankind as having arrived at a historical moment when we should now finally be able to understand that all humankind is one—we are all crew on spaceship earth, our lives are interdependent, and our fate is in our collective hands. He sees an emerging consciousness around the world that we are all heirs to the entire religious history of the human race. Therefore, we must begin to theologize, or intellectualize our faith, in terms of that entire history and not just in relation to our own tradition, whether it is Christianity, Judaism, Islam, Hinduism, Buddhism, Greco-Roman humanism, or something else. In this era, we must be doing *world theology.*

One of the reasons is that we now know how religions have been deeply intertwined for thousands of years, even though that fact isn't always recognized when practicing one's own tradition. Take the Roman Catholic devotional practice of using the rosary, for instance. Christians lived for a thousand years without the use of prayer beads, but then adopted them from the Muslims around the time of the Crusades. As any visitor to the Middle East knows, the Islamic use of prayer beads remains widespread now. But the earliest documented use of these kinds of beads was actually in India among Hindus. Buddhism, which began around 500 B.C. in India, then picked up this practice and took it eastward through Tibet and China to Japan. (The Tibetan Buddhist Dalai Lama came to Stanford with prayer beads in his hands.) Later, Muslims picked up the practice from Hindus and moved it westward into the holy lands of Palestine, where the Christians eventually adopted it as the rosary.[42]

Religions have been intertwined in their ideas as well as their practice. For example, the idea of the devil has a world history,[43] having first arisen in Zoroastrianism in sixth-century B.C. Persia. This destructive fiend, according to Zoroaster, was able to defile the good lord's creation, and human beings were caught in a continuous cosmic battle between good and evil. The idea of the devil made its way into Judaism, where it's seen, for example in the book of Job. As described in the last chapter, Satan kills Job's animals, servants, and children and then inflicts Job himself with terrible sores from head to foot—all in a challenge to God that this blameless and upright man's faith can be broken. Later in Christianity, the devil takes on other names—Lucifer and Beelzebub. The devil is then incorporated into Manicheanism in the third century A.D. By the time of the Islamic Qur'an in the seventh century A.D., the tempter of Eve is described explicitly as Satan,[44] rather than as the serpent that was used in the pre-Zoroastrian story of the Garden of Eden in Genesis.[45]

Emerging in the modern era is a more generalized awareness of the history of other religious communities and of world history as a whole. Smith expects that eventually each group will self-consciously participate in the religious history of humankind as the context for faith. Christians will not cease to be Christians or Buddhists to be Buddhists, but will understand the dynamic concept of a Christian strand or a Buddhist strand in the religious history of the world; hence, they will participate self-consciously as Christians and Buddhists in a world process of religious convergence. They will participate in what is ultimately the only true community—the worldwide and history-long community of humankind.

Therefore, a world theology cannot be a Christian or Hindu or Muslim theology of the "other religions." On the one hand, it would not be valid if it were not at least Christian, Hindu, Muslim, etc., although it must be more. This world theology must be written by theologians who know people from all traditions as members of one community—a community in which he or she also participates. The task of such a theology is to interpret and to intellectualize our multiform faith.[46]

This may seem like pie-in-the-sky as Jewish Israelis battle Muslim Palestinians and vice versa, as Hindus and Buddhists continue to war with one another in Sri Lanka, and as different kinds of Christians have butchered each other in Europe—most recently in Northern Ireland and the former Yugoslavia. This world theology is not very realistic, it might be said, when you think concretely about Friday afternoon Muslim prayers, Saturday morning Jewish services, and Sunday mass. Very academic. Very heady—head in the clouds, that is.

Please note, however, that theology has never been the province of the majority of religious people. First of all, in practical terms it's always been unrealistic for any Christian to suppose that he or she could write a theology acceptable to all Christians, even within a particular denomination. Or for a Muslim to write a theology acceptable to all Muslims, even within a particular sect like the Sunni or Shiite. Generally it has only been academically oriented Christians and Muslims who have read or studied theology anyway. Nonetheless, writing a theology intended for all Christians or all Muslims has been valid as an ideal. Similarly, a world theology, when constructed, should be cogent for and acceptable to all humankind as an ideal.[47]

We now live in a thoroughly pluralistic reality, radically different from that of many of our ancestors, who never knew much beyond their Shinto or Taoist or Christian contexts. As Smith notes, "We are learning each other's languages, both literally and figuratively."[48] We have an increasingly common consciousness of the world around us. We are faced with the challenge to collaborate in building and saving a world very much at risk[49] from environmental desolation and nuclear destruction, not to mention various holy wars and genocides. It's ultimately global suicide for us to speak in terms of "we" versus "they," rather than in terms of a worldwide "we" (albeit within "we" there's enormous and precious diversity). It's no longer possible to develop a Christian theology or a Muslim theology or a Hindu theology without taking into account the other traditions and their understandings and insights.

How do we do this? It has to emerge from dialogue among the traditions and not from one person embedded (regardless of their openness to others) within his or her own tradition.[50] And a world theology can't come from people who aren't religious practitioners within some tradition themselves, because subjective insight is as critical as objective knowing. One must have a personal life of faith to understand faith more broadly, one must know what it's like to worship God to explore how others do so, and one must have participated in ritual to speak about its role in human life. Otherwise, this would be like developing a theory of art without ever experiencing a painting or piece of sculpture, explaining music without ever singing or playing an instrument oneself, or at least hearing a piece performed. Objective knowledge—about the history of one's own religious traditions and those of others, about the psychology of religious experience, about the relationship of religion to politics, to name a few areas—is important as well. Knowledge in the domain of the humanities develops through the constant interplay of the subjective and the objective.[51]

The way that Smith encourages us to develop a world theology can be seen by what he did in the religious centers he started and directed. When he founded the McGill Institute of Islamic Studies in 1952, Smith insisted that half of the students and faculty be practicing Muslims and that the other half come from other traditions.[52] This was radical in two ways. In the early 1950s, almost all of the study of Islam in North America was being done by non-Muslims. Decrying "orientalism" long before Palestinian scholar Edward Said,[53] Smith insisted that Islam couldn't be understood without active dialogue, day in and day out, with practicing Muslims. On the other hand, he felt it was important that all traditions be held up to objective analysis by outsiders as well. So, Muslim students and scholars needed the perspective of non-Muslims to understand their faith fully. Subjective and objective must go hand in hand. Every afternoon at four o'clock, Smith would ring a bell and call all members of the institute to assemble for tea. It was a mandatory gathering. There East and West met to discuss Islam and resolve misunderstandings.[54] Similarly, when he directed Harvard's Center for the Study of World Religions, he established a "common room" where students of different religions and nationalities were asked routinely to gather and discuss their worldviews together.[55]

A world theology must emerge from within a concept of a global "we," even though "we" have very different individual and community-based forms of faith. "Not they, not you, but some of *us* are Buddhist, some Muslim, some Jewish, some skeptic, some confused."[56] On the other hand, a world theology must be recognizable within each of the traditions, without trying to displace them with some sort of transcendent universalism. It must emerge from genuine dialogue among practitioners and scholars of the various religions, and it cannot be created by any one of them outside of that interaction.[57] The verification principle for a world theology would be twofold: (1) Does it do justice to the objective facts of human religious history in general? (2) Does it do justice to the particular faith, experience, and insight of Buddhists, Zoroastrians, Confucians, Jews, and the others?[58]

What does this mean practically and pragmatically for Christians today? First, Smith asks us to remain firmly rooted in our own traditions, learning as much about them and practicing them as fully as we can, while at the same time understanding ourselves as part of a global "we," rather than separating ourselves from the "other" or the "outsider" as a "them." Most people in the world have a basic experience of "faith" as a common human attribute of finding sense, purpose, and meaning in life. Yet, like love, it comes in very different forms. We need to be steeped in our own way. But then, we can benefit in our own faith from learning about different forms of faith, just as we can benefit from reading love poetry or stories from many different cultures.

Second, a basic way to engage in dialogue with people of differing traditions is through empathetic listening. Put yourself in the other person's shoes as much as possible as you hear what they have to say, or try to participate in their practices. In an exchange, be able to summarize what your discussion partner or partners said to you well enough that they could say, "Yes, that's it. You've understood me (or us)." Modeling careful listening creates a context for oneself to be understood as well.

Third, take the process of developing a world theology seriously, for in it may lie the salvation of this earth and all who live on it. The world has grown too small for us to live in ignorance of and lack of respect for each other. Violence has grown too brutal, and with nuclear weapons too terminal, to allow it to be used as a way to resolve our problems and differences. Religion is too important and too precious to allow it to divide us rather than to build community, to degrade us rather than to make us fully human. In the words of the Finlandia hymn, "For other hearts in other lands are beating with hopes and dreams as true and high as [ours]...For other lands have sunlight too, and clover, and skies are everywhere as blue as [ours]."[59]

SEVEN

TALKING TO ATHEISTS AND CHRISTIAN CONSERVATIVES

You will know the truth, and the truth will make you free.

—John 8:32

Do not judge, so that you may not be judged.

—Matthew 7:1

Blessed are the peacemakers, for they will be called children of God.

—Matthew 5:9

The atheists I've mentioned also have faith, in my view, and should be part of the process of developing a world theology. Richard Dawkins has a strong sense of awe for the natural order; he speaks of the "transcendent wonder" of the universe.[1] Daniel Dennett explains that letting one's *self* go—letting one's "own mundane preoccupations...shrink to *proper* size, not all that important in the greater scheme of things"—may be one of the best secrets of life.[2] Sam Harris writes that "Each of us has to get out of bed in the morning and live his life, and we do this in a context of uncertainty, and in the context of terrible certainties, like the certainty of death. This positive disposition, this willingness to set a course in life without any assurance that things will go one's way, is occasionally called 'faith'...Let me state for the record that I see nothing wrong with this kind of faith."[3]

American liberal Christians need to find a way to bridge the gap in what's so often described in our press as the culture war between the religious right and the secular left. We need to have meaningful dialogue with atheists, just as we do with Christian conservatives. There's a lot that people at each end of this spectrum have to say that's important to hear. That includes criticism aimed directly at liberal Christians.

CHRISTIAN RESPONSIBILITY FOR VIOLENCE

Sam Harris in his book *The End of Faith* claims that "The greatest problem confronting civilization is not merely religious extremism: rather, it is the larger set of cultural and intellectual accommodations we have made to faith itself. Religious moderates are, in large part, responsible for the religious conflict in our world, because their beliefs provide the context in which scriptural literalism and religious violence can never be adequately opposed."[4] Daniel Dennett in his *Breaking the Spell* claims that religious liberals are maintaining an "attractive nuisance," like a swimming pool in one's back yard which is dangerous in its potential to attract and kill children: "Those who maintain religions, and take steps to make them more attractive, must be held similarly responsible for the harms produced by some of those whom they attract and provide with a cloak of respectability...Al Qaeda and Hamas terrorism is still Islam's responsibility, and abortion-clinic bombing is still Christianity's responsibility...and the fact that you don't belong to a congregation or denomination that is offending doesn't excuse you: it is Christianity and Islam...that are attractive nuisances, not just their offshoot sects."[5]

I'm afraid there's a lot of truth in these atheist claims. In *The End of Faith,* along with criticizing Islamic extremism, Sam Harris delineates horrendous details of the Spanish Inquisition, English and American witchhunts, and the Nazi Holocaust, chronicling religious justifications for them in the name of Christ.[6] In a later book, *Letter to a Christian Nation,* Harris exclaims, "If you think that Jesus taught only the Golden Rule and love of one's neighbor, you should reread the New Testament."[7] One biblical passage he quotes, taken from Paul's second letter to the Thessalonians, explains what will happen upon Christ's return to earth in the second coming "when the Lord Jesus is revealed from heaven with his mighty angels in flaming fire, inflicting vengeance upon those who do not know God and upon those who do not obey the gospel of our Lord Jesus. These will suffer the punishment of eternal destruction."[8] Bracing, eh?

But that passage has to do with the second coming. What about Jesus' first coming—his life here on earth 2,000 years ago? Here's one of his claims in the gospel of Luke: "I came to bring fire to the earth...Do you think that I have come to bring peace to the earth? No, I tell you, but rather division...father against son...mother against daughter."[9] The parallel passage in the gospel of Matthew reads: "I have not come to bring peace, but a sword. For I have come to set a man against his father and a daughter against her mother...and one's foes will be members of one's own household."[10]

What worse kind of division, violence, and suffering could be contemplated than members of one's own family and household being set against one another, by Jesus Christ no less? And, of course, this has actually happened many painful times since Jesus uttered those words. So, Sam Harris's words have an urgent and compelling ring when he says, "That so much...suffering can be directly attributed to religion ... is what makes the honest criticism of religious faith a moral and intellectual necessity."[11]

When I consulted a biblical commentary to help make sense of Jesus as a sword-wielding family destroyer, here's some of what I found: "One cannot have the kind of fidelity to truth [that Jesus called for]...and not find oneself at odds, and sometimes at war, with the world[12]...[Jesus'] doctrine is either true or untrue...Neutrality is not possible: We are either for him or against him, and between the two camps there is inevitable clash. Why should not the gospel come peaceably? Because...antichrist is always intent to defeat Christ...[Jesus's] gift is...not peace by compromise or evasion. It is peace by strife (strife between the good and evil in us and in our world)."[13] So, it's not surprising that hymns are sung in Christian churches with lyrics like this: "Onward, Christian soldiers, marching as to war, with the cross of Jesus going on before. Christ, the royal Master, leads against the foe; forward into battle see his banners go!"[14] Even better known is the "Battle Hymn of the Republic" by Julia Ward Howe:

Mine eyes have seen the glory of the coming of the Lord;
He is trampling out the vintage where the grapes of wrath are stored;
He hath loosed the fateful lightning of His terrible swift sword;
His truth is marching on.
Glory! Glory! Hallelujah!...His truth is marching on.[15]

We don't need to be historians to recall the rise of the triumphal Christian church behind Constantine's sword,[16] the bloody Crusades in which Roman Catholics slaughtered Orthodox Christians and Jews as well as Muslims,[17] and the use of Christian just war doctrine to rationalize countless conflagrations, including President Bush's justification of the war in Iraq.[18] In his 2003 state of the union address, two months before the U.S. invasion, George W. Bush delineated Christian just war criteria and ended his speech with these words: "We Americans have faith in ourselves, but not in ourselves alone. We do not know, we do not claim to know, all the ways of Providence, yet we can trust in them, placing our confidence in the loving God, behind all of life and all of history. May he guide us now, and may God continue to bless the United States of America."[19]

Of course, it's often said that religion is merely a smoke screen used to cover actions taken for political, economic, social, cultural, racial, and ethnic reasons. It's claimed that you can't blame religion for natural human tendencies toward greed and domination on the one hand and fear and defensiveness on the other. Yet, there's solid academic evidence that religion is itself a root cause of conflict and violence.[20] For example, a group of scholars led by David Little at the U.S. Institute of Peace concluded that "One must see contemporary religious violence as an expression of tendencies always present in the religious life of humanity."[21] It's no excuse to say that religion gets manipulated and perverted to violent ends by false prophets and unholy followers, nor that its original essence has been lost when it becomes violent.

Instead, Little and others ask us to look at how part of religion's special genius lies in its ability to provide persons and groups with a sense of identity or a "place in the universe." In doing this, though, religion frequently divides human communities into an "in" group and an "out" group. In conflict situations, distinctions between those who are "in" and those who are "out" are often heightened to the point of demonizing the other. Sunni and Shiite Muslims in Iraq have both said that the other can never be trusted, nor can the non-Muslim Americans. Abetted by their clergy and religious communities, many tell stories of appalling atrocities and acts of torture targeting them by the other supposedly heretical and alien groups. Violent action then becomes legitimated in struggles with these "others," almost always framed in defensive terms even though it might look thoroughly aggressive to an objective observer. This action becomes accentuated when connected to land, to the need or "right" to dominate within a given territory, like a Greater Serbia for Orthodox Christians, a Buddhist Sri Lanka, a Jewish promised land of Israel, a Muslim Saudi Arabia, and a Protestant Christian America—as it used to be said—united coast-to-coast through a doctrine of Manifest Destiny. There have been historical occasions when both Christians and Muslims have made religious claims to the entire world, and in direct conflict with each other at that.[22]

As Sam Harris explains, and certain gospel passages would seem to confirm, "The danger of religious faith is that it allows otherwise normal human beings to reap the fruits of madness and consider them *holy*. Because each new generation of children is taught that religious propositions need not be justified in the way that all others must, civilization is still besieged by the armies of the preposterous. We are, even now, killing ourselves over ancient literature. Who could have thought something so tragically absurd could be possible?"[23] How could we not agree with Harris that this is absurd and tragic?

So what do liberal Christians, who are not biblical literalists or religious exclusivists, make of Jesus saying that he came not to bring peace but a sword? First, let me place the statement in the context of its own apocalyptic era. For at least two hundred years before and after Jesus, many in the ancient Middle East wrongly thought the world was coming to an end very soon, within a generation.[24] There was a particular and peculiar urgency, then, to live in the proper way oneself so as to be part of the imminent coming of the kingdom of God, even if one's parents, children, and other household members had a different moral code or religious orientation. Second, Jesus's words need to be understood within his dominant message, still critically relevant today. That message is manifest in many other things he said much more often as the Prince of Peace, including these words from the Sermon on the Mount, for example:

Blessed are the meek, for they will inherit the earth...Blessed are the merciful, for they will receive mercy...Blessed are the peacemakers, for they will be called children of God...[I]f anyone strikes you on the right cheek, turn the other also...Love your enemies and pray for those who persecute you, so that you may be children of your Father in heaven...[I]f you forgive others their trespasses, your heavenly Father will also forgive you...Do not judge, so that you may not be judged...Why do you see the speck in your neighbor's eye, but do not notice the log in your own eye?...In everything do to others as you would have them do to you; for this is the law and the prophets.[25]

As noted in chapter 2, Jesus's great innovation in the history of religion was the central emphasis he put on love—what it means to love unconditionally, even unto death; how to love not just one's neighbor but one's enemy and persecutor; how not to take an eye for an eye and a tooth for a tooth;[26] what it means to reach out to hated foreigners, tax collectors, adulterers, lepers; why one should feed the hungry, welcome the stranger, clothe the naked, care for the sick and visit the prisoners. It would be radically unfair to claim that Jesus advocated divisiveness, violence, or bigotry in the name of his religion.

Here's more of what the biblical commentary I cited earlier says: "We are reminded by this passage of the paradox that the peacemaker may, despite all of his efforts, be the occasion of conflict. Jesus is...above all the peacemaker, the reconciler [and yet he is horribly tortured and then crucified]...The Christian who faithfully bears witness to Christ will be the victim of an inescapable amount of misunderstanding and hostility, no matter how gentle and tactful he may be, and in some periods and crises he will face actual persecution...But there is no justification here for the war method—not while the Sermon on the Mount remains."[27]

Yet, Sam Harris reminds us, it's more than partially true that "The most monstrous crimes against humanity have invariably been inspired by unjustified belief. This is nearly a truism."[28] An enormous amount of discrimination, brutality, inhumanity, and suffering could be eliminated by the end of faith, as Harris calls for, by eradicating religion from the earth once and for all. There are two small problems, however. The human species seems to be wired for religion. And much of what's most positive in life is also a product of religion. Harris admits both of these points, but he still thinks on balance we should work tirelessly to try to abolish religion, as we've largely been able to do with slavery and other once-common human institutions. My answer, instead, is to try to build up the positive elements of religion and weaken the negative. Practically speaking, I have no confidence that religion will ever disappear. Look at what's happened in countries that were officially atheist during the Soviet era and now have burgeoning religious communities. There are plenty of us who are sustained and fulfilled to our core by our religion. So the answer to bad religion can only be good religion.

What's good religion? Harris himself understands it: "We must find ways to invoke the power of ritual and to mark those transitions in every human life that demand profundity—birth, marriage, death—without lying to ourselves about the nature of reality . . . There is more to life than simply understanding the structure and contents of the universe . . . Jesus and the Buddha weren't talking nonsense when they spoke about our capacity as human beings to transform our lives in rare and beautiful ways."[29] Elsewhere, Harris writes, "Faith enables many of us to endure life's difficulties with an equanimity that would be scarcely conceivable in a world lit only by reason . . . [S]piritual experience, ethical behavior, and strong communities are essential for human happiness."[30] I'm quoting Harris out of context here since he has a "but" for each of these statements that sends him back to atheism, even as I interpret his statements as the positive side of religion itself.

Yet, Harris distinguishes between spirituality, in which he feels he can personally participate as an atheist and a rationalist, and religion, which he feels is cultic and irrational. The foundational dimension of spirituality is the mystical consciousness that contemplatives have nurtured for thousands of years. A lot of evidence has been amassed about this kind of consciousness—neurological, philosophical, and literary. Mystical awareness helps us extinguish our own petty human egos while connecting us with the universe as a whole. He writes: "Man is manifestly *not* the measure of all things. This universe is shot through with mystery. The very fact of its being, and of our own, is a mystery absolute, and the only miracle worthy of the name." On the other hand, Harris sees religion as connected to various legends and folklore, which we don't need for a sense of awe and wonder in the universe. As he explains, "No tribal fictions need to be rehearsed for us to realize, one fine day, that we do, in fact, love our neighbors, that our happiness is inextricable from their own, and that our interdependence demands that people everywhere be given the opportunity to flourish."[31]

As a Christian minister, I look to Jesus, of course, to learn how to love, be nonviolent, and be happy. But I also look to modern Christian exemplars like Rosa Parks, Cesar Chavez, Delores Huerta, Dorothy Day, Desmond Tutu, Mother Teresa, and Joan Chittister. Ultimately, as it turns out, Sam Harris looks to the Buddha and other contemplatives who have their origin in India. This has gotten him in trouble with other atheists who claim he's religious after all. Harris insists that his own spirituality or even mysticism is thoroughly rational, empirical, and scientifically based.[32] I believe mine is too—as well as mythical and storied and poetic.

I hope that a bridge can be built between liberal Christians and thoughtful, articulate atheists like Sam Harris on the issue of religious violence. Then we can spend less time defining and defending our spiritual or religious territory and much more time doing what's truly important: together standing up to religious extremism, religious violence, and religious terror, so that we can help save the world for all of us.

RATIONAL RELIGION

Part of the problem is that religion is so often seen as irrational by those inside it as well as by those on the outside. Daniel Dennett's *Breaking the Spell* is dedicated to breaking the spell of religion that, he believes, holds much of the world captive to preposterous and often dangerous irrationality. He subtitles his book *Religion as a Natural Phenomenon* and attempts to trace its evolutionary history, with both negative and positive adaptive value for the human race. He calls for elimination of *super*naturalism in religion, which he believes is the enemy of truth, of rational dialogue between people, and ultimately of human and ecological harmony for the earth as a whole. In the end, Dennett's project has to do with saving the world, plain and simple. I think it's critically important that we listen to much of what he's recommending.

I knew Dennett, a philosophy professor at Tufts University near Boston, and I had personal conversations with him about religion during the sixteen years that I was the university chaplain there in the 1980s and 1990s. I was particularly fascinated by his 1991 book, *Consciousness Explained,* and used to kid him that it proved he was actually a closet Buddhist.

Dennett is deeply bothered, to the point of exasperation, by people who unapologetically take things on blind faith, without subjecting them to logical, scientific, and historical confirmation. He observes that "blind faith secures its own perpetuation by the simple unconscious expedient of discouraging rational inquiry,"[33] thereby rendering the ideal of truth-seeking and truth-telling its victim. Blind faith also often leads to fanaticism that injures others. Furthermore, he asks, how could any God worth worshipping possibly be pleased by unreasoning veneration when we humans have been given the most advanced brains on the planet and the capability of using them?[34]

Similarly, Rev. William Sloane Coffin Jr. used to condemn blind belief by saying, "It is right to be stabbed by doubt...It's wrong to require certitude to the point of blind stupidity. And it is dangerous. If God is like a marine sergeant who has been handed a bunch of hopeless recruits, then those who believe in such a God will become soldiers prepared to do almost anything they're told, no matter what, no matter to whom."[35] Coffin went on to say that "Christians have to listen to the world as well as to the Word—to science, to history, to what reason and our own experience tell us. We do not honor the higher truth we find in Christ by ignoring truths found elsewhere."[36]

In fact, in all three gospels in which Jesus repeats the part of the Shema[37] (the daily Jewish prayer) relating to loving God, he makes a significant addition. The traditional formulation found in the Torah reads "You shall love the Lord your God with all your heart, and with all your soul, and with all your might,"[38] to which he adds the words "with all your mind." Jesus was not the first Jewish teacher to note that one must use one's mind in relation to God, not just one's heart, soul, and might. Rabbi Hillel, for example, the greatest spiritual and ethical leader of his generation, who died twenty years before Jesus's ministry began,[39] insisted that "An ignorant man cannot be saintly."[40] Faith cannot be blind.[41]

Dennett compares religious faith to falling in love.[42] "But, sad to say, even if it is true that nothing could matter more than love, it wouldn't follow from this that we don't have reason to question the things that we, and others, love. Love is blind, as they say, and because love is blind, it often leads to tragedy."[43] He asks us to imagine loving music more than anything else: "I [then] should be able to live my life in pursuit of the exaltation of music, the thing I love most, with all my heart and soul." But that love and life pursuit do not endow him with the right to compel his children to practice musical instruments, or to impose musical education on everyone, or to threaten others who do not share his love of music. Dennett continues, "If my love of music is so great that I am simply unable to consider its implications objectively, then this is an unfortunate disability, and...I cannot rationally participate in the assessment of my own behavior and its consequences."[44] In other words, love should not compel us to abandon reason.

Dennett has been criticized for not recognizing that he has the kind of faith in science that many religious people have in the dogma of their tradition. For example, he desperately wants people to understand and accept evolutionary theory because he believes "that their salvation may depend on it" by alerting them to "the dangers of pandemics, degradation of the environment, and loss of biodiversity, and...some of the foibles of human nature." But he sees a major difference between his belief in evolution as the path to salvation and belief in a religion. "We who love evolution do not honor those whose love of evolution prevents them from thinking clearly and rationally about it!...In our view, there is no safe haven for mystery or incomprehensibility. Yes, there is humility, and awe, and sheer delight, at the glory of the evolutionary landscape, but it is not accompanied by, or in the service of, a willing (let alone thrilling) abandonment of reason."[45]

Similarly, Dennett explains that beliefs about the truths of physics, from theories about gravity to atoms to relativity, is "a place where the rubber meets the road" by comparison to claimed religious truths. Some religious people may believe that they've been made miraculously invulnerable to arrows or may give all their belongings away in anticipation of the imminent End of the World. But beliefs in physics must be relied upon to build bridges that don't collapse and to construct spacecraft that can fly people safely to the moon and back.[46] Rationality is critical to human life and its flourishing.

So, where does this leave religion? Dennett reminds us that "Many deeply religious people have all along been eager to defend their convictions in the court of reasonable inquiry and persuasion...Every religion—aside from a negligible scattering of truly toxic cults—has a healthy population of ecumenical-minded people who are eager to reach out to people of other faiths, or no faith at all, and consider the moral quandaries of the world on a rational basis."[47] He cites, for example, those who gathered at the Parliament of World Religions in Barcelona in 2004, carrying on a tradition that goes back to the first such meeting at the Chicago World's Fair in 1893.[48]

Dennett also reminds us how religious commitment has led to many good deeds throughout history, including ministering to the sick, feeding the hungry, and helping the suffering. Religion also provides community, which is particularly important for those who would otherwise be isolated, lonely, and alienated. This is not just a matter of charity for the needy. Religion has helped change the world as a matter of social justice.

There is also considerable evidence of religion being good for individual and public health, both physical and mental, from lowered heart attack rates to effects on eating disorders like anorexia and bulimia. Dennett cites "growing evidence that many religions have succeeded remarkably well on this score, improving both the health and morale of their members, quite independently of the good works they may have accomplished to benefit others...Moreover, the defenders of religion can rightly point to less tangible but more substantial benefits to their adherents, such as having a meaning for their lives provided!"[49]

Yet, the central and critical point that Dennett insists upon remains: Religion is the most prolific source of the "moral certainties" and "absolutes" that zealots depend on. Throughout the world, "people are dying and killing" in the name of blind faith and unapologetic irrationality.[50] Science and scientific methods, which among other things could lead to medical advances and ecological solutions, are under fire from scriptural literalists. Supernaturalism is creating false and dangerous reliance on supposed divine intervention through miracles and providential events, rather than encouraging human beings to roll up their sleeves and work together as stewards of the creation that we ourselves are destroying.

All of us—bright atheists and committed religionists—need to wake now and hear the earth call, in the words of one of my favorite hymns.[51] We need to give and receive as love shows us how, join with each pilgrim who quests for the true, give heed to the voices of the suffering, awaken our consciences with justice as our guide, and work toward a planet transformed by our care.

RECOVERING A SENSE OF WONDER AND AWE

One of the most successful of the best-selling atheist books has been *The God Delusion* by evolutionary biologist Richard Dawkins. He claims to be appealing to "lots of people out there who have been brought up in some religion or another, are unhappy in it, don't believe in it, or are worried about the evils that are done in its name." He believes that the living world is explained with great elegance by Charles Darwin's evolutionary theory of natural selection. And he asserts that "a proper understanding of the magnificence of the real world...can fill the inspirational role that religion has historically [held]."[52]

Dawkins admits that his atheistic scientific viewpoint has been seen by many as "empty and purposeless." He's been accused of presenting "a cold, bleak, joyless message of barren desolation."[53] This is not a new critique, as he points out in another book, *Unweaving the Rainbow*. He cites these lines from a poem by John Keats from the year 1820:

In the dull catalogue of common things.
Philosophy will clip an Angel's wings,
Conquer all mysteries by rule and line,
Empty the haunted air, and gnomed mine—
Unweave a rainbow[54]

Yet, Dawkins claims personally to be overwhelmed by the "transcendent wonder" of the universe.[55] He's concerned that so many religious people seem to have lost this sense of awe and wonder in the universe, replacing it with dry, mechanical ritual. "Why do humans fast, kneel, genuflect, self-flagellate, nod maniacally toward a wall, crusade, or otherwise indulge in costly practices that can consume life and, in extreme cases, terminate it?"[56] His words seem an echo of the transcendentalist Ralph Waldo Emerson, who wrote about the church of his day: "The doctrine of inspiration is lost...In how many churches...[are we] made sensible...that the earth and heavens are passing into [our] mind...We shrink as soon as the prayers begin, which do not uplift, but smite and offend us...The faith should blend with the light of rising and setting suns, with the flying cloud, the singing bird, and the breath of flowers. But now the priest's Sabbath has lost the splendor of nature; it is unlovely; we are glad when it is done."[57]

Dawkins points out how much of religion is devoted to dogmas, doctrines, and creeds that divide people from each other and from the natural world, to rituals that are exclusionary rather than inclusive, to belief in miracles that interfere with the natural order rather than the ability to glory in that order as it is. He's particularly concerned with the threat of biblical literalism to science education in our schools: "Fundamentalist religion is hell-bent on ruining the scientific education of countless thousands of innocent, well-meaning, eager young minds."[58] Understandably, this is an area in which he has a lot of passion: "As a scientist, I am hostile to fundamentalist religion because it actively debauches the scientific enterprise. It teaches us not to change our minds, and not to want to know exciting things that are available to be known. It subverts science and saps the intellect."[59]

I've spoken from the pulpit of the Stanford Memorial Church of how I'm filled with awe at the natural order of the universe. The fact that there are natural laws at all, which are discoverable through the scientific method and which are consistent and trustworthy and binding, fills me with feelings of amazement and gratitude and confidence. Those are religious or spiritual sentiments for me. Science is not the enemy but the companion and enabler of my faith in that natural order. What's not religious or what belittles the creation and its order for me is the claim that every so often a Supreme Being breaks in and violates the natural order of the universe for this or that reason (say, suspending gravity or reversing it so that someone who's jumped out a skyscraper window flies back in, or reversing time so that an accident that's already occurred never happened). What's awe-inspiring to me is the regularity and trustworthiness of the natural order, not periodic claims that it's been interrupted and altered for my benefit or yours, for this compelling reason or that.[60] It's atheists like Richard Dawkins that are doing the heavy lifting on this perspective now, and I'm grateful to them.

Liberal Christians need to reaffirm and publicize our understanding of scriptural passages that promote a deep sense of awe and wonder in the universe. We can start with the creation story in Genesis that ends with "And God saw that it was good."[61] The fifteenth chapter of Genesis uses the image of the array of all the stars in the sky, "if you are able to count them."[62] The Psalms are full of magnificent appreciation of the natural order in passages like this: "The heavens are telling the glory of God; and the firmament proclaims his handiwork."[63] Jesus uses imagery of naturally growing lilies of the field, explaining that "even Solomon in all his glory was not clothed like one of these."[64]

Yet, Dawkins, the atheist, pushes Christian liberals further as he cites astronomer Carl Sagan: "How is it that hardly any major religion has looked at science and concluded, 'This is better than we thought! The Universe is much bigger than our prophets said, grander, more subtle, more elegant?...A religion, old or new, that stressed the magnificence of the Universe as revealed by modern science might be able to draw forth reserves of reverence and awe hardly tapped by the conventional faiths."[65] Physicist Albert Einstein didn't believe in God as a supernatural person who intervened in the daily life of the world, but he said that "it suffices to stand in awe at the structure of the world, insofar as it allows our inadequate senses to appreciate it."[66] Dawkins is willing to call himself religious in this sense too, but he wants to be clear that he's a naturalist, not a supernaturalist.[67]

Dawkins wishes that he had written William Blake's famous stanza celebrating nature:

To see a world in a grain of sand
And a heaven in a wild flower
Hold infinity in the palm of your hand
And eternity in an hour.[68]

Yet, Dawkins explains that "The stanza can be read as all about science, all about standing in the moving spotlight [of the present moment], about taming space and time, about the very large built from the quantum graininess of the very small, a lone flower as a miniature of all evolution. The impulses to awe, reverence and wonder which led Blake to mysticism (and lesser figures to paranormal superstition...) are precisely those that lead others of us to science."[69]

I've personally been very moved to see how an atheist family I'm close to spends countless hours together—in what I can only call reverential awe and wonder—watching video after video of the Discovery Channel and BBC productions "Planet Earth," "The Life of Mammals," and "The Life of Birds." By contrast, I think of how much biblical literalists miss, for example, by claiming that the universe is only about six thousand years old. As Dawkins enthuses, "It is the inhuman age of fossils that knocks us back on our heels. We pick up a trilobite and the books tell us it is 500 million years old. But we fail to comprehend such an age, and there is a yearning pleasure in the attempt. Our brains have evolved to grasp the time-scales of our own lifetimes...We can cope with centuries. When we come to millennia—thousands of years—our spines begin to tingle...Epic myths of Homer...the Jewish heroes Abraham, Moses and David...Yet, on the time-scale of our trilobite, those vaunted antiquities are scarcely yesterday."[70] I wonder what my own childhood would have been like without spending countless hours studying and imagining the Jurassic world of the dinosaurs 200 million years ago?[71]

Dawkins laments that poets have largely "overlooked the goldmine of inspiration offered by science."[72] He cites the Romantic poet William Wordsworth who looked forward to a time when "The remotest discoveries of the chemist, the botanist, or mineralogist, will be as proper objects of the poet's art as any upon which it can be employed."[73] So I congratulate Richard Dawkins on his enthusiasm, awe, and wonder forged as an atheist in the realm of science alone. We religious people need more of his spirit. He's condemned by many believers simply because he's an atheist, supposedly trying to persuade others through a joyless message of barren desolation that life is meaningless.[74] He actually sees the world so differently: "Isn't it a noble, an enlightened way of spending our brief time in the sun, to work at understanding the universe and how we have come to wake up in it? . . . To put it the other way around, isn't it sad to go to your grave without ever wondering why you were born? Who, with such a thought would not spring from bed, eager to resume discovering the world and rejoicing to be a part of it?"[75]

DIALOGUE WITH CHRISTIAN CONSERVATIVES

Atheists often feel alienated and condemned by mainstream American culture, but I've certainly found that conservative Christians can experience alienation and condemnation of their own, especially in a university context like Stanford's. For one thing, there are those who claim such Christians don't have intellectual respectability. An article in the *Atlantic Monthly* at the beginning of this millennium, entitled "The Opening of the Evangelical Mind," explained that "Of all America's religious traditions, evangelical Protestantism, at least in its twentieth-century conservative forms, ranks dead last in intellectual stature."[76] Conservative Christianity has, of course, played its own role in this, going back to the Reverend Billy Sunday's famous statement that "When the word of God says one thing and scholarship says another, scholarship can go to hell."[77] Yet, as the *Atlantic* article explains, in recent years there's been a "determined effort" by a number of evangelical Christian institutions like Wheaton and Calvin Colleges, Pepperdine, Baylor, and Valparaiso Universities, and

Fuller Theological Seminary to "create a life of the mind."[78] Moreover, a number of evangelical scholars have left those institutions to find full academic acceptance at mainstream institutions like Yale, Harvard, and Princeton.[79]

Another reason evangelicals have felt marginalized and discriminated against in the context of higher education is that their beliefs can run them up against university policies with which they feel they cannot in good conscience comply. For example, the author of the *Atlantic* article, Alan Wolfe, described a class he attended in which a student "was close to tears as she talked about the efforts of student government at Tufts University to defund a conservative Christian organization because it excluded gays and lesbians from leadership positions."[80] This happened, incidentally, when I was the university chaplain at Tufts. As a liberal who's committed to academic freedom, freedom of belief, and freedom of association, I defended the conservative Christian group's right to exist on campus and receive funds, even though I adamantly opposed their stand on homosexuality.

But there's another group of Christians these days on campus who often feel disrespected and abused. They are liberal Christians. The Reverend Jim Burklo, long a campus minister at Stanford and now at the University of Southern California, wrote a book entitled *Open Christianity: Home by Another Road*. The first story he tells is about a Stanford student who e-mailed Jim that he needed some time to talk about some religious questions. "I transferred to Stanford because it's a long way from the college where I started out as a freshman. I needed to get away to keep my sanity," the e-mail said.

The student wasn't exceptionally religious. He supposed that he really wasn't all that much of a Christian. His roommate, however, was a fundamentalist, and invited him to a fellowship group. The student enjoyed the fellowship's company, and liked thinking about the soul. But he found it difficult to believe in the physical resurrection, to believe that every word of the Bible was literally true. After going to fellowship for a year, he came to believe that the group was right, that the "only way to salvation was through faith in Jesus as shown in the literal truth of the Bible." He believed that he was "damned to hellfire for eternity" because he would never be able to "step outside my rational mind and take that leap of faith."

The student was in crisis. He felt that he was having a kind of nervous breakdown. He "became depressed, obsessed with the damnation" of his soul. He struggled to study, to sleep, to eat. "Why bother with anything if I was going to hell anyway?" He felt that he was losing his mind. Eventually he made the bold decision to make a major change and transfer away from this decision that was causing him so much pain. He came to Stanford. But even though his life was now better in many ways, and some of the pressure had eased, he still felt confused. He wrote that "Faith still matters to me, but I don't know what to do about it."[81]

In his counseling with this student, Jim assured him that there was another understanding of Christianity—liberal or open Christianity—that didn't threaten him with damnation. Jim presented the Christian view of God in Jesus as a compassionate presence and as a liberator. He emphasized personal experience—outside in nature and inside in silent meditation, out in the world in social service work and back at Stanford in a small, nonjudgmental fellowship group—over a set of beliefs insisted upon by particular religious authorities (in this student's case, a doctrine that imperiled the student's very life, not only now but for all eternity). Jim also raised up intellectual doubt and rational inquiry as God-given capacities for approaching the world. He explained that Jesus was singularly uninterested in the doctrinal purity of the people he encountered along his road. Liberal Christianity, as Jim understands it, holds that the way we treat one another is much more important than the way we express our beliefs.[82]

How ironic that these two groups of Christians who feel disrespected and abused, conservatives and liberals, together represent most of Christianity! How ironic that each group feels oppressed primarily by the other group. Evangelical or conservative Christians often speak of the continuing hegemony of liberal Christians in centers of power in America, especially in higher education where evangelicals feel themselves silenced. Liberal Christians often speak of the power of the Christian right, especially in politics where liberals feel conservative values are being legislated against them from the local to the national level. Each group generally dislikes and distrusts the other, which it caricatures, if not demonizes, in the process. The lines between Christian denominations are barely important anymore by comparison to the lines within each denomination between conservatives and liberals. Often you'll find members of one group within a denomination saying that people in the other group aren't real or true Christians.

What would Jesus say about all this? His church was founded with the intent that his followers become one body of Christ in the world. Instead, Christian history has seen many Christian saints and prophets martyred at the hands of other Christians. War upon war has been fought with each side praying to Jesus Christ for the destruction of the other. Yet, the principal sacrament that Jesus left us, Christian communion or Eucharist, started around a common table and was given to us as a gift by which we might remember Jesus together. As Paul said in his first letter to the Corinthians: "Because there is one bread, we who are many are one body, for we all partake of the one bread."[83] The most important Christian sacrament is meant to bring all of us together in communion as Christians, body and soul, evangelical and liberal. So can't we stop beating up fellow Christians? Can't we stop insulting and wounding and throwing each other out? Can't we stop killing each other, literally and figuratively? Unfortunately, that's easier said than done. A lot of this probably seems like platitudes. What's the practical route to reconciliation between conservatives and liberals?

The first step, I'd say, has to be empathetic listening. That means starting out *not* by telling the other person what *you* think, but by listening carefully to what the *other* thinks, and feels, and does. Only after you've listened in this way should you speak, with the hope that the other person can put himself or herself completely into your shoes as well. Honest, often tough, dialogue follows. Hopefully each party will then know where they stand—without being susceptible to the likes of Christian killers such as David Koresh or Jim Jones, for there really are wrong ways to be a Christian. But for real dialogue to take place, I believe partners must leave at least 5 or 10 percent of themselves open to be deeply influenced, indeed changed, by the other.

This became clear in a series of dorm conversations that the Stanford Office for Religious Life and Stanford Associated Religions ran on campus after the release of Mel Gibson's film, *The Passion of the Christ*. It quickly became evident that students were seeing completely different films based on their own theological starting points. Many liberal Christians couldn't see beyond the violence that they felt they were working hard against in their daily lives. Conservative Christians were deeply moved by the portrayal of Christ's sacrifice on their behalf. Jews were offended by what they experienced as anti-Semitism in the film. Secularists wondered why anyone would find anything attractive in Christianity in the first place if this is what it's all about. We sent teams of one Christian and one Jewish professional into each dorm to guide student discussions.

What worked well were some basic ground rules that helped people to hear each other deeply, without judging or arguing or closing up. As a result, most students learned something new about the movie and also left with a more sensitive and nuanced understanding of other people's perspectives. Specifically, we asked that each participant briefly summarize the prior speaker's comments before contributing herself or himself, and not begin until the prior speaker affirmed that he or she had been understood. And we asked people to use only "I" statements in their own reactions. We made it clear that this was not a debate or a time for pointing fingers to criticize others. However, we did want students to express their own feelings, beliefs, and values clearly. Generally this seemed to work in creating and maintaining a respectful sense of community, allowing people to express themselves freely, and maximizing learning across significant difference.

A second step is respectful dialogue—how one refers to and speaks about another. A wonderful example of this kind of conversation between liberal and conservative Christian scholars is Marcus Borg's and N.T. Wright's book *The Meaning of Jesus: Two Visions*. They write that their book grew out of a decade and a half friendship pursuing "the fascinated study of Jesus within his historical context." They both went to Oxford University and studied under the same biblical scholar. They share Christian faith and practice. They have prayed together and taken Communion together. And yet they've been puzzled and disturbed by some of what they've found each saying about Jesus from their liberal and conservative perspectives. One thing they do agree on is this: "Debate about Jesus has recently been acrimonious, with a good deal of name-calling and angry polemic in both public and private discourse...we hope, and indeed pray, that in this book we will be able to model a way of conducting public Christian disagreement over serious and central issues that will inspire others to try the same sort of thing." In the end they say: "Though we have not, of course, reached agreement, we are satisfied that we have eliminated misunderstandings, that is, that neither of us has misrepresented the other. We offer the result to the reader as the celebration of shared friendship, faith, and scholarship."[84]

Borg and Wright constantly take account of each other in their individual chapters of the book, and they do so respectfully: "Like Marcus...," "Tom and I begin...," "My disagreement with Marcus is more oblique than head on...," "Of these two options, Tom chooses the first, I choose the second," "We disagree about a particular historical judgment," "If Tom is saying... then I have to demur," "Marcus does not, of course, hold an extreme position...," "Tom is right that...," "Marcus expressed the issue between us as...," "As I understand Tom's position, he sees... On the other hand, I see...," "We make different probability judgments...," "At this point we stand shoulder to shoulder..." They don't shy away from confronting big issues for Christians, like "Was Jesus born of a virgin?" "Was he physically, bodily, raised from the dead?" "Will he come again?" and "Was he God?" Not surprisingly, their conclusions are quite different, and yet they remain in active dialogue, trying to understand and be fair to each other's perspectives.

Liberal Christians can and should talk to conservative Christians. As much as possible. And liberal Christians can and should find as many opportunities as possible to talk to atheists. The watchwords for dialogue are fundamental liberal values: tolerance, respect, openness to learn, and willingness to change one's mind. Modern atheists have lots to teach liberal Christians about religiously based violence, rationality, and the wonders of the natural world. Conservative Christians have lots to teach liberals about taking the Bible seriously, a personal relationship with Jesus, and living fully in the Christian master story. Only by keeping the channels of dialogue open can we hope for the life of abundance that Jesus proclaimed.

PART TWO

A Liberal Christian Questions Society

EIGHT

THE GREAT SOCIAL ISSUES

Poverty, Bigotry, War,
and Environmental Destruction

Go, sell what you own, and give the money to the poor.

—Mark 10:21

Let justice roll down like waters, and righteousness like an ever-flowing stream.

—Amos 5:24

Deliver my soul from the sword, my life from the power of the dog!

—Psalm 22:20

God saw everything that he had made, and indeed, it was very good.

—Genesis 1:31

Gary Vance, the evangelical Southern Baptist minister quoted in my preface to this book, seems to equate religious liberalism and political liberalism in relation to Jesus. He declares that Jesus "aligned Himself with the poor and the oppressed...He liberated women and minorities from oppression...Jesus was the original Liberal...His Liberalism lives on today and the issues have not changed much." Vance asserts that no average American would have a fair wage today if it weren't for the work of liberal Christians with the early twentieth-century labor movement. Liberal Christians played an active role in the civil rights movement, and they still fight against conservative America for racial equality and gender equality. Jesus advocated nonviolence (which presumably would have kept us out of Iraq). Liberal Christians have fought for clean air and water standards instead of favoring industrial polluters and short-term profiteering.[1]

I don't want to make any easy associations between religious liberalism and political liberalism, however. There are many theologically conservative Christians who have worked in the front lines against poverty, bigotry, war, and environmental destruction. At the same time, there are plenty of theologically liberal Christians who have done nothing about these great social issues. However, at the outset of this chapter, I want to lay out some clear distinctions that I see between liberal Christians and conservative Christians.

This is important first of all because there are many who use the word "liberal" as the very opposite of "Christian." To them, "liberal" by definition means "secular" or "antireligious." Gary Vance claims that the contemporary definition of liberal has been altered to the point that "Conservatives use it as a profane word. They use it to paint a political opponent as anti-God." An example is conservative commentator Ann Coulter's book *Godless: The Church of Liberalism,* in which it's claimed that "liberalism rejects the idea of God and reviles people of faith." [2]

On consulting a mainstream resource, the Encyclopedia Britannica, one finds an entry headed "Liberalism, theological" that traces liberalism's modern history back to the mid-seventeenth century. Christian liberalism is described as "an important influence in Protestantism" and has gone through three primary phases: Cartesian Rationalism, Romanticism, and Modernism. An important American Christian liberal mentioned is Walter Rauschenbusch (1861–1918), leader of the Social Gospel movement. [3]

Christian liberals (as distinct from political liberals) have generally opposed the authority of religious tradition, defended individual conscience, honored reason as a mode of religious insight, underlined humans' goodness in being created in the image of God, and been confident that human beings could make genuine progress through their own moral and spiritual efforts. Christian conservatives, by contrast, have tended to uphold religious tradition, insisted on the teaching authority of the church, prioritized belief over reason, accentuated original sin, and stressed that history is ultimately in the hands of God. Christian liberals have prized tolerance, while Christian conservatives have given priority to truth. [4]

There can be, and should be, political implications that follow from religious liberalism, but not all religious liberals turn out to be politically liberal. A number of them incline toward libertarian politics, which puts them on the conservative side of the ledger in many people's political estimation. Others take a classical liberal position, which today is labeled as politically conservative: advocacy of free market capitalism, strong private property rights, and limited government. A robust connection was drawn for many in the late nineteenth and early twentieth centuries, though, between religious liberalism and modern political liberalism through the Social Gospel movement.

With the publication of *Christianity and the Social Crisis* in 1907, the Reverend Walter Rauschenbusch became the leading voice of the "Social Gospel." He spoke to the issues of inhumane living conditions for the working poor and the underclass in urban slums. Describing unbridled capitalism as inherently evil, he asked Christians to build a "kingdom of God on earth," referring back not only to biblical injunctions but also to the Puritan idea of building "a city on a hill" in the New World of America.[5] His influence has been durable; for example, Martin Luther King Jr. described *Christianity and the Social Crisis* as "leaving an indelible imprint on my thinking." Although King criticized him for "unwarranted optimism concerning human nature" and coming "perilously close to identifying the kingdom of God with a particular social and economic system," King insisted that "Rauschenbusch gave to American Protestantism a sense of social responsibility that it should never lose." It was Rauschenbusch who taught King that "Any religion that professes to be concerned about the souls of men and is not concerned about the slums that damn them, the economic conditions that strangle them, and the social conditions that cripple them is a spiritually moribund religion awaiting burial."[6] Let's examine the great social issues from a liberal Christian perspective, starting with poverty.

POVERTY

I was part of a congregation of tens of thousands when Pope John Paul II preached on the Boston Common back when I was thirty years old. I remember it well to this day. It was a gray and drizzly morning in October of 1979, but the pope began by exclaiming, "I greet you, America the beautiful."[7] In his sermon, he explicated the story of the young rich man, which is reported in three of the four gospels.[8] Jesus instructs this young man who has faithfully followed the Ten Commandments since his youth that he needs to do one thing more: "Go, sell what you own, and give the money to the poor." At the time I was a young lawyer and minister, providing free legal services to the poor on a church salary in a low-income neighborhood of Boston. So I was glad that the pope had come to America the Beautiful and America the Richest Nation on Earth to talk about our obligations to the poor.

I'd become frustrated after four years of battling banks foreclosing on my clients' mortgages in economic hard times, hospitals refusing to provide free care to those with no money to pay, utility companies shutting off the heat in the middle of the winter when people were behind on their bills, big landlords evicting families whose breadwinner had lost his or her job, and welfare and social security administration offices tying up eligible recipients with bureaucratic red tape. I felt I was like the prophet Amos, crying out of the wilderness: "Ah, you that turn justice to wormwood . . . you [who] trample on the poor and take from them levies of grain, you have built houses of hewn stone, but you shall not live in them; you have planted pleasant vineyards, but you shall not drink their wine."[9]

That day the pope *did* talk about America's obligations to the poor, both domestically and around the world. He spoke powerfully. Yet, he also started speaking very personally to me and everyone else on the Boston Common. What if I was a good person who had tried to follow the commandments not to steal, or bear false witness, or defraud anyone? The pope reminded me that when the rich man told Jesus that he'd always kept the commandments, Jesus looked at him and loved him.[10] The implication was that Jesus loved him for his sincerity as well as for his good deeds. I wanted to be loved by Jesus too.

Then came the crux of the story. When Jesus tells him to give everything he has to the poor, the young rich man is shocked. "What!" he must have been thinking. "Sell everything I own? That's what's required to follow in Jesus's footsteps? Really? How can I possibly do that? Can't I just keep my wealth, but make sure that I'm following all of the Ten Commandments all the time?" So, what does the young rich man do? Instead of following Jesus, "When the young man heard this word, he went away grieving, for he had many possessions."[11]

As I sat there on a wet blanket in the rain on the Common, huddled under a poncho, I began to ask myself about my own life. Sure, I was doing some good works for the poor. Sure, I had some systemic knowledge and political awareness of what was going on in the Richest Nation on Earth, and I was trying to act on it daily. Yet, was I willing to sell everything that I personally owned and give the proceeds to the poor in order to follow Jesus? I was on a church salary, but I had other resources. I had a car and an apartment. I had money in the bank. I came from a family of means that had put me through college and two professional schools, and from whom I might inherit more money someday. What would giving all my money and possessions away mean for starting my own family? Could I get married and have children? Jesus actually goes on in this set of Bible passages to talk about leaving behind one's home, brothers and sisters, mother and father, and even wife and children for his sake and for the sake of the good news of the kingdom of God.[12]

As I sat there thinking through the implications of what this great Christian leader, Pope John Paul II, was saying to me—Rev. Scotty McLennan, the poverty lawyer—about what was truly required to follow Jesus, I began, shockingly, to cry. Just like the young rich man in the gospel story, I began grieving, openly and increasingly unashamedly, in the midst of the multitudes. For it was clear to me that I just wouldn't sell all that I owned and give the proceeds to the poor. That seemed to mean that I couldn't be a disciple of Jesus, whom I take to be my Lord and my Savior. That seemed to mean I had no chance of entering the kingdom of God. In a much more immediate way, it seemed to mean I was a hypocrite in my legal ministry to the poor. Give a little charitable service to those in need, sure, but maintain a comfortable lifestyle for myself. Pretty soon I was sobbing uncontrollably.

But luckily the pope was a pastor as much as he was a prophet that day. He went on to the end of the gospel lesson, beyond the point when Jesus explains "It is easier for a camel to go through the eye of a needle than for someone who is rich to enter the kingdom of God"[13]—another passage that wasn't helping my grief. The disciples challenge Jesus at this point, asking who then *can* actually be saved. Jesus responds by saying, "For mortals it is impossible, but not for God; for God all things are possible."[14] The pope emphasized that God is love and that Jesus came with a special message of love.

Jesus had looked at the rich man and loved him—not just for what he had done, but also for what he was trying to do. Presumably Jesus already knew that this man wasn't ready to sell everything and follow him.[15] Jesus loves him anyway. The rich man had not gone away angry, like many others who didn't like Jesus's answers throughout the New Testament. The young rich man had gone away sad. His sincerity was intact, even though he was not a saint. The Bible does seem to describe a "preferential option for the poor,"[16] and yet God's love, as manifested through Christ, is broad enough and deep enough to extend to rich people who are sincere, even if they aren't able to respond fully to what Jesus asks of them.

The paradigm case of a young rich person selling all to follow Jesus is that of Saint Francis of Assisi (1182–1226). He grew up in the family of a rich cloth merchant. At the age of 22, he gave up every stitch of expensive clothing and everything else he owned to live a life of complete renunciation of worldly goods, trusting in God to provide for all his needs as he served his fellow human beings, animals, and nature itself.[17] Saint Francis took entirely to heart Jesus's words in his Sermon on the Mount: "Do not worry, saying 'What will we eat?' or 'What will we drink,' or 'What will we wear?'...Strive first for the kingdom of God and his righteousness, and all these things will be given to you as well."[18] It became very clear to me on the Boston Common, however, that Scotty McLennan was a long way from being a saint and probably never would be. Like the young rich man, I seek to follow Jesus, but in all sincerity I can't see my way to selling everything and leaving my family as well to do so. I hope and pray that God's embracing arms of love are wide enough to take me in anyway.

I certainly don't understand this to mean that I can forget about the poor, however. I recognize that I have a special responsibility—"from everyone to whom much has been given, much will be required"[19]—to roll up my sleeves and be helpful, as well as to study and try to articulate the systemic and political reasons why poverty exists in America and in a globalizing world. At the time of my installation as Stanford's dean for religious life early in 2001, I spoke about my vision of marshalling the unparalleled intellectual resources and pioneering spirit of this great university to address the growing worldwide disparity between rich and poor, starting in California's Silicon Valley. There are ways that all of us, without necessarily giving away everything we own to the poor, can make a real difference. I speak to myself here as much as to you, my reader, because I worry about my own hypocrisy, fearing I'm becoming too complacent and comfortable at my wonderful university in sunny California.

I've admired the courage and determination of students who have twice fasted for a week at Stanford as a way of demanding the institution of a code of conduct for labor practices on campus, with special concern for the poorest of the poor who work at the university. They addressed wage and benefit levels, working conditions for temporary employees, and the outsourcing of jobs. They also followed spiritual disciplines in the process—not just Christian, but also Muslim, Jewish, Buddhist, and Hindu. The first group of students set up an altar in the midst of where they were fasting in the public square on campus, White Plaza, and invited clergy and other religious representatives to take part in daily worship with them. They negotiated with Stanford's president to set up an advisory committee with student and employee members. The second group to fast successfully advocated for implementation of a number of the committee's findings.

In my local community, I've been happy to join with students, faculty, and staff along with many community residents who were instrumental in establishing the $24 million Palo Alto Opportunity Center in 2006. It provides housing and drop-in services for the homeless. The center is the successor to the Urban Ministry of Palo Alto, which for 16 years had offered outdoor assistance to the unhoused population in our area. The Urban Ministry—supported by many local churches, other religious organizations, and interfaith associations—had long been directed by the liberal United Church of Christ minister, Jim Burklo, described in the last chapter.

On the state and national levels, Christians need to understand and act upon the systemic and political reasons for the increase of poverty in our country. According to Northwestern University professor of economics Rebecca Blank, who runs the Joint Center for Poverty Research, during the economic expansion of the 1980s, real wages of workers in the poorest 10 percent of the population fell.[20] Economist Barend de Vries, in a Georgetown University study, cites increasing inequities in the distribution of wealth during the 1980s and the 1990s, so that by 1998 almost 60 percent of net wealth in the United States was held by the top 10 percent of families. During the 1990s, the richer families also reaped three-quarters of the nation's real income gain, while the bottom 60 percent of the population actually lost ground.[21]

It appears that the Bush tax cuts in the new century averaged just over $300 per year for the bottom 60 percent of Americans, while the average for those making over $1 million was over $100,000.[22] By the year 2010, when the cuts were slated to be fully in place, it has been estimated that 52 percent of the total cuts would go to the richest 1 percent of

Americans. That is, of the $234 billion in tax cuts originally scheduled for that year, $121 billion would go to just 1.4 million taxpayers.[23] The Bush administration also wanted to eliminate all estate taxes, a change that would primarily benefit only the rich.[24] This all occurred while welfare programs for the poor were being cut back. Christians need to advocate for effective across-the-board government responses to economic realities, especially with the economic crisis that began in the fall of 2008, and not just rely on the private sector and church charitable operations for adequate responses to poverty.

Finally, there's the problem of increasing worldwide poverty in the face of globalization. It appears that the rich have been getting richer and the poor are getting poorer abroad as well—in particular in developing countries.[25] De Vries reports that worldwide more than one billion people, one out of five, now "live in the kind of abject poverty which makes human life hardly worth living."[26] Christians must pay attention and become part of the solution and not part of the problem with the kind of policies we promote.

The prophet Amos asks that "justice roll down like waters, and righteousness like an ever-flowing stream."[27] We may not be able to or wish to sell everything we have to benefit the poor, but it is our Christian obligation to be clearly committed to the needs of the poor and to make a real difference in their lives. Otherwise, the force of scripture—Old and New Testament alike—drives in the direction of our disinheritance: We will not drink the wine of our own vineyards let alone enter the kingdom of God.

One of the greatest risks that churches face, however, is that they will provide mere charity and not the economic justice that the prophet Amos calls for. Rev. William Sloane Coffin Jr. used to criticize trickle-down economics and faith-based social services with this image: Charity is finding a baby drowning in a stream and pulling it out; charity is pulling out a second baby and a third baby that come floating down the stream; but justice is going upstream, finding out who's throwing the babies in, and stopping the evil at its source. "Had I but one wish for the churches of America I think it would be that they come to see the difference between charity and justice. Charity is a matter of personal attributes; justice a matter of public policy. Charity seeks to alleviate the effects of injustice; justice seeks to eliminate the causes of it. Charity in no way affects the status quo, while justice leads inevitably to political confrontation."[28]

According to Census Bureau reports in late 2007, well before the economic crisis that began in late 2008, the number of Americans living in poverty was approaching 40 million people, or more than one-eighth of our population. The figures for children were even worse, with almost one-fifth of children under the age of 18 living in poverty. The number of people without health insurance was approaching 50 million.[29] For the Census Bureau, a family of four was considered to be living in poverty in 2008 if their combined family income dipped below $21,200 annually.[30]

One area I know a fair amount about personally from my work as a poverty lawyer is homelessness. I was doing a lot of housing law in the 1970s when there was virtually no homelessness problem in Boston or anywhere else in the nation. It was a major issue, though, by the time I left my law practice to go to Tufts as the university chaplain in the mid-1980s. A political decision had been made that reduced the federal housing budget from $33 billion annually to $7 billion. This was accompanied by political decisions nationwide to deinstitutionalize mental patients, without the willingness to fund the community mental health centers required in local neighborhoods to house those patients as had been promised. A lot of mentally ill people were simply discharged to the streets. As a direct result of these two political decisions, in Boston and all over America suddenly there were homeless people everywhere, sleeping in subways, in parks, on heating grates.

Strangely, this was all happening at the same time as new governmental incentives were being implemented for business along with general tax reductions. Both fiscal policies helped fuel an economic boom in the 1980s that resulted in enormous increases in wealth for the already well-to-do, but not for the poor. Churches and other charitable organizations were asked to step in, to provide shelters and food pantries, and to help the homeless and hungry at dramatic new levels. Certainly "the churches have to feed the hungry, clothe the naked, and shelter the homeless," as William Sloane Coffin Jr. puts it. "But they have also to remember that the answer to homelessness is homes, not shelters."[31] Coffin explains this in a wider context:

> Many of us are...eager to respond to injustice, as long as we can do so without having to confront the causes of it...There's the great pitfall of charity. Handouts to needy individuals are genuine, necessary responses

to injustice, but they do not necessarily face the reason for injustice. And that is why...so many business [and governmental] leaders today are promoting charity; it is desperately needed in an economy whose prosperity is based on growing inequality. First these leaders proclaim themselves experts on matters economic, and prove it by [themselves] taking the most out of the economy! Then they promote charity as if it were the work of the church, finally telling us troubled clergy to shut up and bless the economy as once we blessed the battleships.[32]

The economic debacle of 2008 has provided some stark examples of where this attitude can lead. It's clear why the prophet Amos cried out to let justice, not charity, roll down like waters: While charity may provide Band-Aids to the effects of poverty, only justice seeks to eliminate its causes.[33]

BIGOTRY

Economic justice is not the only kind Christians are called on to promote; equally important is social justice. The Reverend Martin Luther King Jr., for example, had no intention of becoming a national civil rights leader. But his call came, as he wrote, when "I was suddenly catapulted into the leadership of the bus protest in Montgomery."[34] Just three weeks before, he'd refused a nomination for the presidency of the Montgomery NAACP, claiming that he needed to devote his time to his church work and his family.[35] Then he was totally surprised when he was asked to lead the boycott and given "only 20 minutes to prepare the most important speech of his life...He had always taken at least fifteen hours to prepare a sermon."[36] He rose magnificently to the occasion, wanting to give the people of Montgomery "a passion for justice."[37] The rest is history.

What are Christians called to do in the face of bigotry, often expressed in the form of racism? How can we prepare to stand up to prejudice, discrimination, and intolerance? A great blueprint is laid out in Dr. King's "Letter From a Birmingham Jail." It was sent in the form of an open letter on April 16, 1963, in response to an open letter in January of that year from eight prominent liberal white Alabama clergy. Those clergy had entreated Dr. King to work in a tempered way for racial justice through the court system, warning him that his active nonviolent resistance campaigns would have the effect of inciting violence in Birmingham.[38]

What strikes me first about this letter is that King's understanding of social justice requires deep respect for the inherent worth and dignity of all other people, including the oppressor. He noted that the largest and best-known Black Nationalist group of his time, led by Elijah Muhammad, referred to white people as incurable "devils."[39] Instead, King saw all people as created in God's image and asked, in Jesus's words, that you "Love your enemies, bless them that curse you, pray for them that despitefully use you."[40] King is genuinely polite to the eight white ministers, calling them "My Dear Fellow Clergymen" at the beginning and begging their forgiveness at the end, "If I have said anything in this letter that is an overstatement of the truth and is indicative of an unreasonable impatience."[41]

On the other hand, he felt that social justice required him to speak the truth clearly and directly. King wrote: "Few members of a race that has oppressed another race can understand or appreciate the deep groans and passionate yearnings of those that have been oppressed, and still fewer have the vision to see that injustice must be rooted out by strong, persistent and determined action." He saw himself as part of a social revolution, and he also expressed gratitude to those white brothers and sisters who had committed themselves to it, "all too small in quantity, but...big in quality."[42]

King had strong words, though, for those "all too many" white clergy who "have been more cautious than courageous and have remained silent behind the anesthetizing security of the stained-glass windows...So here we are, moving toward the exit of the twentieth century with a religious community largely adjusted to the status quo, standing as a taillight behind other community agencies rather than a headlight leading people to higher levels of justice."[43] I hear those words now as continuing condemnation and not only because Sunday morning remains the most segregated time in America. So many churches remain likewise willing to dogmatize, excuse, and promote institutional homophobia, reducing sexually active gays and lesbians to sinners, defectives, or second-class citizens, even as those churches claim to be working on institutionalized racism. They are taillights, from my perspective, rather than headlights leading people to higher levels of justice.

The call to justice is not just local. King was criticized as an "outside agitator" interfering in local affairs. In response, he referred to the prophets of Israel who "left their little villages and carried their 'thus saith the Lord' far beyond the boundaries of their hometowns."[44] He described the apostle Paul leaving his village of Tarsus to carry "the gospel of Jesus Christ to practically every hamlet and city of the Graeco-Roman world." King explained that he is "cognizant of the interrelatedness of all communities and states." Therefore, he "cannot sit idly by in Atlanta and not be concerned about what happens in Birmingham." These words from his letter have been often quoted: "Injustice anywhere is a threat to justice everywhere. We are caught in an inescapable network of mutuality, tied in a single garment of destiny."[45] Similarly, I believe we're now called to be concerned about injustices like the genocide in Darfur, the destruction of Tibetan culture and religion by China, new forms of anti-Muslim and anti-Jewish fascism in Europe, and the racial dynamics of capital punishment in the United States.

The call to social justice requires direct action, always nonviolent in King's view but always assertive when negotiations have broken down. Direct action for him included boycotts, demonstrations, sit-ins—and lots of other creative activities short of destruction of property and harm to other human beings. But it's intolerable to stay with words alone when promises have been broken, when negotiations are not in good faith, when justice delayed becomes justice denied. In other famous words, King explained that "We know through painful experience that freedom is never voluntarily given by the oppressor; it must be demanded by the oppressed."[46]

That may also mean that laws need to be broken. Civil disobedience has a long and proud tradition going back to biblical martyrs in both the Old and the New Testaments, although King insisted on certain conditions. First, the law itself must be unjust, which for King meant out of harmony with the law of God or with moral law that can be universalized. The classic example he gave was Nazi law: "We can never forget that everything Hitler did in Germany was 'legal.'" King would have wanted to aid and comfort his Jewish brothers and sisters at the time even though it was illegal.[47] Second, breaking an unjust law must be done openly. (Obviously, he might have put this differently outside of the modern U.S. civil rights context—as with the underground railroad for slaves in the nineteenth century or with protection of Jews during the Second World War.) Third, one must be willing to accept the penalty. Then, going to jail and arousing the conscience of the community over the law's injustice actually expresses the highest respect for law. So, for example, in recent memory there have been many in South African prisons who challenged apartheid laws, environmentalists in American prisons who challenged laws that protect or encourage environmental degradation, and dissidents in prisons around the world who challenged laws that curtail freedom of speech and assembly. King himself was in jail in Birmingham because he peacefully protested without a parade permit, which was denied to him in violation of his First Amendment rights.[48]

The call to confront bigotry as part of the call to discipleship of Christ is never easy. I remember reading King's Birmingham Jail letter in 1963 as a white suburban high schooler and finding it much too radical to affirm myself. In fact, it made me deeply uncomfortable, defensive, and resistant. What am I ready for now? We honor the life and work of Rev. King because he was called, he answered, he acted, and he gave his life at the age of 39 in the understanding that injustice anywhere is a threat to justice everywhere. May we not rest until we can share in his vision.

WAR

Warfare may be the greatest perennial threat to social justice. Christianity has historically taken three different positions on war: pacifism, which held sway for the first three centuries of the Christian era when the church was persecuted within the Roman Empire;[49] just-war theory, which was articulated by Saint Augustine, among others, after the Emperor Constantine converted to Christianity in the fourth century;[50] and crusade, first initiated by Pope Urban II in 1095 to liberate Jerusalem and the Christian Holy Lands from the Muslims, whom the pope called wicked, accursed, and alienated from God.[51] The dominant Christian position in the modern era has become just-war theory.

President George W. Bush clearly had Christian just-war principles in mind when he gave his 2003 State of the Union address. He proclaimed that the United States of America will "defend the peace and confound the designs of evil men," referring to disarming Saddam Hussein. He assured the American public that if it comes to war, "We will fight in a just cause and by just means." President Bush ended the speech by asking for God's guidance.

"Declaring a Just War?" was the title of an op-ed article of mine published in the *San Francisco Chronicle* five weeks before the United States invaded Iraq in 2003.[52] On the basis of traditional Christian just-war principles, I argued that we must not go to war. I enumerated the six basic principles that must be fulfilled before resorting to military force and explained that we had not met a single one of them.

First, just cause for Christians has traditionally required a defensive response to grave and certain harm to the nation. The Bush administration had not made the case that Iraq's intention or capacity to use weapons of mass destruction was likely, much less certain. There were also no proven high-level Iraqi links to al Qaeda or other international terrorists targeting the United States.

Second, going to war was not a matter of last resort. Containment and deterrence of Hussein's regime had been effective for 12 years following the Gulf War, although with extreme hardship for the civilian population. Political and military sanctions could have been continued. There were U.S.-patrolled no-fly zones. Surveillance and intelligence gathering were at a high pitch. If we could continue negotiating with a more dangerous North Korea rather than going to war, why not with Iraq?

Third, President Bush didn't have clear legitimate authority to act. The majority of Americans were then against the war, according to polls, and Vietnam should have taught us not to prosecute a war without the backing of the American people. The president claimed that the previous year's UN resolution gave him all the authority needed for a war against Iraq, but the Security Council disagreed.

Fourth, the probability of success was far from assured. I wrote that "America is strong militarily, and Iraq is not, so we may well be able to defeat their armed forces within a couple of months. But this criterion fails when we consider how long we would have to be tied down in Iraq in order to win the peace." I cited claims that some 50,000 to 75,000 U.S. troops would be required for many years to restore civil order under fire and to defend Iraq's borders. "There would be continuing casualties, costs would probably run in the hundreds of billions of dollars, and that would have a dramatic impact on providing services at home to U.S. citizens." (The U.S. troop level at the time of this writing, more than five years after our invasion of Iraq, is over 130,000;[53] the Pentagon-estimated cost of the war to date is close to $600 billion.[54])

Fifth, a war would not meet the Christian test of proportionality. There was the very real potential of creating greater evil by going to war than by not. I asked, "Is it not likely that such a war will infuriate much of the Muslim world and solidify them against us?" I suggested that "The world becomes more dangerous if the United States is seen as an aggressor nation engaged in preemptive war. Why should everyone else not abandon the UN charter to pursue their own preemptive strikes where they feel at risk, from Kashmir to North Korea?" And I explained that "concentrating our resources on a war in Iraq could well mean that al Qaeda and related terrorist groups...are emboldened as we have less resources and less attention to pay to those potentially greater threats."

Sixth, and finally, Christian principles require that great care be taken to avoid injury to civilians in any war. I asked, "Would innocent men, women and children be spared in a war against Iraq? The United States has precision smart bombs, but what if we end up in door-to-door fighting in Baghdad? What about civilian death and suffering based on destruction of Iraq's infrastructure?" I noted that UN estimates at the time were of the potential for 500,000 civilian casualties, directly and indirectly due to a war, with some 2 million civilians displaced. (Subsequently, the World Health Organization [WHO] and the Iraqi Health Ministry released a joint survey estimating that no less than 151,000 Iraqis died violently from March 2003 through June 2006,[55] while a study published in the *Lancet* estimated over 650,000 deaths for the same period.[56] Those are not true casualty figures, since they do not include deaths by indirect causes nor the much higher number of injured civilians. The UN Refugee Agency reported in 2007 that more than 4 million Iraqis had been displaced by violence at that time.[57])

I ended the article, "Basic moral and spiritual values are the lifeblood of this country, and without them the American way of life itself is in grave peril. We must not go to war with Iraq."

I've also expressed my Christian convictions concerning our country's use of torture during the wars in Iraq and Afghanistan. In the late spring of 2004, news reports began circulating of Americans' torture of Iraqis at the Abu Ghraib prison in Baghdad. On June 20, 2004, Father's Day, I preached a sermon in the Stanford Memorial Church which began: "Torture is wrong, always. Period. I shouldn't have to be preaching a sermon about this. There should be universal agreement about the impermissibility of torture, and that should be the end of it." I read from Psalm 22: "Dogs are all around me; a company of evildoers encircles me. My hands and feet have shriveled; I can count all my bones. They stare and gloat over me; they divide my clothes among themselves . . . Deliver my soul from the sword, my life from the power of the dog!"[58]

I reminded the congregation how President Bush, in his State of the Union Address before the start of the Iraq War, described what he called the "torture chambers" of that country, which used methods such as forced confessions, electric shock, and rape. As he famously said, "If this is not evil, then evil has no meaning."[59] Then after Saddam Hussein's military had been defeated, President Bush—in emphasizing the ethical underpinnings of the war—called "on all governments to join with the United States and the community of law-abiding nations in prohibiting, investigating, and prosecuting all acts of torture." He added, "We are leading this fight by example."[60]

But then we graphically learned what Americans did when they took over Saddam Hussein's torture chambers at Abu Ghraib: yes, forced confessions, electric shock, and rape; yes, isolation, beatings, attack dogs, starvation. And add to that intentional humiliation, sleep deprivation, sexual abuse, and homicide. In our names, by service men and women and agents of our United States of America. This happened despite the fact that a bright line had been drawn on torture in the U.S. Army Field Manual precisely at the time our Abu Ghraib abuses were taking place. In addition to more serious abuses, the manual prohibited pain induced by bondage, forcing an individual to stand, sit, or kneel in abnormal positions for prolonged periods of time, and food deprivation. Under mental torture, the Army Manual prohibited mock executions and sleep deprivation.[61]

Unfortunately, I noted, there had been an August 2002 Justice Department memo advising the White House that torturing terrorists abroad may be justified, arguing that "necessity and self-defense could provide justifications that would eliminate any criminal liability later."[62] Addressed to White House Counsel Alberto Gonzalez, the memo also defined torture in a much more limited way than the Army Manual. It claimed that moderate pain does not constitute torture. Torture, the memo says, "must be equivalent in intensity to the pain accompanying serious physical injury, such as organ failure, impairment of bodily function, or even death."[63]

I stated in my sermon that I didn't want to be heard to be making a partisan political statement. I explained that I was making a moral statement, based on Christian religious principles, including our understanding that all human beings are created by God, in the image of God, and we're all called upon to do unto others as we'd have them do unto us. I noted that I had been preaching for almost thirty years, through both Democratic and Republican administrations, and I've always felt it my duty to criticize certain actions of each and every one of them from a moral and religious perspective. Torture has been as much of a concern on moral and religious grounds to conservative Republicans like William F. Buckley Jr. who served on the board of Amnesty International in the 1970s, as to liberal Democrats like Jimmy Carter, who made no secret of his Christian faith and spoke and acted from the White House to promote freedom from torture worldwide.

"My God, my God, why have you forsaken me?" cries the tortured Jesus on the cross,[64] quoting the beginning of Psalm 22. Asks the psalmist, "Why are you so far from helping me, from the words of my groaning?"[65] In the Psalm, one who has been stripped naked, tormented by snarling dogs, starved, surrounded by gloating evildoers, and put to the sword cries out to God without experiencing any response. By the end of Psalm 22, though, God is seen as standing with and comforting the tormented and the tortured: "For God did not despise or abhor the affliction of the afflicted; he did not hide his face from me, but heard when I cried to him."[66]

In the gospel story in the Christian lectionary for June 20, 2004,[67] a naked man named Legion, kept under guard and bound with chains and shackles, was freed by Jesus. He was tormented by internal demons, we're told, as well as external. When Jesus first approaches him, he begs Jesus not to torment him too. True to his nature throughout the gospels, though, Jesus comes to liberate, not to torment. This couldn't have felt like a safe situation for Jesus. Legion was a dangerous man who might even have been seen by some as a mad terrorist, although the story gives no indication that he'd ever killed anyone. Jesus steps into the midst of the danger with courage and an orientation toward healing and transformation, rather than treating Legion as anything less than a fellow human being. He calls the demons out of Legion, and they run away in swine to be drowned in the lake. As a result, Legion ends up going away, proclaiming how much Jesus has done for him. However, the rest of the people then manage to transfer their fear to Jesus. Jesus is asked by them to leave the area, so he gets into a boat on the lake and departs.

To act like Jesus in the world is not necessarily to become popular. Most of us respond more easily out of our fear than out of our desire to heal and transform. And it seems like a particularly dangerous world these days. But it becomes more dangerous when America abandons the moral high ground and leads by its example in exactly the wrong direction. When others equate our methods with Saddam Hussein's, then the world will indeed see, in President Bush's words, "If this is not evil, then evil has no meaning."

I ended my sermon lamenting how haunted I felt as an American on that Father's Day. A particular photograph had recently been widely publicized in the press that showed an Iraqi mother and her son holding a photograph of his father's bloodied, plastic-wrapped corpse at Abu Ghraib. In that photo, a female American soldier leaned over his head with a big smile on her face and a thumbs up. I ended the sermon with these words: "I shouldn't have to be preaching this sermon in America. Especially on Father's Day."

ENVIRONMENTAL DESTRUCTION

Thankfully, environmental preservation seems to be a growing area of interfaith cooperation across the country. It certainly is for the more than thirty diverse student groups that make up Stanford Associated Religions, from liberal to conservative Christians, Muslims, Jews, Hindus, Buddhists, Baha'is, and Unitarian Universalists. Many religious people have been concerned about this for a long time, at least as far back as the first Earth Day in 1970. By now it's become crystal clear that the time has come for people of conscience to act. As an example, starting in 2007 Earth Day has also been designated as a National Campus Day of Prayer on Global Warming, based on efforts of students at the University of Chicago and Stanford. As I said in our campus interfaith service in 2007, the central religious question now seems to be how we can live righteously within a society that appears to be politically and economically bent on doing fundamental violence to God's creation and to people living within it. How do we go about our lives, for example, knowing that our use of energy leads directly to permanent harm for the developing world, our own communities, and the future that we bequeath to our children and grandchildren?

When I was at Tufts University, I twice taught a course on environmental ethics. The preface of the text we used explained that our current environmental crises are not just scientific, technological, or political problems. They "raise fundamental questions about what we as human beings value, about the kind of beings we are, about the kinds of lives we should live, about our place in nature, and about the kind of world in which we might flourish." The book's preface continued: "This text seeks to provide students with a systematic introduction to these philosophical issues."[68]

But these are religious as well as philosophical issues. Although there were a dozen pages in the text in which religion was mentioned, it unfortunately was seen more as part of the problem rather than of the solution to environmental devastation. A prime example of this orientation is a seminal article that appeared in the journal *Science* in 1967. Entitled "The Historical Roots of Our Ecological Crisis," written by UCLA historian Lynn White Jr., it claims that a particular Judeo-Christian perspective or worldview underlies our present environmental crisis.[69] White cited biblical verses like this one in the very first chapter of Genesis: "God created humankind in his image...male and female he created them. God blessed them, and God said to them, 'Be fruitful and multiply, and fill the earth and subdue it; and have dominion over the fish of the sea and over the birds of the air and over every living thing that moves upon the earth.'"[70]

This biblical passage depicts humans in a privileged position, literally lording it over all the rest of creation. Humans are created separate from and superior to nature and have been commanded by God to subdue and dominate it. "Especially in its Western form, Christianity is the most anthropocentric religion the world has seen,"[71] as White put it. By contrast, "In antiquity every tree, every spring, every stream, every hill had its own *genius loci,* its guardian spirit...By destroying pagan animism, Christianity made it possible to exploit nature in a mood of indifference to the feelings of natural objects."[72] White shows how these kinds of attitudes lead to environmental degradation and destruction. Compare these words attributed to Chief Seattle from the Native American tradition: "This we know. The earth does not belong to us; we belong to the earth. This we know. All things are connected...We did not weave the web of life; we are merely a strand in it."[73]

The Parable of the Good Samaritan[74] is what many consider the high-water mark of Christian ethics. Yet, the high-water mark of Christian ethics is about man's humanity to man—about a particular man's humanity to another particular man. It's still very much in the anthropocentric worldview that began with the creation story in Genesis. As White put it, "More science and more technology are not going to get us out of the present ecological crisis until we find a new religion, or rethink our old one."[75]

White does not think that the hierarchical, human-centered view is the only or the most reasonable interpretation of Jewish or Christian theology though. He goes on to suggest an alternative biblical view associated with St. Francis of Assisi that would support a much more environmentally friendly relationship with nature.[76] More recent authors[77] have seen the Hebrew Bible or Old Testament primarily as a story of a people and their relationship to the land. The promised land of Israel is understood to belong to God and to be valued by God as good. It is given to the Jewish people as a divine gift on the condition that they care for it as responsible stewards and live according to the divine law of the Torah. Many passages in the Hebrew Bible counsel compassion for animals, and kosher rules reveal profound respect for living beings that sustain human life as our food.

In his great farewell address to the Israelites before they entered the Promised Land, after 40 years of wandering in the barren wilderness, Moses explains that they will be blessed if they follow God's commandments, including those related to environmental stewardship, and cursed if they don't. If they are faithful, God will make them "abundantly prosperous...in the fruit of your livestock, and in the fruit of your soil."[78] Earlier in the address Moses warns that if the people don't follow the commandments he received from God at Mount Sinai, the result will be devastation of the land: "all its soil burned out by sulfur and salt, nothing planted, nothing sprouting, unable to support any vegetation."[79]

Saint Francis of Assisi is celebrated in the Christian tradition for his close relationship to nature. A well-known hymn attributed to Saint Francis has him praising the sun, moon, wind, water, and fire. He asks us to sing alleluia to "Dear mother earth, who day by day unfoldest blessings on our way," including "the flowers and fruits that in thee grow."[80] Francis even counseled treating worms and wolves with kindness. In the famous prayer attributed to him, he asserts that it is in giving that we receive, and this is as good advice in approaching our natural environment as in approaching other human beings.[81]

A twentieth-century Christian thinker, Albert Schweitzer, continued this tradition by defining the moral person this way: "He accepts as being good: to preserve life, to raise to its highest value life which is capable of development; and as being evil: to destroy life, to injure life, to repress life which is capable of development. This is the absolute fundamental principle of the moral. A man is ethical only when life, as such, is sacred to him, that of plants and animals as that of his fellow man, and when he devotes himself helpfully to all life that is in need of help."[82]

The Jewish thinker Martin Buber was in some ways more radical than Schweitzer. Author of *I and Thou*, widely read by liberal Christians in my experience, he argued that "every thing and being" should be respected as a Thou, an end in itself, and not merely as an it, a means to an end external to itself. He described I-thou relations with trees, rocks, and soil as well as with human beings. God is encountered not as someone apart from the world but in and through I-thou relations with beings and things that make up the world.[83]

An earmark of religious faith has always been its ability to help the individual transcend him or herself and awaken to new possibilities of cooperating, sharing, and loving. In this age of ecological crisis as well as increasing global community and interfaith dialogue between the world's religions, there's an opportunity for religion to help the human race immeasurably in the evolution of its consciousness. Philosophical ethics concerning the environment can be aided greatly by religious ethics that lie deep in the hearts and minds of so much of humanity.

Nature seen as sacred trust is a dramatically different perspective from nature seen as object of human subjugation and domination. That religious vision of sacred trust can be found in the Native American tradition as well as in Hindu, Buddhist, Taoist, and other eastern religions. Yet, Christians and Jews also have ancient strands of their tradition to draw upon in fashioning a modern environmental ethic that can help resolve the ecological crises of our day.

Religious worldviews make a very real, practical difference in how we act, not least of all because they run so deep in so many peoples' assumptions and so often drive our actions without our being aware of them. Hope lies in perspectives like this, taken from a Jewish prayer: "How wonderful, O Lord, are the works of your hands!...The sun and the stars, the valleys and hills, the rivers and lakes all disclose Your presence...the beasts of the field and the birds of the air bespeak Your wondrous will. In your goodness You have made us able to hear the music of the world...A divine voice sings through all creation."[84] To that may we say Amen.

NINE

CHURCH AND STATE

Render unto Caesar the things that are Caesar's, and unto God the things that are God's.

—*Matthew 22:21*

RELIGION AND POLITICS

After the 2004 presidential election, I heard a National Public Radio commentator describe it as a contest between the religious right and the secular left. Earlier in the show author Alain De Boton had explained, from a European perspective, how dangerous he thought it was for religion to be involved in politics, noting that historically it leads to the likes of the Spanish Inquisition.[1] After the election I received a hand-delivered letter from a Stanford colleague who complained that the outcome of the presidential election was tainted by religious bigotry, and suggested that I was personally complicit in a threat to American freedom that comes from firmly held religious dogma. It seemed that Christianity in America was being widely portrayed as right wing, bigoted, leading to a new Inquisition, and threatening American freedom. And apparently, as the Stanford dean for religious life and as a committed Christian, I was complicit in all of this.

It is true that broadcaster Pat Robertson, founder of the Christian Coalition, had stated a year before the election, "I'm hearing from the Lord it's going to be like a blowout election in 2004. The Lord has just blessed [George Bush]... It doesn't make any difference what he does, good or bad..."[2] Rev. Jerry Falwell said in 2004, "It is the responsibility of every... evangelical Christian, every pro-life Catholic... to get serious about re-electing President Bush."[3] A Roman Catholic bishop in Colorado stated that in deciding how to vote in the election, for Christians "abortion outweighs every other issue."[4]

But I'm a professing Christian, one among many who is pro-choice on abortion and in favor of marriage for same-sex couples. I don't think our presidents are blessed no matter what they do, good or bad. I don't consider myself either a member of the religious right or the secular left. But I do think religion has an important role to play in the public square. During my formative college years in the 1960s, I was religiously motivated by the likes of Dr. Martin Luther King Jr. and Rev. William Sloane Coffin Jr. to get involved in the civil rights and antiwar movements. Where's my place as a liberal Christian in American political life? As a politically active Christian, am I part of a threat to American freedom, leading inexorably to a new Inquisition?

We had a baccalaureate speaker at Stanford a few years ago who has been an enormous help to me in negotiating these questions—the Reverend Jim Wallis, editor of *Sojourners* magazine. Subsequently he has written books entitled *God's Politics*[5] and *The Great Awakening*.[6] Wallis was the main mover behind advertisements and bumper stickers leading up to both the 2004 and 2008 elections that read, "God is not a Republican or a Democrat."[7] Accompanying the bumper stickers were issue guides that supported the importance, for Christians, of looking at the presidential candidates through Christian lenses. The guides reminded us as well that sincere Christians can conscientiously choose to vote for either a Republican or Democratic candidate for reasons deeply rooted in their faith. Responsible Christian citizenship involves identifying all the religious issues that have political implications, getting thoughtfully involved in the election process, and avoiding becoming a single-issue voter.

Abortion, for example, was placed in the context of seven broad areas discussed in a nationally run ad in 2004: "We believe that a consistent ethic of human life is a religious issue. Do the candidates' positions on abortion, capital punishment, euthanasia, weapons of mass destruction, HIV/AIDS—and other pandemics—and genocide around the world obey the biblical injunction to choose life? (Deuteronomy 30:19)." The other six broad areas that the ad encouraged Christians to consider were caring for the poor, protecting the natural environment, being peacemakers in the face of war, truth-telling, defending human rights (especially relating to torture), and responding to terrorism without using language of righteous empire or seeing evil only in our enemies but not in our own policies. The 2008

Sojourners issues guide had seven similarly broad areas, renamed somewhat to give greater emphasis to racial justice and strengthening families.[8] In the area of abortion, *Sojourners* in 2008 called for "common-ground policies that dramatically reduce the abortion rate by preventing unwanted pregnancies," along with other measures. Strengthening families was seen as a national priority, but "without scapegoating gay and lesbian people for the breakdown of the family."[9]

Tens of thousands of Christians endorsed *Sojourners'* principles by signing online petitions. And they weren't only liberal Christians like me. There were plenty as well from organizations like the National Association of Evangelicals (NAE), founded in 1942, and now representing millions of conservative and moderate Christians across the country. Jim Wallis himself identifies as an evangelical Christian. In 2004 the NAE issued an unprecedented "Evangelical Call to Civic Responsibility."[10] Noting that evangelical Christians now make up fully a quarter of all voters in the United States, the document calls for shaping public policy in ways that could improve the well-being of the entire world. It decries single-issue voting and restricting political concerns only to matters in the private and domestic spheres, reminding us that Jesus followed in the tradition of the Hebrew prophets in announcing a kingdom of God "which would be marked by justice, peace, forgiveness, restoration and healing for all."

The Evangelical Call to Civic Responsibility looks at a *process* for Christian engagement in politics, as well as areas of *substance* that Christians should be concerned about. For example, it states that "As Christians engaged in public policy, we must do detailed social, economic, historical, jurisprudential, and political analysis if we are to understand our society and wisely apply our normative vision to political questions." It explains that social problems can't just be addressed by personal choices; unjust systems must be challenged and wise structural changes made, for example, by legislation to increase economic opportunity for all. It recognizes that evangelicals will differ with other Christians and with non-Christians over the best policies. Therefore, it counsels, "we [evangelicals] must practice humility and cooperation to achieve modest and attainable goals for the good of society. We must take care to employ the language of civility and to avoid demonizing those with whom we disagree." It recognizes that power tends to corrupt and that all people, including Christians, often abuse power for selfish purposes. It therefore commends a decentralized constitutional system that includes the separation of powers. It affirms the principles of religious freedom and liberty of conscience and declares pluralism to be foundational to the religious liberty of all.

In terms of substance, it makes some rather strong statements (with which I agree as a liberal Christian) on economic and social justice:

- "God identifies with the poor [and]...God measures societies by how they treat people at the bottom."
- "Our primary allegiance is to Christ...not to any nation."
- "Reduction of global poverty [should be] a central concern of American foreign policy."
- "Because the Creator gave human beings liberty...people must be free to express their vision for a just social order without fear of torture or other reprisal."
- "America has a tragic history of mistreating Native Americans... [of] slavery...segregation and exploitation...To correct the lingering effects of our racist history, Christians should support well-conceived efforts that foster dignity and responsibility."
- "God did not call Christians to bring in God's kingdom by force...We urge governments to pursue thoroughly nonviolent paths to peace before resorting to military force...We urge followers of Jesus to engage in practical peacemaking locally, nationally, and internationally."
- "We affirm that God-given dominion is a sacred responsibility to steward the earth and not a license to abuse the creation of which we are a part."

So, what about those concerns on religion and politics with which I began this chapter—as expressed on National Public Radio by Alain De Boton and by the letter I received from a member of the Stanford community? Here are my personal responses.

First, there's no doubt that religious bigotry has an impact—perhaps a critical impact—on elections. It's the duty of all of us, religious and nonreligious alike, to resist and overcome that bigotry. To talk longingly of America as a "Christian nation" is to deny the pluralism and freedom of conscience that is our national heritage. It is factually inaccurate and a great disservice to all of us to see the political right as religious and the political left as secular.

Second, religion must speak its ethical vision in the public square, on the right and on the left, because pastoral care and liturgy and religious education behind closed doors are not enough. We've always needed the voice of the public prophet, from Amos to Jesus to Martin Luther King Jr., to tell us when we're enslaving and oppressing each other. These voices also encourage us to act in the world and to help bring about what the prophet Isaiah calls a new heaven and a new earth, where no more weeping shall be heard.[11]

But, third, false prophets must be named and countered. No president or other leader should ever think he or she has been given divine sanction—been blessed by God—no matter what he or she does, bad or good.

Fourth, when Christians develop public policy, they must make sure they are doing so on the basis of detailed social, economic, historical, jurisprudential, and political analysis, not just on Christian ideals. When engaging in public dialogue, religious perspectives must be translated into a common civic language and made subject to challenge and debate by those with other religious, as well as nonreligious, perspectives. Religion should never be a trump card or a voting block. The "other" must never be demonized, which can be a special challenge if you are convinced that he or she is literally going to hell.

Yet, even after all of this has been done, we Christians need to be aware of Jesus's prediction that we will be hated, persecuted, and denounced.[12] Unfortunately, that will come at the hands of fellow Christians of different stripes, perhaps more than from anyone else. But it will also come from certain people in other religious traditions, from certain people who identify themselves as secular, and from certain people who are unapologetically antireligious. We will also find that our most heartfelt personal commitments and visions for the world are regularly denigrated, devastated, and demolished. Then, our solace must be in Jesus's words of hope: "By your endurance you will gain your souls."[13] For as the prophets have always promised in the name of God: "Be glad and rejoice forever in what I am creating: for I am about to create Jerusalem as a joy, and its people as a delight...They shall build houses and inhabit them; they shall plant vineyards and eat their fruit... They shall not hurt or destroy on all my holy mountain, says the Lord."[14]

RENDER UNTO CAESAR THE
THINGS THAT ARE CAESAR'S

But what about the gospel passage that's often cited as the biblical authority for the separation of church and state: "Render unto Caesar the things that are Caesar's, and unto God the things that are God's"?[15] Jesus is asked whether Mosaic law, which binds Jews together as a covenanting people, allows paying taxes to a hated foreign occupying power in Judea. Jesus in effect says "yes"—separate church and state.

In this biblical account, the Pharisees, with Herodians by their side, were challenging Jesus within the sacred walls of the temple in Jerusalem. The Pharisees were a Jewish intellectual elite, distinguished by their learning, strongly attached to studying and explicating the Mosaic law.[16] The Herodians were overt supporters of the Roman regime that had placed the local Jewish king, Herod, in charge of territory in Judea.[17] The Pharisees resented the Roman tax, but they wouldn't go as far as the radical nationalists, the Zealots, and publicly resist its payment. The Herodians supported paying the tax.[18] So these two groups put Jesus on the spot. Would he support tax payment and look like an apologist for Rome in the eyes of the Jewish nationalists, or would he counsel against paying the taxes and thereby make himself subject to arrest for violation of Roman law?

Jesus responds in a very clever way. It turns out that Roman taxes can only be paid with Roman coins, and most of them had an image and an inscription considered sacrilegious by many Jews: Translated, it read in part, "Tiberius Caesar...son of the divine Augustus..." So Jesus asks them for the kind of coin used for the tax. They bring him a Roman denarius, a small silver coin.[19] Note that this means that these Jewish biblical teachers, the Pharisees, are being forced to produce, within the most sacred context of the temple, a Roman coin with its idolatrous image and inscription, proclaiming Caesar divine. Jesus then asks his opponents to identify whose likeness and inscription is on the coin, and they, of course, respond "Caesar's." Now Jesus can defuse the incendiary issue of paying tribute to an occupying power by making it merely a matter of property:[20] "Render therefore unto Caesar the things that are Caesar's." But then, he adds a zinger: "And unto God the things that are God's."[21] By those words, Jesus makes it crystal clear that Caesar is not God, and that what's really important are those things that are God's, not some coins of foreign oppressors. Later in the same chapter of Matthew, in answer to another question by the Pharisees, Jesus answers explicitly what belongs to God, and it's a lot: "You shall love the Lord your God with all your heart, and with all your soul, and with all your mind...And you shall love your neighbor as yourself. On these two commandments hang all the law and the prophets."[22]

Paying taxes to an occupying force in no way violates Mosaic law, so the Pharisees, with all their learning, could not actually have trapped Jesus theologically.[23] But their aim and intent was solely pragmatic and political anyway. As stated earlier in Matthew: "The Pharisees went out and conspired against him [Jesus], how to destroy him."[24] By their challenge on taxes, they hoped terminally to alienate him either from the masses of oppressed Jewish people or from the Roman authorities. They asked him a political question, really, not a theological one. He responded with an unexpected answer that had both political and theological implications.

Another way of putting it is that Jesus was operating religiously in a highly charged political environment. And he never shrank from doing quite publicly what he felt was religiously correct in that political environment, even unto his own death.

It's a misreading of this passage to see it as a proof text for the separation of church and state. Jesus was regarded as a prophet,[25] and the prophets of Israel were always deeply involved in challenging kings, principalities, and powers and the political order in the name of the higher authority of God. Jesus began his ministry by identifying himself with the prophet Isaiah: "The Spirit of the Lord is upon me, because he has anointed me to bring good news to the poor...to proclaim release to the captives...to let the oppressed go free."[26] He said these words in the synagogue in his hometown of Nazareth. His fellow congregants were so dubious of his authority that he retorted, "Truly I tell you, no prophet is accepted in the prophet's hometown."[27] Jesus's very last lesson to his disciples before he died, according to Matthew, was also prophetic in its instruction to his followers to be worldly activists, to direct their attention to the very least of those around them: They were to feed the hungry, welcome the stranger, clothe the naked, care for the sick, and visit the prisoners.[28]

How does this translate to America, where we claim to have separation of church and state? My first answer comes from my experiences in several months of travel through five totalitarian communist countries in the early 1980s. At that time the constitution of Romania guaranteed freedom of religion so long as its exercise did not harm public morals and order. In practical effect, though, that outlawed all commentary from church pulpits that related religious principles to political life in any critical or prophetic way. Not only was any suggestion of social change emanating from the churches prohibited, so was much of what we would call charity. As a pamphlet on religion I picked up in the Soviet Union explained, "Charitable activity is not directly related to the performance of religious rites...[and therefore it is] prohibited. Neither is there any practical need for such activity. Poverty, famine and unemployment have long been done away with in the Soviet Union. The socialist state undertakes responsibility for social security." So much for the religious duty of feeding the hungry, clothing the naked, and caring for the sick, as Jesus called his followers to do.

James Luther Adams, for many years professor of Christian ethics at the Harvard Divinity School, insisted that churches must bear a hefty share of the blame for Hitler's rise to totalitarian power in Nazi Germany, because they were so lacking in political concern and prophetic consciousness that they created a moral vacuum in their society into which a powerful charismatic leader could march with his Brown Shirts. When Hitler did come to power, he reduced the life of the church to the minimum allowed in totalitarian communist countries: personal piety, worship permitted only in registered churches that swore loyalty to the state, and no challenges to the existing social order.[29]

I breathed a big sigh of relief when I returned to America and its religious pluralism: historically engaged in politics on both the left and the right, a major contributor to civil rights and antiwar movements just as surely as to pro-life campaigns and opposition to same-sex marriage. As U.S. constitutional scholar Lawrence Tribe has put it, "The attempt to silence the clergy on matters political or ... to silence politicians on matters religious is fundamentally and deeply inimical to the First Amendment and to its underlying spirit."[30]

Yet, how should we respond when a Yale Law School graduate, clergyman, and politician named Pat Robertson claims that "The Constitution of the United States is a marvelous document for self-government by Christian people. But the minute you turn the document into the hands of non-Christian and atheist people, they can use it to destroy the very foundation of our society, and that's what's been happening."[31] Or when the Reverend Jerry Falwell asserts that "We must have men and women elected to office at every level who believe...in the right of little children to pray in their schools...Biblically sound textbooks must be written for every school child in every course of study."[32] This is where the other side of Professor Tribe's perspective is helpful. No, we should never silence clergy on matters political, nor politicians on matters religious, but the United States Constitution is equally clear that "neither religion nor politics may become an arm of the other," for "when those arms embrace, the result may be the suffocation of freedom."[33]

The most hopeful document I've ever seen for addressing the proper extent of church-state separation was published in 1988 as the Williamsburg Charter.[34] It was the result of a summit meeting composed of both conservative and liberal Protestants, Roman Catholics, Eastern Orthodox Christians, and Jews, along with members of Congress, academics, media people, business leaders, and various other representatives. Signatories included the likes of Jimmy Carter and Gerald Ford, Billy Graham and Coretta Scott King, Bob Dole and Michael Dukakis, William Rehnquist and Warren Burger, Norman Lear and Phyllis Schlafly, Robert Bellah and Peter Berger, Bill Bennett and Lane Kirkland. The charter noted that "Justifiable fears are raised by those who advocate theocracy or the coercive power of law to establish a 'Christian America'...At the same time...interpretations of the 'wall of separation' [between church and state] that would exclude religious expression and argument from public life also contradict freedom of conscience and the genius of the [first amendment]." It went on to identify "a growing philosophical and cultural awareness that all people live by commitments and ideals, [and] that value-neutrality is impossible in the ordering of society...Politics is indeed an extension of ethics and therefore engages religious principles."

So, concretely speaking, how do we decide what to render unto Caesar and what to render unto God, according to the Williamsburg Charter? First of all, public policy should be developed through vigorous religious and nonreligious contention, but within an atmosphere of political civility. This means that "Arguments for public policy should be more than private convictions shouted out loud. For persuasion to be principled, private convictions should be translated into publicly accessible claims…[This should be done] for two reasons: first, because they must engage those who do not share the same private convictions, and second, because they should be directed toward the public good." I understand the Williamsburg Charter to be calling for us to be well grounded in our own religious and philosophical perspectives, but in the public sphere to make arguments from those perspectives that have been translated into a language of civil discourse that can be rationally articulated and readily understood across traditions.

Second, the Williamsburg Charter implores us not to allow the needed dynamic tension between church and state to deteriorate into ideological warfare in which individuals, motives, and reputations are impugned. "Too often," the Charter tells us, "religious believers have been uncharitable, liberals have been illiberal, conservatives have been insensitive to tradition, champions of tolerance have been intolerant, defenders of free speech have been censorious, and citizens of a republic based on democratic accommodation have succumbed to a habit of relentless confrontation." Instead, what we should be working toward is "neither a naked public square where all religion is excluded, nor a sacred public square with any religion established or semi-established." The ideal is "a civil public square in which citizens of all religious faiths, or none, engage one another in the continuing democratic discourse."

Jesus was forced to deal with religious and political enemies who were plotting to entrap him in what he said about church-state conundrums and ultimately to have him killed. We seem to be living in a difficult age now too, with high stakes religiously and politically, if not all-out struggles unto death. What does Jesus teach us to show us the way through? The Pharisees are actually right in their disingenuous comment that Jesus is sincere and teaches God's ways without either partiality or deference to anyone. May we be careful as we engage religiously in public life to be sincere, impartial, and nondeferential ourselves. May we also not make idols out of worldly pursuits like material wealth and personal power, remembering to render only unto God those things that are God's: like ultimacy (that is, what's really and finally important, beyond having to make the next tax payments); like gratitude for our very lives on this glorious earth of which we are stewards; and like devotion to others in return for the unconditional love that is the enduring law of the universe, even after all has seemingly gone wrong.

ONE NATION UNDER GOD

There are many liberal Christians, however, who feel it's entirely inappropriate that the Pledge of Allegiance includes the words "one nation under God." I feel differently. We need to look at much more in our civil life than the pledge in addressing this dimension of church-state relations. Indeed, look at a patriotic song like "America the Beautiful," with its words "God shed His grace on thee." The second verse is: "O beautiful for pilgrim feet, Whose stern, impassioned stress, A thoroughfare for freedom beat Across the wilderness! America! America! God mend thy every flaw, Confirm thy soul in self-control, Thy liberty in law."[35] Or look at another of our great patriotic songs: "My country, 'tis of thee,—Sweet land of liberty, Of thee I sing...Long may our land be bright, With freedom's holy light; Protect us by thy might, Great God, our King."[36] It's critical to note, though, when we look carefully at these songs, that they don't assume that God blesses America in some special way; instead, they beseech God to bless America—including mending our flaws and helping us preserve our freedom. As Abraham Lincoln explained, we should never assume that God is on our side; instead, we should pray and worry earnestly about whether we are on God's side.[37]

There's a long national history behind God language in our civil life, and it's surely not enough to say that the critical moment was a Republican congress's decision in 1954, at the height of McCarthyism, to add "under God" to the Pledge of Allegiance. Nor is it enough to note that "In God we trust" was also officially made the national motto during Dwight Eisenhower's first term as president.[38] The story begins back with those seventeenth-century Pilgrims and their stern, impassioned stress. The European emigration to America began with certain religious people seeking freedom to practice their religion. As Alexis de Tocqueville, the great early-nineteenth-century French observer of America, so aptly put it: "It must never be forgotten that religion gave birth to Anglo-American society. In the United States, religion is therefore mingled with all the habits of the nation and all the feelings of patriotism, whence it derives a peculiar force."[39]

There's a book by Stanford graduate and Unitarian Universalist minister Forrest Church that I've found particularly enlightening on this matter. It's called *The American Creed*. Church was the son of the late liberal democratic Senator Frank Church, and the book is dedicated poignantly to Church's four children. Forrest writes to them: "I wonder...whether I have imparted to you just how much I love our county...You have often heard me criticize the policies of our government and the actions of our leaders...You might conclude that, in today's world, America creates more problems than it solves. When we exercise our power wantonly, we *can* do great damage. But...ours is a good nation that sometimes does bad things. To be mindful of the latter and forget the former is both cynical and wrong...Note especially how the song lines of faith and freedom play throughout [our history]."[40]

Forrest Church sees the 1776 Declaration of Independence, written by liberal Christian Thomas Jefferson, as the centerpiece of America's claim to be "one nation under God." In its preamble all of the foundational American values that we still treasure are crystallized: "We hold these truths to be self-evident, that all men are created equal, that they are endowed by their Creator with certain unalienable Rights, that among these are Life, Liberty and the pursuit of Happiness." This is the American creed, which includes commitments to equality, liberty, and rights-based justice—not merely as a matter of human desire or principles of good government, but as having a transcendent source in the Laws of Nature and of Nature's God.

Oh how we stand under God's judgment, though, for our shortcomings in fulfilling our creed! African American slaves were not considered men at the time a slaveholder wrote the Declaration of Independence; it took the long, bloody Civil War to settle that issue. Women were not included in the term "men," and women's equality, in terms of suffrage alone, took another 144 years. Much of this country was stolen outright from its indigenous inhabitants, who were herded as supposedly sovereign nations onto reservations. Martin Luther King Jr. had to invoke the Declaration of Independence almost 200 years later at the Lincoln Memorial, along with explicit biblical references, to talk about a dream of freedom not yet achieved.

So what does our modern, pluralistic nation—with plenty of agnostics and atheists among us—gain now by calling ourselves "one nation under God?" One result is that our creedal commitment to liberty as an inalienable right, as interpreted through the constitutional Bill of Rights, protects atheist and agnostic liberty not to be coerced by believers. Our American creed also protects liberty from itself, from its becoming such thoroughgoing individualism that we forget the transcendent referent that calls us together in a covenanting community, that helps us to see ourselves as one nation, not just many individuals living in the same place—*e pluribus unum,* "out of many, one."

The American creed should ideally help us in the face of particularist religious fundamentalisms that challenge the alleged amorality or materialism or self-centered excesses or spiritual emptiness of certain forms of modern secularism. As the English author G. K. Chesterton put it, "America is the only nation in the world that is founded on a creed," one set forth "with theological lucidity in the Declaration of Independence." That creed can both face down sectarian fundamentalist attempts to impose a different creed upon the body politic and also coexist with many different forms of sectarian religion, which can be freely exercised as long as they don't try to become the established religion of the state. If we didn't have a common vision of being one nation under God, we'd be much more vulnerable to specific fundamentalist challenges to remake our nation in their image. We've seen this, for example, in the religious revolution in Iran that toppled the secular government of the Shah and imposed its own sectarian authority, not to mention the twentieth-century problems with secular fundamentalisms like Marxism-Leninism, Stalinism, and Maoism.[41]

Our American creed has given rise as well to a robust and respected tradition of civil disobedience, from Henry David Thoreau's refusing to pay war taxes to Martin Luther King's refusal to obey Jim Crow laws. Calvin Coolidge once said, you may "speak of natural rights, but I challenge anyone to show where in nature any rights existed."[42] As Coolidge saw it, that's what positive laws established by legislatures are all about. Laws create rights, and they do not exist otherwise. That would mean that rights could just as easily be eliminated by legislators. Of course, the Holocaust perpetrated by Nazi Germany was in large part based on duly passed laws, carefully administered by legally authorized agents of the state. Coolidge was wrong. The genius of the American creed is that it produces moral checks and balances to positive law, whether created by legislators or by judges in the common-law tradition. It's on the basis of inalienable rights with which we're endowed by Nature's God that Martin Luther King could write from the Birmingham City Jail, "There are two types of laws: there are *just* and there are *unjust* laws...A just law is a man-made code that squares with the moral law or the law of God...An unjust law is a human law that is not rooted in eternal and natural law...All segregation statutes are unjust because segregation distorts the soul and damages the personality. It gives the segregator a false sense of superiority and the segregated a false sense of inferiority."[43] As I look at King's statement, all of the basic values of the American creed are implicated here, including equality, liberty, and rights-based justice, each with a transcendent source.

In addition, our American creed has given rise to a powerful tradition of social service and social justice work. Equality, liberty, and justice are ideals to strive for as part of our national duty. Abraham Lincoln in his second inaugural address toward the end of the Civil War calls his newly reunited Americans to respond in this way: "With malice toward none, with charity for all, with firmness in the right as God gives us to see the right, let us strive on to finish the work we are in, to bind up the nation's wounds, to care for him who shall have borne the battle and for his widow and his orphan—to do all which may achieve and cherish a just and lasting peace among ourselves and with all nations."[44] In 1848 at Seneca Falls, New York, Elizabeth Cady Stanton and Susan B. Anthony, in their struggle for women's equality, rewrote Jefferson's words to say: "We hold these truths to be self-evident: that all men and women are created equal; that they are endowed by their Creator with certain inalienable rights."[45] President John F. Kennedy in his inaugural address, after noting that "the same revolutionary beliefs for which our forebears fought are still at issue around the globe—the belief that the rights of man come not from the generosity of the state but from the hand of God," went on to say that "the trumpet summons us again...[to] struggle against the common enemies of man: tyranny, poverty, disease and war itself."[46]

Finally, our American creed has served as a source of solace and strength when our nation was under attack. Our religious institutions were filled after September 11, 2001. In the public square, as one Episcopal bishop noted, in diners and in bait and ammo shops, signs reading "God Bless America" outnumbered those for hot coffee.[47] The creed supported pluralism as well: Americans of many faiths expressed deeper kinship with their Muslim neighbors, even though the attack had been at the hands of Muslim extremists. Despite some hate crimes around the country, a Reuters poll found that the number of Americans viewing Muslims favorably went from 45 percent before 9/11 to 59 percent two months after 9/11. The change was most pronounced among Republicans, whose favorable opinion of Muslims more than doubled, from 29 percent to 64 percent.[48]

No matter what one may think of the words and actions of President George W. Bush at the time, I think he got the spirit of our "one nation under God" right in a speech he gave at a university in Beijing, China, five months after 9/11:

Faith points to a moral law beyond man's law and calls us to duties higher than material gain. Under our law, everyone stands equal. No one is above the law, and no one is beneath it... Faith gives us a moral core and teaches us to hold ourselves to high standards, to love and to serve others and to live responsible lives... In a free society, diversity is not disorder. Debate is not strife. And dissent is not revolution. A free society trusts its citizens to seek greatness in themselves and their country... The United States has its share of problems, and we have our faults... We're on a long journey toward achieving our own ideals of equality and justice. Nonetheless, there is a reason our nation shines as a beacon of hope and opportunity.[49]

So that's why I believe America is, and should be, one nation under God. May we not be ruled by gods of materialism, military power, selfishness, and greed. May we not be ruled by any particular sectarian religion's notion of what's good for us. May we remain the land of the free and the home of the brave. May we glory in our pluralism, including, of course, those who believe in no God at all. *E pluribus unum.* Out of many, one. One nation committed to the God-given, inalienable rights of equality, liberty, and justice for all.

THE AMERICAN SOUL

But how does America really hold together given our enormous diversity and our commitment to pluralism? We're constantly absorbing new immigrant populations. Many countries are held together by an ethnic identity of being, say, Japanese or Turkic, or Chinese, or Russian, or Serbian, or even French or German. Although America has arguably historically been a melting pot into a white, Anglo-Saxon, Protestant reality, that hasn't been our conscious self-image. Instead, we've pledged ourselves to "liberty and justice for all," and we have sung of "crowning thy good with brotherhood from sea to shining sea." That spirit of hospitality is picked up in the inscription on the base of the Statue of Liberty. Written by Emma Lazarus, a noted nineteenth-century poet and essayist, it reads: "Give me your tired, your poor, Your huddled masses, yearning to breathe free, The wretched refuse of your teeming shore. Send these, the homeless, tempest-tost to me, I lift my lamp beside the golden door!"[50]

America is not an ethnicity, or even a people with a common history. As Jacob Needleman in his book *The American Soul* exclaims, "America [is] an *idea!* What other country can say that?"[51] I had the pleasure of interviewing Needleman once at Stanford for our "Aurora Forum" lecture series, which is dedicated to exploring democratic ideals and inspiring social hope. He explained that American identity has been forged through the idea of this nation being the hope of the world. That hope includes material prosperity, yes, but also the promise of freedom and equality of opportunity. It includes working together for common safety and security, yes, but much more importantly, for a vision of what humanity is and can become in terms of its potential, individually and in community.[52] Needleman sees all the rights guaranteed by the United States Constitution as based on a vision of something within ourselves that is higher than the all-too-human desires for personal gain and satisfaction or the instinctive loyalties to family and tribe.

Of course, the idea of America is far from being fully realized. To say "God bless America," as presidents and presidential candidates seem inevitably to do in ending their speeches, is hopefully always a trembling statement of supplication, not an assumption of fact. It's not "America has

God's blessing and we deserve it," but instead "*May* you, God, please bless America, by showing us your ways" and "*May* you shed your grace on us, sinners that we are, and help us to move closer to you." In Irving Berlin's 1938 song "God Bless America," God is asked to stand beside America and to guide her.

I suggest that America is really not a nation divided in the sense of conservatives and liberals. We are really not two separate countries in the United States, a Republican country and a Democratic country. Our nation's soul is not divided either. Instead, we have a central idea of America that binds us together. Like any great myth or symbol, the idea of America has layers of meaning, and it's capable of holding opposites in creative tension. We are held together by a few basic values inherent in the idea of America—liberty, equality, hope for the future, and faith that nature and nature's God have endowed us with certain unalienable rights as human beings. Of course, we differ deeply over a number of political issues like abortion, marriage for same-sex couples, the war in Iraq, and levels of taxation. Yet, we usually base our arguments with each other on this set of deeper values that make up the idea of America. We have the same reference points for our disagreements.

Abortion has to do with women's reproductive freedom and/or with the fetus's inherent right to life. Marriage for same-sex couples has to do with the inherent freedom of each individual to choose exactly whom to marry, or with a sense of what is natural and what's meant to be (or not) in the order of the universe. Disagreements over the war in Iraq are a matter of both how best to protect the sanctity of life and how best to promote freedom at home and abroad. Taxation debates often weigh liberty rights for individuals and groups against interests in social equality and equality of opportunity.

Great symbols and myths work by incorporating dichotomy and paradox, by having the breadth to embrace past, present, and future, and by providing a hopeful vision of transformation on the horizon. From a Christian perspective, as the apostle Paul explained in his second letter to Timothy, the word of God is not chained. It is always transformational. Perhaps activist and statesman John Gardner, beloved by both Republicans and Democrats, put it best when he exclaimed that America consists of "a shared vision, shared norms, expectations, and values...If we care about the American Experiment, we had better search out and celebrate the values we share...That we have failed and fumbled in some of our attempts to achieve our ideals is obvious. But the great ideas still beckon—freedom, equality, justice, and the release of human possibilities...We are capable of so much more than is now asked of us. The courage and spirit are there, poorly hidden beneath our surface pragmatism and self-indulgence...I'm saying that the moment has come."[53]

PART THREE

Living the Liberal Christian Life

TEN

CHRISTIAN DOCTRINE

The Trinity, Communion, Being Born Again, the Apocalypse, and the Sabbath

Baptize them in the name of the Father, and of the Son, and of the Holy Spirit

—Matthew 28:19

We who are many are one body, for we all partake of the one bread.

—1 Corinthians 10:17

No one can see the kingdom of God without being born again.

—John 3:3

Repent, for the kingdom of heaven is at hand.

—Matthew 4:17

Observe the Sabbath day and keep it holy.

—Deuteronomy 5:12

If church and state issues aren't hard enough, there are a number of Christian doctrinal issues that can be very difficult in discussions among Christians and nearly impenetrable for those outside of Christianity. Some of them were discussed in earlier chapters of this book: What does it mean to say that Jesus was the Son of God? Does God miraculously intervene in the world to alter natural laws? In what sense is the Bible the actual Word of God? Is faith different from belief? This chapter examines five more tough ones. Of course, there are many more to consider, but these five may be some of the most divisive or incomprehensible. How exactly can God be three in one and one in three? What does it mean to eat and drink the body and blood of Jesus together as the central ritual of Christianity? How is it that I can be "born again" as a Christian, and do I actually want to? Is the apocalypse coming, and how will it affect me? Is keeping the Sabbath really important enough to be one of the Ten Commandments? Hopefully shedding some light on these matters of Christian doctrine will be helpful to liberals and promote constructive conversations with others.

THE TRINITY

What's the meaning of the Trinity? How can Christians seem to have three gods in one? At the very end of the gospel of Matthew, after the resurrected Jesus has first appeared to Mary Magdalene and another woman outside the tomb in Jerusalem, Jesus meets with his eleven male disciples in Galilee more than 100 miles away and gives them the "great commission."[1] He says, "All authority in heaven and on earth has been given to me. Go therefore and make disciples of all nations, baptizing them in the name of the Father and of the Son and of the Holy Spirit."[2] The *HarperCollins Study Bible* has a note that says, "This explicit Trinitarian formula is rare in the New Testament and probably derives from early Christian worship."[3] In fact, there is no developed doctrine of the Trinity in the Bible.[4] It comes later, as the Christian community develops, and ultimately it's the result of the decisions of theologians at the Councils of Nicaea and Constantinople in the fourth century A.D.[5]

At least since that time, many Christians have understood God to be three in one, and one in three—a triune God.[6] The Nicene Creed, which many Christians still regularly repeat today, begins this way, "We believe in one God, the Father, the Almighty, maker of heaven and earth." It goes on to say, "We believe in one Lord, Jesus Christ, the only Son of God, eternally begotten of the Father, God from God, Light from Light, true God from true God, begotten, not made, of one Being with the Father." Finally, it references the third part of the Trinity: "We believe in the Holy Spirit, the Lord, the giver of life, who proceeds from the Father and the Son. With the Father and the Son he is worshiped and glorified. He has spoken through the Prophets."[7]

Now, for my own Unitarian Christian forebears, this seemed rather complicated. They emphasized the monotheistic God of the Old Testament, and they claimed that the early Christian church in fact saw the Father as superior to the Son, in general giving *him* the title of God, as distinguished from the Son.[8] As for Jesus, the Son, they saw him as a unique moral exemplar and teacher, helping human beings reach their full dignity and ability to love.[9] Unitarian minister Ralph Waldo Emerson spoke of the Holy Spirit as a metaphor for the heavens passing into the human mind, as the human ability to drink from the soul of God, as the courage to love God directly—without any mediator or veil. Yet, Emerson was clear that while God may enter into each of us in important ways, only God is God, and God is one, not three.[10]

There are many verses in the New Testament that Unitarian Christians point to, demonstrating that Jesus never considered himself identical with God. For example, Jesus distinguishes himself from God when a man addresses him as "Good Teacher." Jesus responds, "Why do you call me good? No one is good but God alone."[11] Jesus instructs his disciples and the crowds, "Call no one your father on earth, for you have one Father—the one in heaven."[12] When Jesus prays in the Garden of Gethsemane on the night before he is crucified, he asks, "My Father, if it is possible, let this cup pass from me."[13] The cup symbolizes his destiny to be executed,[14] and Jesus does not want to die. But then, realizing none of this is in his hands, only in God's, he says, "Yet, not what I want but what you want." Or, as he's quoted in the gospel of Luke, "Yet, not my will but yours be done."[15] Even the Roman Catholic *Jerome Biblical Commentary* notes that Jesus's prayerful struggles in the Garden of Gethsemane "constitute a problem for anyone 'defending' the divinity of Jesus."[16] So what can liberal Christians make of the doctrine of the Trinity?

As I have underscored throughout this book, the great Christian innovation among the religions of the world is seeing God first and foremost as love.[17] To properly explicate love, one needs to see it not just abstractly as a natural law of the universe emanating from the creator God. There's also a need for a flesh-and-blood human exemplar of love incarnate. It's also important to have a sense of love shared in community, imaged as a kind of breath or wind that moves among us and unites us all. So, we can say Father, Son, and Holy Spirit. Or, avoiding patriarchal imagery: parental mother-father love, friendship unto death, and beloved community. These are different ways of seeing the one God—in the universe and in our world. The Trinity constitutes three different windows on the one God of love.

There are a few other biblical bases for the church's doctrine of the

Trinity. Early in the gospel of Matthew, when Jesus himself is baptized by John, the text reads: "Suddenly the heavens were opened to him and he saw the Spirit of God descending like a dove and alighting on him. And a voice from heaven said, 'This is my beloved Son, with whom I am well pleased.'"[18] All the elements are there: The Father showing his love for his Son not only through words but also through the medium of the Holy Spirit alighting on the Son. When he is no longer on earth, Jesus explains, "the Holy Spirit, whom the Father will send in my name, will teach you everything, and remind you of all that I have said to you."[19] There's the link between the love of the parent, the love of the companion-mentor, and the love that builds community over time. Then, sure enough, the Holy Spirit does descend on the disciples in wind and fire on Pentecost, as reported in the second chapter of the book of Acts. Paul later ends his second letter to the Christian community in Corinth by saying "The grace of the Lord Jesus Christ, the love of God, and the communion of the Holy Spirit be with all of you."[20]

The creator's infinite love, the grace of the human incarnation, Jesus, and the sense of communion with each other that the Holy Spirit continues to provide—all these aspects come together to form a complete picture of the power of the one God in our lives. Perhaps another way of seeing through these three windows to God is to think of the transcendent God of the universe (out there as the creator of all we know in nature), the God who walks by our side in human form—both rejoicing and suffering along with us (having known suffering in the extreme of crucifixion)—and the God who is deep within our own souls but also working as the force that ties us together in community with each other. This is one God, but one who can feel quite different in an operational sense, like three modes of being.

As Daniel Migliore explains it in his introduction to Christian theology, the doctrine of the Trinity

did not fall down from heaven, nor was it etched in tablets of stone. It is the product of the reflection of the church on the gospel message over many centuries. The doctrine of the Trinity is second-order reflection on the workings of divine love attested in Scripture and experienced by the Christian community. In other words, the starting point of Trinitarian faith is the good news of the love of God in Christ that continues to work transformingly in the world by the Holy Spirit.[21]

Migliore, who teaches at Princeton Theological Seminary, claims that what he calls "the dance of Trinitarian love" has far-reaching implications: God the creator—God the parent—is experienced not as a God of absolute power and rule of force, but as one who gives both life and love, as one who empowers by pointing to caring family relationships. God in human form befriends the poor and forgives sinners. We are all redeemed through the direct experience of unconditional love played out on the human stage; that's the compassion for the hungry, the estranged, the homeless, the sick, the imprisoned which Jesus consistently showed. And then we are sustained by a vision of genuine, inclusive community and just sharing of the earth's resources that moves us beyond all petty divisions of race, nationality, class, and gender and provides a positive sense of solidarity, a sense of being one in the spirit.[22]

I experienced this in concrete form during the last five years that I lived in Boston, just before moving to California in 2001. I used to meet every two weeks with three other Unitarian Universalist Christian ministers and a Catholic spiritual director for Bible study, prayer, and personal development. We found a constant interplay between our awe in the face of the transcendent creator of the universe, our appreciation for the loving accompaniment we felt from Jesus as one who knew suffering and joy at infinite levels, and our comfort in being bound together by a force that felt so much stronger than anything that could threaten to tear us apart. I remember one time in particular when one of us had to face the gunfire death of a fifteen-year-old boy who had been in her inner-city church's summer work program. As so often happens, he was a good kid, friendly, cooperative, hardworking, bright. He was just hanging around with the wrong people at the wrong time. A huge emotional funeral gave some release and some sense of hope to her parishioners. Yet, behind the scenes, my fellow minister was devastated. In fact, she was deeply discouraged and depressed. Our group came together around her, expressing how our hearts ached with hers. We verbalized our anger: "Children should not die, and we adults should not make available the tools of destruction, which kids can neither control nor comprehend." We cried with her and sat in silence with her. Jesus on the cross was the pervasive image for us in our prayers. Yet, we also spoke of the creator God's ultimate goodness and unconditional love. Paraphrasing Martin Luther King Jr., the universe bends toward justice and toward love. And we remembered all the time that

God was with us and among us in spirit; we were bathed by love for each other and joined to the larger community that we hoped someday could become truly beloved.[23]

There we were, Unitarians living out a Trinitarian understanding of God. The triune God had us in his grip, or her grip, just as surely as our espoused theology would have said that God is one, God is one, God is one. As the old Christian hymn affirms, "Holy, Holy, Holy, merciful and mighty! God in three persons, blessed Trinity."[24]

COMMUNION

Trinitarian love can be expressed in a particularly poignant, ritualized way: communion. The earliest description of it comes from the Apostle Paul, writing about 55 A.D.[25] He was likely referring to what happened during Jesus's last Passover seder with his disciples before he was executed by the Romans: "Jesus on the night when he was betrayed took a loaf of bread, and when he had given thanks, he broke it and said, 'This is my body that is for you. Do this in remembrance of me.' In the same way he took the cup also, after supper, saying, 'This is the new covenant in my blood. Do this, as often as you drink it, in remembrance of me.'"[26]

What exactly is the meaning of communion? It's been central to the worshiping life of Christians back to the very beginning. We do it twice a month at University Public Worship on Sunday mornings in the Stanford Memorial Church. Yet, what are we really doing? Communion literally means "sharing." It's breaking bread together. The word comes from the King James Bible translation of the Greek word for "sharing" that Paul used in describing the taking of bread and wine as the body and blood of Christ.[27] The Latin root is *communis,* meaning participation by all. The same root is used for the words common, community, and communicate.[28] It's supposed to bring everyone together as one body. As Paul says in his first letter to the Corinthians, when speaking of sharing bread as the body of Christ, "Because there is one bread, we who are many are one body, for we all partake of the one bread."[29]

"One bread, one body," and yet an argument over whether to use leavened or unleavened bread in communion was a principal basis for the split between the Church of Rome and the Eastern Orthodox Church in the eleventh century.[30] "One bread, one body," and yet my Protestant father, who lovingly went to mass with my Catholic mother every Sunday, was never allowed to take communion together with her there. "One bread, one body," and yet Protestant reformers Luther and Zwingli argued bitterly and split over whether the bread and wine were the actual flesh and blood of Christ or merely symbolized his body and blood, an argument that persists today.[31]

Of course "communion" is not the only word used to describe this Christian ritual. Paul also calls it "the Lord's Supper."[32] Another term is "the Eucharist," meaning "thanksgiving," and while there's no indisputable biblical use of this word to describe the bread and wine ritual, "Eucharist" was frequently used by Christian writers from the second century on.[33] It was the Greek word used for giving thanks or blessings over food,[34] as in "Jesus took a loaf of bread, and when he had given thanks, he broke it."[35]

The fullest biblical account that we have of communion as it was practiced in the early Christian church is in Paul's first letter to the Corinthians. At that time it was part of a full-scale meal, apparently in the home of a member of the Christian community in Corinth.[36] Paul criticizes the Corinthian Christians, however, because they have come to observe communion as a highly individualized, privatized matter: "For when the time comes to eat, each of you goes ahead with your own supper, and one goes hungry and another becomes drunk."[37]

Paul also seems to be concerned that there were significant distinctions being made between rich and poor: "You show contempt for the church of God and humiliate those who have nothing."[38] As one biblical commentary puts it, wealthy people were apparently invited earlier for the choice food and drink, and poorer Christians came later to "find, along with tipsy co-worshipers, leftover food at best."[39] Obviously this violated the radical social vision of equality that Jesus continually promoted. So Paul calls each member of the Christian community at Corinth to self-examination before partaking of the Lord's Supper.[40] When they come together to eat as a church, he asks them to wait for one another[41] and then to break bread together in explicit remembrance of Jesus, as he instructed at his own Last Supper.[42]

The larger Christian church subsequently formalized communion (or the Lord's Supper or the Eucharist) and made a small ritual meal part of worship services. What remains absolutely central to the ritual, however, is the concept of community, the idea of overcoming distinctions and barriers, the coming together as one body to share in the one bread. Jesus came with a clear understanding of human solidarity that he symbolized again and again, in the face of fierce criticism, by breaking bread with tax collectors and sinners and outcasts,[43] by breaking bread with the multitudes.[44] This language from the gospel of John sounds familiar, doesn't it, describing how he fed 5,000 people by the Sea of Galilee: "Then Jesus took the loaves, and when he had given thanks, he distributed them to those who were seated."[45] He didn't ask if all those people were his followers, or were merely curious about him, or in fact were doubtful. He didn't distinguish between rich and poor, male and female, Jew and Gentile.

Communion is not just a matter of ingathering in unity. It should also nourish us for an outpouring of love in the world. Jesus always did both. He gathered people to break bread together, and then he sent them out to feed and clothe and comfort others: "I was hungry and you gave me food, I was thirsty and you gave me something to drink, I was a stranger and you welcomed me, I was naked and you gave me clothing, I was sick and you took care of me, I was in prison and you visited me...Just as you did it to the least of these [my brothers and sisters]...you did it to me."[46]

Catholic priest Henri Nouwen wrote this Eucharistic prayer:

Dear Lord...Isn't my faith in your presence in the breaking of the bread meant to reach out beyond the small circle of my brothers to the larger circle of humanity and to alleviate suffering as much as possible? If I can recognize you in the Sacrament of the Eucharist, I must also be able to recognize you in the many hungry men, women and children [in the world]. If I cannot translate my faith in your presence, under the appearance of bread and wine, into action for the world, I am still an unbeliever. I pray, therefore, Lord, deepen my faith in your Eucharistic presence and help me find ways to let this faith bear fruit in the lives of many. Amen."[47]

A church I used to belong to in inner-city Boston was located on what was called Meetinghouse Hill. People who knew what went on in the church, though, called it "Eating House Hill." The minister, Rev. Jim Allen, always had a huge pot of stew or chili or soup cooking on the stove in the kitchen and lots of fresh bread. Many people came by that church during the week asking for help paying their rent or utilities. They came to discuss problems with the welfare office or the Social Security Administration or local merchants. They came because their children had just been taken away for alleged neglect, or because they couldn't get health care, or because they were about to be deported as "illegal aliens."

This minister never passed the buck. He always seemed to provide cash when needed, and he got on the phone and called people he knew in the agencies and businesses with which people were having trouble. All the time he was ladling out stew and bread. Most of these people in need didn't come to church on Sunday and therefore didn't formally take communion, although some of them sent their children to Sunday school. No matter, though. They experienced communion. For half an hour or more they were able to come in out of the cold and find a warm and welcoming human face who asked them to break bread with him and the others who happened to be around that kitchen table each day. Not only did they fill their stomachs and get concrete assistance with their problem, they filled their souls. And privileged people like me did too, simply by being at that table.

Carl Scovel, another minister I knew in Boston, once preached about soul food, starting with the African American tradition developed during slavery—with turnip and collard greens and chitlins and hog's knuckles— and ending with the soup and bread that this minister's own father was able to get him when they were in a concentration camp together.[48] He talked about soul food coming from a time of trial, but also about it being a sign of affection on the part of those who actually prepare it and serve it. To refuse such food is to refuse love. He gave J.D. Salinger's *Franny and Zooey* as an example, when Franny is obsessed with looking for God, trying to repeat the Jesus prayer properly, over and over again: "Lord, Jesus Christ, have mercy on me." Increasingly she withdraws from her family and friends, her work, and her everyday life until her brother Zooey gets through to her:

> I'll tell you one thing, Franny. One thing I know. And don't get upset. But if it's the religious life you want, you ought to know that you're missing out on every single religious action that's going on around this house. You don't even have sense enough to drink when somebody brings you a cup of consecrated chicken soup, which is the only kind of chicken soup Bessie ever brings anybody around this madhouse. So just tell me, buddy. Even if you

went out and searched the whole world for a master, some guru, some holy man, to tell you how to say your Jesus prayer properly, what good would it do you? How [the heck]…are you going to recognize a legitimate holy man when you see one if you don't even know a cup of consecrated chicken soup when it's right in front of your nose?[49]

As Carl Scovel, explained, "Soul food is an act of love…Bread and wine are the soul food of the Christian. They come from a time of trial, [and] they are invested with love."[50]

I hope the time will come when Christian communion is a true sharing, when Christians are united by this ancient ritual in remembrance of Jesus, rather than divided by it, when Christians reach out beyond their own community to break bread with tax collectors and sinners and outcasts—indeed, with the multitudes. Christian communion to me should stimulate an outpouring of love for others, especially those who suffer, and just as importantly an acceptance of love for oneself. Through communion, ideally we commemorate the life and death of Jesus and then celebrate his true spiritual presence with us now, and every day.

BEING BORN AGAIN

Being born again is another way of talking about actively living in the spiritual presence of love that Jesus represents in the world. Four out of ten American adults these days identify themselves as "born again Christians."[51] The Greek phrase translated "born again" appears in the Bible only at the beginning of third chapter of John's gospel, but the concept has had a lot of staying power! It's generally been used as a marker for evangelical or conservative Protestant Christians, as opposed to liberal Protestant Christians, to Roman Catholic Christians, and to Eastern Orthodox Christians. Indeed, many Americans who so identify would claim that members of these other denominations are not Christian at all if they haven't been "born again" in this conservative Protestant sense. And, typically, that means having gone through a sudden, powerful personal conversion experience.[52]

John Stott, a prominent evangelical spokesman, prefers the term "regeneration" to "conversion." Conversion for Stott implies consciously repenting one's sin and turning to Christ, accepting him in faith as one's Lord and Savior. Regeneration emphasizes new birth as solely the work of God; it is indeed sudden and utterly transformational, but it cannot be self-generated through a personal sense of moral reformation. We might not even be conscious that it's happened, just as we were not conscious of our own birth experience and would not know our birthday unless our parents told us.[53]

Let's look at what's actually said, though, in the third chapter of John's gospel. A Jewish religious leader named Nicodemus comes to Jesus, honorifically calls him rabbi, and then rather courageously says, "We know that you are a teacher who has come from God; for no one can do these signs that you do apart from the presence of God."[54] He has come secretly to Jesus at night, presumably because his Pharisee community would not be pleased to hear him saying that Jesus had come from God; yet, he's doing his own independent thinking and bringing it directly to Jesus. He sounds almost as if he wants to become a disciple of Jesus, and in fact later he does.[55] Jesus responds to Nicodemus indirectly, but in a way that implies he doesn't want to be followed as a mere miracle worker: "very truly I tell you, no one can see the kingdom of God without being born again."[56] Nicodemus takes him literally and asks how to enter one's mother's womb a second time. Jesus's answer is that in order to enter the kingdom of God one must be born of water and Spirit.[57]

Here's where the commentators I've read start splitting in various directions. Does water and Spirit mean baptism, being born again through baptism? This has historically been the Roman Catholic position, as well as that of more liturgical Protestant denominations like Episcopalians and Lutherans.[58] As we say in the sacrament of baptism performed in the Stanford Memorial Church, "We thank you, Father, for the water of Baptism...Through it we are reborn by the Holy Spirit." Paul explains in his letter to the Romans that through baptism we rise with Christ to walk in newness of life.[59] In fact, in the next chapter of John, after the exchange with Nicodemus, Jesus goes out into the Judean countryside with his disciples to baptize people.

However, the contrary view is that Nicodemus the Pharisee is listening to these words of Jesus without any knowledge of Christian baptism, and he may well be hearing that new life will link physical birth (the breaking of a mother's waters) with spiritual rebirth:[60] "No one can enter the kingdom of God without being born of water *and* Spirit."[61] This reading from a Protestant commentary seems confirmed in the next sentence of the gospel text: "What is born of the flesh is flesh, and what is born of the Spirit is spirit."[62] Yet, my Catholic commentary sees this very sentence as a gloss on the power of baptism. Being born of the flesh is not enough; it's only the outward manifestation of life. True life comes from the Spirit of God transforming the inner life, which begins for Christians in the initiatory sacrament of baptism.[63] Hence, the importance of a priest, or even a nurse, baptizing a defective newborn who is expected to die soon after physical birth.

However, John Stott, the evangelical, insists that baptism, important as it is, must never be confused with the kind of new birth that Jesus was presenting to Nicodemus: "The new birth is a deep, inward, radical change, worked by the Holy Spirit in the inner recesses of the human personality." Baptism is a sign of new birth, but it does not operate mechanically to bring about what it signifies. Stott quotes a seventeenth-century archbishop's statement that infant baptism or any baptism is not fully effected until one believes, until one actually lays hold by faith of what God has mercifully granted us through the gift of his son, Jesus Christ.[64]

And how many angels can dance on the head of a pin? These kinds of intricate theological debates, that have so split the Christian church and that have ultimately led to so much hatred and bloodshed down through the centuries, may thankfully not be of great interest to liberal Christians. Frankly, not quibbling unto death over theological minutia is one of the great strengths of liberal Christianity, often distinguishing it from conservative Christianity. But is there anything else about being born again that might prove helpful in thinking about our spiritual lives?

In the gospel of John, Jesus uses another image for being born again: "The wind blows where it chooses, and you hear the sound of it, but you do not know where it comes from or where it goes. So it is with everyone who is born of the Spirit."[65] Jesus's offer of a new birth here is connected with wind. It doesn't sound like something one can grab hold of by conscious intent. The proper attitude would seem to be more like gratitude for an undeserved gift, and a radical openness to the variety of ways it chooses to envelop and massage us.

The gospel writer continues, in one of the most memorized verses of the New Testament, to explain the greatest undeserved gift of all—God's love for the whole world, manifested by the presence on earth of Jesus: "For God so loved the world that he gave his only Son, so that everyone who believes in him may not perish but may have eternal life."[66] For me, the new element here in understanding what it means to be born again is the enveloping love of God. Not only do we receive the physical gift of life in this world through our perishable bodies, but also our lives take on ultimate meaning beyond physicality through redeeming love. Our job is to receive that love unconditionally and joyfully from the spiritual wind that blows around us, and then to become channels of love ourselves to other people. Jesus is our exemplar. He shows us the way, the truth, and the life of genuinely selfless love, even unto death. We are born again as we let go and let the love of God and love for our fellow human beings overwhelm us and transform our lives.

So, what might it look like to be born again in our time and place, especially for those of us who wouldn't usually describe ourselves as "born again Christians"? I have a favorite John Cheever short story called "The Housebreaker of Shady Hill" that might explain it.[67] A 36-year-old New Yorker, well bred and well heeled, with a wife and four children, has come on hard times with his own business after he's left a major firm. He becomes ill tempered with his family and friends and seems headed for a divorce, after he breaks into a house in his wealthy residential neighborhood and steals cash to support his lifestyle. He describes what happens one night as he's heading toward a second house to rob.

While I was walking toward the Pewters', there was a harsh stirring in all the trees and gardens, like a draft on a bed of fire, and I wondered what it was until I felt the rain on my hands and face, and then I began to laugh. I wish I could say that a kindly lion had set me straight, or an innocent child, or the strains of distant music from some church, but it was no more than the rain on my head—the smell of it flying up to my nose—that showed me the extent of my freedom from . . . the works of a thief . . . There were ways out of my trouble if I cared to make use of them. I was not trapped . . . And it was no skin off my elbow how I had been given the gifts of life so long as I possessed them, and I possessed them then—the tie between the wet grass roots and the hair that grew out of my body, the thrill of my mortality that I had known on summer nights, loving the children and looking down the front of my wife's dress . . . It is not, as someone once wrote, the smell of corn bread that calls us back from death; it is the lights and signs of love and friendship.[68]

He's able to get his old job back, and then, with an advance on his salary, he breaks back into the first house late one night, for the last time, to return the money he stole.

So there's being "born again" in this Cheever story, with all the elements of deep, inward, radical change—baptismal water, wind blowing,—worked by the Spirit in the inner recesses of the human personality—and of undeserved gifts of life and love, if only we can appreciate them. There's no self-generated moral reformation. There's no conscious repenting of one's sin and turning to Christ. Just sudden regeneration, out of the blue, utterly transformative. It's in that sense I hope for all of us the experience of being born again.

APOCALYPSE

Sudden regeneration has another major biblical referent. The prophet Isaiah cries out, "O that you would tear open the heavens and come down, so that the mountains would quake at your presence!"[69] Jesus speaks of a future when, "in those days, after that suffering...the stars will be falling from heaven...Then they will see 'the Son of Man coming in clouds' with great power and glory."[70] There's lots of apocalyptic language in the Bible. The quoted words were written some 2,500[71] and 2,000 years ago respectively. But apocalyptic words have been very much the order of the day in the twenty-first century as well. Witness the phenomenal success of Tim LaHaye's and Jerry B. Jenkin's "Left Behind" series, based on this kind of vision: "Driverless cars careen out of control. Terrified people watch their loved ones vanish. Some say it's an alien invasion, but Rayford Steele knows that his wife's warning has come true—Christ has raptured believers and he's been left behind."[72]

As they've sold more than sixty million copies of best-selling novels and related books about "the earth's last days," LaHaye and Jenkins have taught that this very generation here on earth now will witness the return of Christ and the end of history.[73] LaHaye and Jenkins are conservative Christians. But a well-known liberal Christian theologian, Walter Wink, spoke apocalyptic warnings from the pulpit of the Stanford Memorial Church a few years back. He catalogued perils that jeopardize the viability of life on earth: global warming; overpopulation and attendant malnutrition and starvation; unemployment; destructions of species; pollution of air, water, and land; errors in genetic engineering; overfishing; nuclear and chemical mishaps and warfare; and more. Together or singly, these dangers, he said, threaten "to catch us unexpectedly, like a trap." [74]

What are we to make of all these claims of an apocalypse now? According to a survey in *U.S. News & World Report,* one third of Americans think the kingdom will be coming soon.[75] What's the lesson for people like me who simply don't believe that the end of time is at hand? I'm not altogether optimistic that we human beings can save ourselves from our own self-destructive tendencies, but I think there's good evidence that the earth will be around for a very long time, including many of its species like cockroaches and ants. And I'm betting that the universe itself will long outlive our planet and our solar system and our Milky Way galaxy.

Let's start with the concept of apocalypse itself. What's it all about? The word, from the Greek of the New Testament, means "uncovering" or "revelation."[76] It refers to the end-time event which will supposedly be marked by the sudden, dramatic, and cataclysmic intervention of God in history—including the judgment of all human beings, the salvation of the faithful elect, and the eventual rule of this set of elect people with God in a renewed and transformed heaven and earth. The concept goes back to Zoroastrianism, founded in Persia in the sixth century before Christ, and it was subsequently developed more fully in Judaism, Christianity, and Islam. There was an apocalyptic literary genre that flourished in the ancient Middle East from about 200 B.C. to 200 A.D., especially in Judaism and Christianity, apparently to give hope to religious groups undergoing persecution or the stress of great cultural upheavals at that time. In the Bible, apocalyptic literature stretches from the book of Daniel in the Old Testament to the book of Revelation at the end of the New Testament.[77]

Jesus himself seems to have been an apocalyptic teacher. The person who sketched the clearest portrait of Jesus in this regard for the modern era was Albert Schweitzer. Schweitzer was not just a medical missionary to Africa and Nobel Prize recipient, but also a towering New Testament scholar. Before he had turned thirty, he had written two books on the historical Jesus (published in 1901 and 1906) that contemporary biblical scholar

Marcus Borg describes as decisively shaping twentieth-century scholarship.[78] Schweitzer explained that Jesus expected the end of the world in his own time. Jesus is reported in the gospel of Mark as having said, "Truly I tell you, this generation will not pass away until all these things have taken place. Heaven and earth will pass away."[79] Earlier in this gospel Jesus had addressed a crowd with these words: "Truly I tell you, there are some standing here who will not taste death until they see that the kingdom of God has come with power."[80] Matthew and Luke preserve similar claims of Jesus.[81] Jesus called people to "Repent, for the kingdom of heaven has come near,"[82] and he presented a radical turn-the-other-cheek ethic in the Sermon on the Mount, about how to live in the last few months or years of the world's existence.[83] Schweitzer's claim that Jesus's message must be understood in an end-of-the-world framework became a near-consensus position in mainstream biblical scholarship in the twentieth century.[84]

Of course, these words attributed to Jesus turned out to be wrong, at least in a literal sense. The world did not end in his time. Heaven and earth did not pass away before the generation who heard him preach died. This caused considerable problems for the early Christian church since the imminent end of the world appears to have been a universal Christian belief in the first century. Only in the second century A.D., when the world still seemed to be carrying on as usual, did the church fathers begin to develop other ways to explain Jesus's words. For example, he must not have meant the end of the world literally but in a spiritual sense.[85] Or perhaps he was speaking of time symbolically, with one day not being literally twenty-four hours but more like a thousand years.[86] Hence, it's ironic that throughout Christian history the claim keeps reemerging that we are in the earth's last days right now and that this very generation here on earth will witness the end of history.[87] Don't we ever learn?

A particularly poignant example of this was a group of end-of-the-world believers studied by Stanford psychology professor Leon Festinger and others during the 1950s. They predicted the exact day that the earth would be ravaged by a series of floods, and they warned that only a faithful few would be saved. Members quit jobs, sold their possessions, and gathered to be saved, only to find that life on earth continued as usual. The classic book that chronicled the lead up and aftermath was called *When Prophecy Fails*.[88] From this work, Festinger developed the theory of "cognitive dissonance," which he presented fully in a book published in 1957.[89] He found that beliefs firmly persist even after their complete invalidation and that proselytizing activities actually increase as believers try to convert others to a failed but then slightly revised belief system.

In this book, Festinger also describes the nineteenth-century Millerites in America. William Miller was a New England farmer who, after a two-year study of the Bible, reached the conclusion in 1818 that the world would end in 1843. Although he was largely ignored for decades, by 1840 a mass movement had developed. As 1843 passed without the world ending, dates were recalculated to 1844. Still, life continued as usual. Proselytizing increased, as did numbers of adherents. Only with a fourth failure of a predicted date did Millerism finally collapse. Meanwhile, many adherents had given away their earthy possessions and experienced relentless ridicule from nonbelievers.[90] However, Millerism gave birth to the Seventh Day Adventists and other Adventists groups that reinterpreted William Miller's original prophecies and have continued as a proselytizing movement with a distinctive doctrine about the imminent end of the world.[91]

So, what exactly is to be gleaned from Jesus's words, if they're not read as a prophecy of apocalypse now, in this generation? I think the key may be found in the biblical passages in which Jesus compares the coming of the kingdom to the growth of a plant from a seed.[92] In the gospel of Luke, Jesus says: "What is the kingdom of God like? And to what shall I compare it? It is like a mustard seed that someone took and sowed in the garden; it grew and became a tree."[93] In Mark, Jesus explains that "The kingdom of God is as if someone would scatter seed on the ground, and would sleep and rise night and day, and the seed would sprout and grow, and he does not know how. The earth produces of itself, first the stalk, then the head, then the full grain in the head."[94]

For me, the seed metaphor is useful because it implies that the spirit of God is already present, working in the world, but that it's not yet fully manifest. Jesus is the harbinger, the seed of divine presence that has been sown with his incarnate life here on earth. It's our job to water and nourish the seed that is among us and within us, to help it grow to full glory. Ultimately, though, as with the life force manifest in growing plants, we really don't know how seeds sprout and grow, and we aren't finally in control.

Nature is. Biblically speaking, we've been called to be good stewards of God's creation, perhaps even cocreators with God.

There's a proclamation that confirms this understanding for me in the book of Luke. It seems to bring us 180 degrees from the notion of signs imminently appearing in the sun, moon, stars, and the Son of Man coming in the clouds with great power and glory. Jesus is asked by the Pharisees when the kingdom of God is coming. He replies, "The kingdom of God is not coming with things that can be observed; nor will they say, 'Look, here it is!' or 'There it is!' For, in fact, the kingdom of God is within you."[95] The Quakers say "There is that of God in everyone."[96] The notion that a divine consciousness of how things might be is both deep within us and among us, longing to grow, is a powerful incentive not only toward respect for the inherent worth and dignity of every person but also toward furthering the goal of world community, with liberty and justice for all.[97] This seed imagery is the link for me between the personal and social imagery in the Bible's apocalyticism. We are called personally to be alert and awake— living as if the full kingdom of God, in all of its social implications, is already inside of us, yearning to come to fruition.

Recognizing that the kingdom of God is somehow accessible within each of us, and then living with an active expectation of its social fulfillment throughout the whole world, requires us to keep attentive, aware, and alive as committed members of the human community. It encourages us to take care of our own spiritual lives as well as to reach out to others in need. There are strong ethical requirements when we're living in the knowledge that the kingdom has already come inwardly in fledgling, seedling form in our hearts and outwardly in Jesus's divine incarnation on earth some 2000 years ago, but has not yet come in all its glory either within us or in the world.

In his Sermon on the Mount, Jesus tells us some of what it means to live within God's kingdom in seedling form: "Do not resist an evildoer...Give to everyone who begs from you...Love your enemies and pray for those who persecute you...If you forgive others their trespasses, your heavenly Father will also forgive you...Do not judge, so that you may not be judged...In everything do unto others as you would have them do unto you."[98] Jesus instructs us for life in this world now, where the kingdom of God is already incrementally breaking into hearts and minds. That's how and why we can keep saying in the Lord's Prayer that Jesus taught his disciples: "Thy kingdom come, thy will be done, on earth as it is in heaven."[99]

THE SABBATH

One of the ways that Jesus was a harbinger for the seedling kingdom of God on earth was through his own healing activities. In the gospel of John he's shown restoring sight to a man who was born blind.[100] John also writes of Jesus's curing a man who had been paralyzed for 38 years and healing a man's whole body.[101] In each of the other three gospels, Jesus is reported to have restored a man's withered hand.[102] Luke adds accounts of healing a crippled woman and a man with dropsy.[103] These seem like magnificent acts, except for one problem. Jesus does all this work on the Sabbath, and certain Jewish authorities of his time challenge him for breaking one of the Ten Commandments: "Remember the Sabbath day and keep it holy. Six days you shall labor and do all your work. But [on] the seventh day... you shall not do any work."[104] The Sabbath is required to be a day of rest, and healing is work.

Jesus was not a biblical literalist, and it's also clear that humane acts came before religious observance for him. We need to be careful in our interpretation here, though. Christians have a special responsibility to avoid anti-Semitic stereotyping of the Pharisees and other religious authorities of Jesus's time as supposedly bound by intolerant legalism. The truth is that Jewish tradition had already decided long before that genuine concern for human well-being takes precedence over ritual observances. Jesus himself cites the prophet Hosea to the effect that God requires steadfast love ahead of sacrifices and burnt offerings.[105] The prophet Amos had famously spoken for God in this way in the Hebrew scriptures more than 700 years[106] before Jesus: "I despise your festivals, and I take no delight in your solemn assemblies... But let justice roll down like waters, and righteousness like an ever-flowing stream."[107]

My New Testament professor in divinity school, Krister Stendahl, used to say that as much as Jesus criticized the Pharisees, he was actually closer to them in his approach than he was to other Jewish groups of his day like the Sadducees, the Essenes, and the Zealots. The Pharisees were a reform group, distinguished by learning and piety, deeply involved in public interpretation of Jewish law as opposed to priestly activities in the temple, quietism, or political agitation against the Romans. The Pharisees' approach greatly influenced the rabbinic movement that grew up after the destruction of the temple in Jerusalem in 70 A.D. and therefore stands directly in the line to modern Judaism.[108]

The Pharisees, like the rabbis who followed them, argued with each other over the proper interpretation of biblical law. Their disputation was as central a part of the social and religious landscape in the Israel of their day as appellate and Supreme Court decision making is now in the United States. Jesus entered into their disputes on their own terms. Hence, the Sabbath stories in the New Testament should be seen as elucidating Jesus's participation in these legal debates as to the proper observance of the Sabbath, rather than as a Christian rejection of "Jewish legalism."[109]

To understand what Jesus was arguing about, it's necessary to say more about the role of the Sabbath in Jewish law and social experience. The Sabbath was felt to be a joy, not a burden. It was a festive day of rest from labor, a day of eating and drinking rather than fasting. It had an explicit dimension of social justice: servants and slaves received a guaranteed day a week of much-needed rest, and the poor and the hungry had a day to relax and to join in the eating and drinking. The words of the Ten Commandments, as recorded in Deuteronomy, required that "You shall not do any work—you, or your son or your daughter, or your male or female slave... or any of your livestock, or the resident alien in your towns, so that [they]... may rest as well as you. Remember that you were a slave in the land of Egypt, and the Lord your God brought you out from there with a mighty hand and an outstretched arm; therefore the Lord your God commanded you to keep the Sabbath day."[110]

Nonetheless, exceptions were recognized to the day-long no-work requirement when they would produce greater social justice and humanitarian benefit. As the rabbinic tradition came to enshrine the principles that were followed, healing could be practiced on the Sabbath if there was danger of death. One was also permitted to render assistance to animals. Jesus can be seen as an advocate in the Pharisees' debates for a more liberal interpretation, that healing the sick and disabled on the Sabbath is ultimately preventing death, even though the healing in those cases was not responding to immediate emergencies and probably could have been delayed for 24 hours.[111] It's telling that Jesus was able to silence his

Pharisee challengers to his healing activities by explicitly referencing the duty to care for thirsty animals[112] and to pull out a child or an ox that has fallen into a well.[113] Jesus was not trying to eliminate the Sabbath or challenge the Ten Commandments or Torah as he entered into these debates. Instead, he was simply trying to remind his antagonists of the requirements of Sabbath law in the context of its real intent—God's mercy for the oppressed, the overworked, the poor, and the hungry.[114]

How about the Sabbath in our day? Blue laws are gone in most states, so stores are open and commerce is in full swing seven days a week. Community and school athletic events for children happen all weekend long, and parents are busy getting them there. Many college students study every day of the week. When are we all getting a festive day of rest from our labors—a day off to share with our families and our friends? Are we breaking it to promote even more social justice and sense of humanity than the Sabbath itself provides? Or are we breaking it in such a way as to lose its social intent and social impact entirely?

Rabbi Harold Kushner, best-selling author of *When Bad Things Happen to Good People,* has written that along with other major and minor contributions to world civilization, Jews invented the weekend. However, it may be an endangered invention: "In the modern world, the issue of slavery is not a question of who owns your body, but who owns your soul and who owns your time." Those who live for their work, or are controlled by it—schoolwork or employment—are slaves. Those who feel they can't take a day a week, free of all school or work-related obligations, are slaves. Those who have trouble getting the time to see a child's Little League game or ballet recital are slaves. Kushner knows that few of us thoroughly control our own time. "But if at least once a week, we can claim a day for ourselves, we can feel free... When we refuse to be beasts of burden, constantly working, when we insist on pausing to take stock of our work and to redefine ourselves by who we are and not just by what we do... we transcend the animal in us and let the godly dimension of our nature emerge."[115]

So, I encourage us to "Remember the Sabbath day and keep it holy. Six days you shall labor and do all your work. But [on] the seventh day... you shall rest."[116] I still don't have this right in my own life—even when I try to take Monday as my uninterrupted day of rest. I'm impressed by how the senior associate dean for religious life at Stanford, Rabbi Patricia Karlin-Neumann, regularly observes the Sabbath from Friday sundown to Saturday sundown with her family and friends. She attests to how transformational it has been in her life by comparison to earlier periods of time when she did not regularly observe the Sabbath.

If you claim you're breaking the Sabbath in order to honor it, then make sure you're doing so as Jesus would have it: to promote a greater sense of humanity than the day of rest already provides. Otherwise, you're just kidding yourself. We should all be taking the words of the psalmist to heart: "The Lord is my shepherd, I shall not want. He makes me to lie down in green pastures; he leads me beside still waters; he restores my soul."[117]

ELEVEN

THE CHURCH YEAR

Advent, Christmas, Holy Week, and Easter

Be on guard so that your hearts are not weighed down with...the worries
of this life, and that day does not catch you unexpectedly.

—Luke 21:34

The people who walked in darkness have seen a great light; those who
lived in a land of deep darkness—on them light has shined.

—Isaiah 9:2

No one has greater love than this, to lay down one's life for one's friends.

—John 15:13

If Christ has not been raised, then our proclamation has been in vain and
your faith has been in vain"

—1 Corinthians 15:14

Christmas and Easter are the greatest holidays of the Christian year.
Can liberal Christians celebrate them with the same enthusiasm,
joy, and engagement as conservatives? How about the periods of
preparation leading up to them—Advent and Lent (and, in particular, Holy
Week)? Many liberals have problems with the idea of the virgin birth of a
baby boy destined for the throne of King David, surrounded by angels singing "Glory to God in the highest." Instead of achieving that throne, Jesus as
a man in his early thirties is torturously executed by the Roman authorities
within a week of triumphantly entering the capital city of Jerusalem. Then
we're confronted with an even more astonishing claim: Three days later he
miraculously rises from the dead, coming back fully to life.

It's hard for many of us not to agree here with scientist Richard
Dawkins's analysis in his book *The God Delusion*. First of all, there are the
scientific questions of how Jesus's mother could have been a virgin at the

time of his birth and how anyone could emerge alive after being dead and buried for three days.[1] Second, there's good evidence that critical elements of the birth story—like the virgin birth, the star in the east, and the veneration of the baby by kings—were borrowed from earlier religions of the ancient Middle East.[2] Perhaps, as atheist Sam Harris and biblical scholar John Dominic Crossan agree, "virgin" is a mistranslation of the Hebrew word for a young woman, *almah*. This was the term used in Isaiah 7:14 of the Hebrew scriptures ("The *almah* shall conceive and bear a son, and they shall name him Emmanuel"—why not name him "Jesus" by the way?) which the birth of Christ was prophetically said to fulfill.[3] And even conservative and liberal biblical scholars like N. T. Wright and Marcus Borg agree that Jesus's resurrection, whatever it may have been, was certainly not the resuscitation of a corpse.[4]

So, how are liberal Christians to wholeheartedly join in singing "Hark, the Herald Angels Sing" at the time of the winter solstice, or "Christ the Lord is Risen Today" at the time of the vernal equinox? How are we to intone the words of ancient and venerable creeds that ask us to believe that Jesus was "conceived by the Holy Ghost, born of the Virgin Mary...was crucified, dead and buried...[and] the third day he rose again from the dead"?[5]

WHAT CHRISTMAS IS REALLY ALL ABOUT

Christmas is all about kindling light in the darkness, literally and figuratively: "The people who walked in darkness have seen a great light; those who lived in a land of deep darkness—on them light has shined."[6] That means Christmas is about hope: "I am bringing you good news of great joy for all the people."[7] The story, true or legendary, relates how a tiny vulnerable baby is brought into a cruel world of kings who kill young children.[8] This baby is born when his parents are traveling, and they can't even get a room in an inn; instead, the baby is born in a barn and bedded down in an animal-feeding trough. But what joy a baby can bring to its parents, no matter what their circumstances! This particular baby is to be called "the light of the world."[9] Yet, all babies bring light as they renew the world by their presence and kindle hope for the future.

Christmas comes at the darkest time of the year in the northern hemisphere—at the winter solstice. Nights are longest and days are shortest. The sun makes its lowest trajectory across the sky, barely surmounting the horizon in parts of northern Europe, Siberia, Alaska, and Canada. It's not coincidental that many religious traditions celebrate festivals of lights at this time of year. There's Hanukkah in the Jewish tradition, with the lighting of the candles of the menorah over an eight-day period.[10] Many in the African American community celebrate Kwanza in late December, lighting a new candle on the *kinara* candleholder for seven days.[11] Even the Indian Festival of Lights, Divali, falls in December for Jains, although most Hindus celebrate it at the time of the new moon preceding November 14.[12] In the ancient Roman world, December 25 was celebrated as the birthday of the god Mithras, who was identified with the sun and called the Sun of Righteousness.[13] Along with his December 25 birth date, the title "Sun of Righteousness" was subsequently transferred from Mithras to Jesus[14] and is preserved that way in the third verse of the Christmas carol "Hark the Herald Angels Sing."[15] In America, and in much of the world, Christmas tree lights abound in December, along with outdoor lights and candles in windows.

So hope abounds on Christmas. No matter how dark it gets, one small candle can pierce that darkness. Then its light can be diffused and spread far and wide. Hope abounds. No matter how short the days and no matter how long the nights, the winter solstice comes with the promise of the steady lengthening of the days ahead, of more light each morning and of more light each evening. Hope abounds. We may be surrounded by cruelty and death in our world, by suffering and grief, but then all of a sudden we light up with new life among us in the person of a newborn baby. That joy is irresistible and spreads through all who gaze upon a newborn. Hope abounds.

The Christian claim is particularly scandalous, though. In the face of tyrants and great empires of the Mediterranean world two thousand years ago, God slips unobtrusively into a small occupied province far from the center of worldly power, in the person of a helpless baby, born to a peasant couple who've not yet married and who are out on the road. In the Christian story, God incarnate identifies from the very start with the powerless, the oppressed, the poor, and the homeless.[16] Hope abounds, because God stands with us in our brokenness.

How can we modern Christians continue to catch that spirit? How can we live filled with that kind of light against the darkness? How especially when Christians are not always seen as so enlightened by others? For Christians have been responsible for inquisitions, witch hunts, holocausts, holy wars, and bigotry of all kinds, as Richard Dawkins, Sam Harris, Christopher Hitchens, and Daniel Dennett never tire of reminding us. Christians can be smug, moralistic, judgmental, myopic, and intolerant. So, here's a modern Christian story that might point the way and be of some inspiration.

Starting in the 1980s, the five-state area of Oregon, Washington, Idaho, Wyoming, and Montana was designated a "white homeland" by the Aryan Nation and affiliated skinhead groups, Ku Klux Klan members, and other white supremacists. As a result, nonwhites, Jews, and gays in those states were targeted for harassment, vandalism, and injury—up to and including murder. Billings, Montana, with a population of about 100,000, experienced a number of hate crimes, including the desecration of a Jewish cemetery, threatening phone calls to Jewish residents, and swastikas painted on the home of an interracial couple. On December 2, 1993, a brick was thrown through the window of 5-year-old Isaac Schnitzer's bedroom. His bed was strewn with shards of glass. The reason for smashing his window was that a menorah had been stenciled on it as part of the family's Hanukkah celebration. As the *Billings Gazette* explained the next day, his mother was not happy with the advice she then received from the investigating police officer. He suggested that she not replace the menorah. Now, how would Tammie Schnitzer explain this to her son, she was quoted as wondering in the article.

A Christian mother in Billings read the newspaper article and immediately telephoned her minister at the First Congregational United Church of Christ. She imagined out loud with him what it would be like, by analogy, to explain to her children that they couldn't have a Christmas tree in their window or a wreath on their door because it wasn't safe. As a result, the minister got on the phone to his Christian clergy colleagues around town, and after their Sunday sermons, menorahs appeared in the windows of hundreds of Christian homes. During the week, one by one, more menorahs went up as the spirit spread. By the end of the week more than six thousand Billings homes were decorated with menorahs. A sporting goods store got involved by displaying these words on its large billboard: "Not in our town! No hate. No violence. Peace on earth." The billboard was shot at. Christian townspeople organized a vigil outside the synagogue during Sabbath services. The first night they did so, bricks and bullets smashed windows at the central Catholic high school, where an electric marquee read "Happy Hanukkah to our Jewish friends." The United Methodist Church put up a public menorah display, and its windows were shattered. Six non-Jewish homes displaying menorahs had their windows broken. The cat of another family exhibiting a menorah was shot and killed by a bow and arrow. The car windows of a Christian family with a menorah were smashed, with a note left on the car that said "Jew lover."[17]

Exactly right! Jew lover. Lover. Lover of humanity. Lover of the persecuted and the oppressed. *This* is what Christian enlightenment at its best is all about. Putting oneself at personal risk in solidarity with those who are targeted by hate. This is what it means to bring light into the darkness. "Light one candle" in the words of Peter Yarrow's song: "Light one candle to bring us together with peace as the song in our heart…Don't let the light go out, it's lasted for so many years."[18] That's the Jewish heritage of light, which Jesus knew as a Jew. What a fitting tribute to that heritage to have Christians at Christmas time place menorahs in their windows all over Billings, Montana.

And, as a result, anti-Semitic incidents in Billings waned in the New Year. And more demonstrations of solidarity ensued. During the Passover holiday the following spring, 250 Christians joined their Jewish brothers and sisters in a traditional seder meal. Although there were only several dozen Jewish families in Billings, many new friendships formed and greater mutual understanding was achieved.[19] Hate overcome by love. Life affirmed in the face of death. A light in the darkness. "The people who walked in darkness have seen a great light; those who lived in a land of deep darkness—on them light has shined."

WHY WAIT? THE MEANING OF ADVENT

The Christmas season now begins the day after Thanksgiving: Christmas gift shopping in high gear in Santa-filled stores, Christmas carol Muzak in elevators, and Christmas lights strung all over downtown business districts and malls. Commercialism and materialism and overwhelming busyness are primarily what it feels like. But in the Christian calendar there's a nearly forgotten period of four weeks before Christmas called Advent. It's a period of waiting, quiet contemplation, and personal preparation for the commemoration of Jesus's birth. The church year actually begins anew with Advent, on the fourth Sunday before Christmas. "Be on your guard," warns Jesus in the gospel of Luke, "so that your hearts are not weighed down with...the worries of this life, and that day [of the coming of the Son of Man] does not catch you unexpectedly."[20] Advent is on the one hand a time of patient waiting for Christmas, for the birth of the Christ child, but it's also a time of waiting for the days to come in our future when, as Jeremiah puts it, there shall be "justice and righteousness in the land."[21]

Advent has always had two sides. It's a time of increasing darkness—literally, as we near the longest night of the year—but it also holds that promise of the coming of the light into the world at Christmas. In many churches there's an Advent wreath where we begin lighting candles against the darkness: one more candle each Sunday of advent, until the glory of full light is achieved on Christmas. Advent has been seen as a period of introspection and penitence as we struggle with the dark side of reality—in our personal lives and in the world at large.

So Advent (which literally, from its Latin root, means "coming"[22]) is a challenge to us personally to think about how we're living: Are we permanently weighed down with the worries of life or are we learning to live in anticipation of better times to come that we're actively working to help bring about?

As a child, wasn't there a period in your life when you found a fireside world of fancy and fantasy—when you found wonderment, imagination, and delight in songs and stories and laughter and the warmth of those around you? I remember how much I liked coming to church to see the crèche—without Mary, Joseph, and Jesus yet present—in the chancel and to sing Advent hymns like "O Come, O Come, Emmanuel." There was an Advent calendar in my house that I savored slowly, day by day, opening one window at a time to a new delight as a narrative developed over 4 weeks' time. Finally, as we got close to the great day, I remember my father reading "The Night Before Christmas" before my sister and I went to bed every Christmas Eve, getting lost in its poetic strains.

Perhaps, part of the key to Advent is to try to experience it once again like a little child. That means trying to spend time around children if at all possible. But if that's not possible, at least trying imaginatively to revisit our childhoods through present experiences. Obviously, one can do this only by snatches and glimpses. Yet, those snatches and glimpses, when deeply experienced through adult consciousness, can be radically transforming. The wide awareness and ability to savor experience as an adult, when combined with childlike vision, can lead at its best to solemn wonder and profound reverence.

Let me suggest several ways to experience Advent that might lead to some of that wonder and reverence. First, music. Really listen, carefully and deeply, to some great music. Hear it as if it were the strains of a heavenly host. Lose yourself, transcend yourself, in that music. And then, if you're in a church service or concert, concentrate on the silence just after it ends. The silence before people begin to move, to cough, to turn the page of their program. Or, the silence before the next piece begins on your CD at home. That silence that falls around you can pull you into recognition that for one brief moment you've known that indescribable experience of divine presence in your heart.

Second, storytelling. A story well told allows us to break out of our fixed places and limited states of consciousness. We can come to imagine ourselves, or our community, or our world as they might be, or might never be but are worth dreaming about anyway. Some of the great stories for this time of year are Charles Dickens' "Christmas Carol," Frank Capra's movie *It's a Wonderful Life,* and Hans Christian Andersen's folk tale "The Little Match Stick Girl." Of course, the story of the birth of Christ is the classic story of the season. The Wonderful Counselor and Prince of Peace[23] is born in transit. Only a few people, like poor shepherds who lived in the fields and, in another gospel account, some wise men or kings, are willing to follow a star over many miles to find this baby and celebrate with his parents. The child turns out to be the hope of the world. We can begin to find our own hope, our own salvation, in the most unlikely of places, if only we remain open to the possibilities.

Third, laughter. Joy through laughter. Families and friends and work colleagues and new acquaintances and strangers—at their best all find commonality and collegiality through laughter. And laughter can be the best medicine even if we're completely alone. Norman Cousins once wrote of being hospitalized with a 104° temperature and a disease that the doctors couldn't diagnose after many tests. One physician wrote in his chart, "We may lose Norman Cousins." So, when Cousins realized that they were preparing him for death, he signed himself out of the hospital, checked into a hotel room, and sent out for a movie projector and an entire set of Marx Brothers films and old reruns of "Candid Camera." As he lay in his hotel room convulsing in laughter, he found that the pain of his illness began to lessen and his vital signs improved. In time he recovered completely. The miracle of laughter, of exulting with great joy.[24]

Finally, I suggest the advent gift of compassion, ideally for and with children. It might be a newspaper story that you respond to. An afternoon spent at a children's hospital or a home for abused or orphaned children. It might be a moment of tenderness with one's own children or nieces or nephews. There may be no more profound moments than those spent responding empathetically to another person in need. And thinking about children and their future can move us toward social action in trying to build a new world of peace and justice.

At minimum, keeping the Christian season of Advent may prevent us from getting totally lost in the busyness of Christmas time—plowing through mail order catalogues, going to shopping malls, buying and wrapping presents, and sending Christmas cards, not to mention endless ongoing tasks like car and home repairs, dentist's and doctor's appointments, returning phone calls and e-mails, and doing laundry.[25] One of my favorite liturgical writers, Rev. Virginia Rickeman, who used to serve my sister's church in Minneapolis, insists that we each be still and quiet for at least some time every day during Advent—listening and waiting and watching—before plunging back into the "thicket of our busy hours." She invites us to count up all the love and health and material comfort that we already do have and pour out our glad thanks. She suggests that we call up "memories buried deep within us...of childhood anticipation and pleasures, remembrances of friends and family members with enduring peculiarities, special talents, and distinctive tastes; thoughts of kitchens and front parlors."[26]

Finally, I suggest putting these words of Rev. Vanessa Rush Southern on a note card and carrying it around with you during Advent:

I couldn't hear myself think above the din of my surroundings and when I finally did, I was surprised by what I heard. I'd lived my life in restless banter, but with a pause I met what had eluded me—the part of me (and Her) that waited to be born. In a flash the voices of my friends, abandoned, AND my children AND my spouse could once again be heard. And I knew then the price of racing, harried, through my life: child, friend, lover, parent, Destiny, God made mute by my deaf ears. No better argument for staying still was ever made to me, nor happiness, in my entire life, more easily found and held than learning to be watchful— listening, waiting, looking—for what watches, waits, and listens to be born.[27]

HOW JESUS ROSE FROM THE DEAD ON EASTER

Actually, Easter is the great holiday of Christianity. Theologically, Christmas doesn't hold a candle to Easter, so to speak. There's no doubt that the resurrection event is the *sine qua non* of the Christian faith. As Saint Paul said, "If Christ has not been raised, then our proclamation has been in vain and your faith has been in vain... We are of all people most to be pitied."[28] The Christian church didn't start, anyway, on the strength of Jesus's virgin birth, insightful words, healing powers, or social or political vision. The Christian church was a nonstarter on Good Friday, with most of Jesus's followers either denying him outright or running for cover—running from the religious leadership in Jerusalem and from the power of the Roman state. What launched the Christian church was news that spread like wildfire in the ancient Middle East: This man called Jesus was crucified, dead, and buried; then on the third day, he rose from the dead and was seen alive again upon the earth. This is the story that eventually transformed the whole Roman Empire that had ruled the Israel of Jesus's time. By our day, Christianity has become the largest religion in the world. Easter is absolutely central to Christianity. Both conservative biblical scholars like N. T. Wright and liberal scholars like Marcus Borg agree on this essential fact: " 'God raised Jesus from the dead' is the foundational affirmation of the New Testament... The only adequate explanation for the rise of Christianity is the resurrection of Jesus."[29]

But was the resurrection a flesh-and-blood photographable event? Most liberal Christians like me can't possibly subscribe to this literalist claim. As I, informed by biblical scholars, read the gospel accounts, this was not a matter of a dead person coming back to his prior life of walking around, eating, drinking, and sleeping like the rest of us. Instead, what's meant by resurrection is that Jesus was transformed into an entirely different level of being, beyond the usual categories of life and death. As various New Testament passages describe, he appeared and disappeared at will,[30] walked through solid objects such as locked doors,[31] and could be heard by one person and not by others in the same place.[32] When Jesus himself is asked to describe resurrection in the gospel of Mark, he says that those who rise from the dead in this way are no longer normal human beings, but become like angels in heaven.[33]

All of this still may not make sense to many modern people, including you, my reader. Still, let's look at it the other way around for a moment, from the perspective of Jesus's followers. A lot of them reported seeing the resurrected Jesus, even if they may not have recognized him at first. Mary Magdalene saw him outside the tomb after first mistaking him for the gardener.[34] Two other followers met him later the same day on the road to Emmaus. They spent the day walking and talking with him, but they didn't recognize him until he broke bread at dinner with them that night, whereupon Jesus immediately vanished from their sight.[35] Likewise, Jesus appeared to Peter, to James, to all of his original disciples together, to five hundred other followers at one time, and to Paul on the road to Damascus.[36] The experience of the early Christian community was that the resurrected Jesus manifested himself to them, and it made all the difference in the world. Of course, that's been true for many Christians throughout history, up to the present time. "Jesus lives," as it's often said, and lots of people report having had a personal experience with Jesus. I'll never forget how vividly my mother once described having encountered Jesus, first sensing his presence fill the room and then feeling his hand on her shoulder, when she was praying intensely one evening at home. That experience provided sustenance for the rest of her life.

So, it seems to me that these are all visions or epiphanies or revelations of Jesus, not meetings with a resuscitated corpse. They are mystical experiences. They are not photographable or recordable events, except as described later by those who have experienced the risen Jesus. Yet, none of this is to say that these experiences are any less real, or powerful, or life changing than meeting a physical, flesh-and-blood person. In fact they may be much more intense and transformational. And they lie at the heart of Christianity—how it began, how it has been sustained, and how it informs the future.

Before Stephen was stoned to death as the first Christian martyr to his faith, we learn from the book of Acts that he had a vision of the heavens opening and seeing Jesus standing at the right hand of God.[37] Pope Gregory I in the sixth century explained that Jesus once appeared to him after the pope was feeding beggars, saying "Ordinarily, you receive me in the poor that assemble at your board, but today you received Me personally." Saint Francis of Assisi reported in the thirteenth century that the risen Christ appeared to him twice. Later, mystics Julian of Norwich and Teresa of Avila described numerous experiences of Jesus in their presence. In the nineteenth century, William Booth recounted that he founded the Salvation Army after he saw Jesus, who rebuked him for his "nominal, useless, lazy, professing Christian life."[38] Former Yale chaplain William Sloane Coffin Jr. stated that he believed "passionately in the resurrection of Jesus Christ, because in my own life I have experienced Christ not as a memory, but as a presence."[39]

This isn't to say that it's a requirement for any of us to have had a direct, personal experience of the post-Easter Jesus to be good, committed Christians. Yet, as Christians, we're part of a religious tradition in which these appearances of the risen Christ have been common and affirmed by others in the community. As Marcus Borg has put it, "the core meaning of Easter is that Jesus continued to be experienced after his death, but in a radically new way: as a spiritual and divine reality."[40] Expanding on this, Borg explains that therefore, "It's not just that his memory lived on or that his spirit lived on, as we sometimes speak of the spirit of Lincoln living on. Rather, he was and is experienced as a figure of the present. In short, Jesus lives."[41]

Each of us can aspire to greater awareness of this sort in our own future. We can know the present manifestation of that Spirit-filled person who walked this earth for more than thirty years, teaching so wisely, healing so effectively, and challenging the worldly powers of his day so dramatically. He's now raised, lives anew, and can continue to influence us deeply. The Easter story is foundational to Christian understanding and Christian action. It's critical that Jesus has been raised and has been experienced as raised. Jesus lives. And as we live in his presence, Jesus saves.

Once resurrection becomes central to one's worldview, death can no longer be the final answer, either after our physical deaths or in our daily lives. Jesus teaches instead that the final answer is love—infinite and eternal love. He teaches that on the cross when he says "Father forgive them; for they do not know what they are doing."[42] He teaches that after his resurrection when he appears to his followers and says "Peace be with you."[43] He teaches that during his life by inspiring people not only to love their neighbor as themselves[44] but also to love their enemies.[45] Love is utterly transforming. As the apostle Paul says, "Love bears all things, believes all things, hopes all things, endures all things."[46] The apostle John puts it in ultimate terms: "God is love, and those who abide in love abide in God, and God abides in them."[47]

The Easter story presents God, through Jesus on the cross, as experiencing human suffering at its most imaginably intense. No matter how bad conditions are for us—whether due to unemployment, war, terror, personal pain, grief, or mourning—and no matter how bad they may get, the Easter message is first that God's love is so great that, as incarnated in Jesus, God completely understands and experiences our suffering with us. Then, through the resurrected Jesus, God remains at our side, as close as the closest friend or lover could be. We can feel unconditionally and eternally accompanied, no matter what and no matter where. The Easter message affirms too that utter transformation is possible on the far side of suffering, not just in a world to come but in this earthly existence as well. Jesus healed continually in his earthly ministry, dramatically altering the course of peoples' lives,[48] and his disciples later did the same.[49] Jesus teaches that by loving God, rather than by loving wealth and status and other earthly idols, we can ease our fears and anxieties dramatically. Like lilies of the field, we don't have to worry constantly about the material details of our lives—what we will drink, and what we will eat, and what we will wear. Striving first to live in alignment with the law of love promises that necessities will be provided in ways we can't now predict or control.[50]

A minister I know used to visit a drug dealer in prison every week for a year—a teenager named Gene who was also a thief and a liar. As the minister described it in writing, "We talked about prison, parents, children; we talked about Darwin, Newton, Einstein; we talked about life, love, hope and truth. We were never aware of the Holy in our midst." Then, "During the final month of prison, [this convict] enrolled as a special student at the Massachusetts Institute of Technology. After his...release, he became a full-time student in chemistry." The minister finished the story and summed it up this way: "When he graduated with honors from MIT, I was thanked by his father, by his mother, and by Gene himself. It was pleasant to receive the accolades. But how the stone had been moved from the cave's entrance was impossible to tell. A resurrection is always a mystery—though it happens every day."[51]

All this minister did was to express his love in action. The transformation for the drug dealer appears to have been love received and accepted. But it was a resurrection, and it happens every day if our hearts are open. Or have our hearts grown too cold? Are we unable to move to the Alleluia of Easter? Does the whole biblical story just seem too remote and too unbelievable for us moderns? If so, here's a final prayerful plea from a great cynical bear of a man I used to know, a now-deceased Unitarian Universalist minister named Clarke Dewey Wells:

> God of Easter and infrequent Spring:
> Announce the large covenant to deceitful lands,
> Drive the sweet liquor through our parched veins,
> Lure us to fresh schemes of life.
> Rouse us from tiredness, self-pity,
> Whet us for use,
> Fire us with good passion.
> Restore in us the love of living
> Bind us to fear and hope again.[52]

DON'T FORGET HOLY WEEK

If that's the Easter message, then why all the suffering leading up to it during the six weeks of Lent that precedes it in the Christian calendar, especially on so-called Good Friday during the last week of Lent, which is liturgically named Holy Week? As a practical matter, many Christians, especially liberals, simply go from the celebration of Mardi Gras or its equivalent just before Lent to the euphoria of Palm Sunday at the beginning of Holy Week to the "day of light and gladness"[53] at Easter—skipping all the doom and gloom along the way. But then something comes along like Mel Gibson's movie *The Passion of the Christ*, and we're graphically reminded that Easter doesn't come easily. The Buddhist tradition tells us in the first of its Four Noble Truths that "all life is suffering." The Christian tradition also seems to put suffering at the very center of its theology and its iconography.

The Stanford Memorial Church has an intensely painful, cruel public execution depicted in the central stained glass window right above the altar: Jesus hanging on the cross. This cross—an instrument of torture and death—has become the primary symbol of Christianity, and it's often worn now as jewelry around people's necks. Mel Gibson's film depicts Jesus's passion in such gory and excruciating detail that I found myself several times wanting to vomit in the theater. I then warned my wife against seeing the movie herself.

Yet, as one evangelical Christian commentator put it: "On more than one occasion as I watched this movie, I had to turn away from the screen. I remember thinking at one point, 'Enough. This is over the top.' And almost immediately I had a second thought, 'That's right...This is over the top, because the death of Christ was, in reality, barbaric and violent.' Maybe what we all need to see is not a cleaned up, sanitized Hollywood version of His death, but a more accurate and graphic look at how He suffered for us."[54]

I don't actually think we all need to see this movie. I definitely don't think children need to see it. We have "R" ratings for a reason. And for adults, like having a good novel ruined by a Hollywood adaptation, there's a risk of this graphic portrayal skewing our understanding of the crucifixion, taking it out of the context of the larger story of Jesus's earthly life and teachings and his resurrected presence for us since.

There's another major problem with Mel Gibson's *Passion: potential anti-Semitism*. As explained by Dennis Prager, the first practicing Jew whom Gibson invited to see the movie before it was released: "For two hours Christians watch their Savior tortured and killed. For the same two hours, Jews watch Jews arrange the killing and torture of the Christians' Savior." Jews see Jewish authorities and a Jewish mob manipulate the Roman overlords, portrayed in the person of Pontius Pilate as morally far more elevated than those Jews before him, "into torturing and murdering a beautiful man."[55] Why does this bother so many Jews so much? Because, as Prager puts it, for nearly 2,000 years, attacked as "Christ killers," countless Jewish men, women, and children were not only tortured and murdered themselves, but saw their families and friends raped, tortured, and murdered. It's not paranoid to worry that "a major movie made by one of the world's superstars [that] depicts Jews as having Christ tortured and killed might arouse anti-Semitic passions."[56]

It is we Christians who need the six weeks of Lent as a time for prayer and meditation, for reflection and introspection, for repentance and the seeking of forgiveness for all that is perverse and fearful and cruel in our own lives. It is we Christians who continually crucify Christ and all that he stands for; we can't just blame it on some distant "other." In the end, actually, the Passion should be understood as the ultimate example of self-giving love. Surely Jesus would want his sacrifice to bring humanity together, not to divide Christians from Jews or anyone else. When asked to illustrate what he means by loving one's neighbor as oneself, Jesus takes as his exemplar of a good neighbor one of the hated "other" peoples of his day, the Samaritans.[57] Similarly, Jesus breaks the social code of his day by speaking with a Samaritan woman near Jacob's well.[58]

Remember that Jesus had plenty of opportunities to leave Jerusalem during that last week when things began to turn against him. He could have just gone back up north to the Galilee region where he was appreciated. Yet, in the Garden of Gethsemane, when his disciples start to defend him against the soldiers' arrest with their swords, Jesus insists on nonviolence.[59] He shows his love even on the cross, not only as he asks that his tormenters be forgiven, but also as he comforts a criminal being crucified beside him by saying, "Today you will be with me in Paradise."[60]

Jesus understood that his loving commitment to bringing good news to the poor, proclaiming release to captives, and letting the oppressed go free[61] was radical. He understood that his triumphal entrance into Jerusalem on Palm Sunday, with crowds welcoming him as a king, as the Son of David,[62] was threatening to both religious and imperial authorities. Yet, he continued—he blessed a poor widow who had contributed two small copper coins to the temple treasury and at the same time condemned scribes who devour widows' houses while saying long prayers for the sake of appearance.[63] He asked that the hungry be fed, the stranger be welcomed, and the sick be taken care of.[64]

Then, for all his loving concern, he's crucified. Jesus is willing to suffer and die for his vision of a humanity reconciled, a humanity at one—literally, atoned for. Those who suffer can see their great comforter suffering unto death himself. An infinitely loving God, through Jesus, transforms the sinfulness and pain of life by experiencing it all himself, and then by being with us always in the midst of our own suffering.

So, may we personally observe those six weeks of Lent, no matter how little or how much we "give up" for it. May we Christians find reconciliation, "at-one-ment," with our Jewish brothers and sisters. May we be as hospitable as Jesus, even treating people who are our foes as our friends. May our prayer life and spiritual disciplines be deepened in contemplation of the cross. And finally, may we ourselves be willing to love unto death, remembering that "no one has greater love than this, to lay down one's life for one's friends."[65]

EPILOGUE

RECLAIMING LIBERAL CHRISTIANITY

THE IMPORTANCE OF THE
"L" WORD FOR CHRISTIANITY

In the fall before the 2008 election, the editor of the 125-year-old publication *Christian Century* wrote, "In the theological arena, *liberal* has become such a negative term that few want to use it."[1] That's a discouraging conclusion from the journal that has probably been the most effective voice for liberal Christianity for over a century. Early in the twentieth century, the magazine was a primary target of the new fundamentalist movement, and by midcentury Billy Graham helped found a new "magazine of evangelical conviction" to oppose it, called *Christianity Today*.[2] But now the editor of *Christian Century* tells us that liberal Christianity is living in exile and that liberal Christians prefer to use other words to describe themselves, like "progressive."[3]

That may be partly a result of the political implications of the word "liberal." I happened to be listening to the radio in September 2008 when a conservative Christian named Mitt Romney was speaking to the Republican convention in support of John McCain and Sarah Palin. I counted more than a dozen times that he pejoratively used the word "liberal" or "liberals."[4] He claimed that liberals are responsible for awarding "Guantanamo terrorists with constitutional rights...putting the interests of the teachers union ahead of the needs of our children...[stopping] nuclear power plants and offshore drilling, making us more and more dependent on Middle East tyrants," and replacing "opportunity with dependency on government largess."[5] And there were a lot more ways that he insisted that liberals have allegedly harmed our country.

Hearing Mitt Romney reminded me of how Michael Dukakis, the liberal governor of Massachusetts, was said to have lost the 1988 election to George H.W. Bush because he was shackled with the "L" word by the Republicans. Worse, perhaps, he refused to defend what was positive about liberalism, even claiming in an interview with television commentator Ted Koppel two weeks before the election, "Ted, I'm not a liberal."[6] A *Washington Post* article in early 2008 explained that Barack Obama was independently ranked as the most liberal United States senator in 2007. Then the *Post* author predicted that in the lead-up to the election he would keep trying to claim that he's "post-partisan," not liberal, even though John McCain, "in his own way, was post-partisan before the term was invented, often working across the aisle on important legislation," defying party orthodoxy far more than Obama had. The *Washington Post* article ended with these words: "The only Democrats who have won the White House in the last four decades have done so by running away from the liberal label. And Obama is certainly a student of history."[7]

By contrast, the *Christian Century* editor claimed that "liberalism is an important thread in the fabric of our political history." He pointed out that "The founders of the republic were Enlightenment thinkers, and in large part philosophically and theologically liberal. The liberal impulse in American politics is responsible for Social Security, Medicare and Medicaid, Head Start and food stamps. Liberals, often in the face of fierce conservative opposition, have been the ones to guarantee equal rights, and they have made laws that help keep our food and automobiles safe and college education affordable."[8]

Liberal Christianity can point to the Old Testament prophets and to Jesus as the original political liberals. As mainstream a resource as the *Encyclopedia Britannica* describes political liberalism as "the culmination of a development that goes back to the Hebrew prophets, the teachings of the pre-Socratic philosophers, and the Sermon on the Mount."[9] Consider, for example, the book of Exodus account of the Jewish people wandering for forty years in the Sinai desert between Egypt and the promised land of Israel, grumbling and complaining. They are depicted as wanting conservatively to go back to the familiar rather than forward to the new—even if going back means slavery under the pharaoh. They confront their leader, the greatest Hebrew prophet of all time, Moses,[10] demanding, "Why did you bring us out of Egypt, to kill us and our children and livestock with thirst?"[11] It's hard to take a progressive view of a different future, of a promised land of milk and honey, especially when the going's tough and you're thirsty right now. Of course, that's natural and understandable; the new can be frightening, the old comfortable. Moses is afraid that they're actually ready to stone him to death. Moreover, they ask the greatest of the existential questions: "Is God among us or not?"[12]

So, Moses reasons with God, asking, "What shall I do with this people?"[13] The answer he's given is that he'll find a spring of water if he strikes a rock with his staff at the recommended place. He does, there's water, the people drink, they quench their thirst, and then they continue their journey without going back to the oppressive country from which they'd come. Note the liberal themes in this story: freedom seeking, progress, and use of reason. The Exodus story as a whole is one of moving forward, not back, of seeking freedom from the slavery of the past, of using human ingenuity and not just unquestioning reliance on God.

Note also how Jesus uses his freedom to oppose conservative religious leaders in his tradition, like the chief priests and elders. For example, there's a story in the gospel of Matthew[14] about these leaders demanding that he tell them by what authority he is acting. Jesus uses a reasoned argument to make his case, posing a question back to them that they're unwilling or afraid to answer: "Did the baptism of John come from heaven, or was it of human origin?" If they won't answer his question beyond saying "We don't know," then he won't answer theirs. They won't answer because Jesus catches them in the logical conundrum of either seeing Jesus's ally as having divine authority to which they should submit, or denying his status as a prophet of God and facing the wrath of the people in the street who do see John as having exactly this divine authority.

Jesus further asserts his freedom from the religious leaders' authority by posing another question to them, this time about two sons who change their minds in opposite directions about working in a vineyard. Their father asks his sons to go work in the vineyard on a particular day. The first says that he won't go, but later he changes his mind and does. The second says that he'll go, but he never does. Jesus asks the chief priests and elders, "Which of the two did the will of his father?" They respond, "The first." Then Jesus confronts them in these words: "Truly I tell you, the tax collectors and the prostitutes are going into the kingdom of God ahead of you. For John came to you in the way of righteousness and you did not believe him, but the tax collectors and the prostitutes believed him; and even after you saw it, you did not change your minds and believe him."[15]

Jesus often asserted that socially despised tax collectors and prostitutes will enter the kingdom of God before esteemed religious leaders. The sinful who make spiritual progress take precedence over the religiously pure who won't recognize any authority but their own. Jesus was known for his commitments to the outcast and the marginalized in society, whom we must never forget have human potential. In this story, as in so many others, Jesus shows himself as tolerant of all sorts and conditions of people, as liberals should be, not doctrinal and dogmatic. Freedom, reason, progress, tolerance. Values to be proud of, not duck because they conjure up the "L" word. And let's not forget the dictionary definitions of "liberal"— as synonymous with generous, bountiful, openhanded, munificent, and abundant.[16]

So what's the future of liberal Christianity—of Christianity marked by commitments to freedom from authority, the use of reason, human progress, and tolerance toward others? There's no future if people aren't willing to stand up for these values and claim the label "liberal" as their own. Jesus was a liberal in substantial and important ways. Christians need to stand up for him in this respect. Why has the liberal voice been so muted in Christianity?

The editor of *Christian Century* reminds us that people living in exile don't get to define the terms of political discourse: "Conservatives have won the rhetorical battle." He also observes that because tolerance is one of the central values of liberals, they "don't like to fight, but instead are always trying to accommodate people, to be inclusive even of those who are trying to exclude them." I must admit that defines me to a T. The *Christian Century* editor concludes "that the first thing on the minds of my conservative brothers and sisters when they get out of bed in the morning is fighting liberals [I think of Mitt Romney and Ann Coulter as quintessential conservatives in this respect], whereas liberals get out of bed trying to figure out how to live with conservatives."[17] Yes, that's what I do most of the time, especially in my role of dean for religious life at Stanford, pledged to "meeting the needs of all faiths by encouraging a wide spectrum of religious traditions on campus,"[18] many of them quite conservative.

But tolerance doesn't mean capitulation. It doesn't mean shying away from expressing liberal Christian values that defend the freedom of all, promote the use of reason, and affirm the human potential to better our-selves and help repair a broken world. There are clear dangers, demonstrated throughout the Bible, and specifically in the Christian gospel, of ceding authority to the religious establishment, cherishing belief over reason, accentuating sin over the human potential for good, and prioritizing alleged truth claims over tolerance.

Liberal Christians constitute at least 20 percent of the U.S. population, according to recent studies.[19] Too many of them choose silence, afraid to use the word "liberal" to describe where they stand. That leaves them lying low, sitting quietly in their pews at church or in private prayer at home, or choosing to identify simply as political liberals, without mentioning their faith commitment. They must reclaim their religious heritage as an independent source of wisdom and courage in their personal lives and in their community involvements. To them, and to myself as one of them, I bellow, "Stand up, stand tall, and proclaim the positive power of liberal Christianity! Do it now, before it's too late!"

WHERE WE GO FROM HERE

It's most effective, of course, to stand up for your beliefs in community with other liberal Christians. Since research shows that we're here in substantial numbers within Catholicism, Eastern Orthodoxy, and mainline Protestant churches, we need to find each other and support each other.

There are many clergy and religious educators who are more liberal than the majority of their congregations, so these professional leaders may be a particularly valuable resource. They've come from seminaries and continuing education with knowledge and resources about biblical research, church history, theology, ethics, and world religions that often aren't shared with lay people in the day-to-day life of the church. So I advise working with them and with church committees to create and promote, for example, Bible study groups on the historical Jesus and his life, reexaminations of church doctrine, forums on church-state relations, discussions of science and religion, and projects in social service and social justice (especially in major issue areas like poverty, discrimination, war, and environmental degradation).

Even with conservative professional leadership, there's a lot that liberal church members can do together to engage in the activities listed above, as well as to promote other opportunities like book groups, social gatherings, women's and men's groups, communal prayer and meditation, retreats, and holiday celebrations.

Regional, state, and national offices of many denominations have projects of particular interest to liberal Christians, as do the National Council of Churches and the World Council of Churches. For example, the 2007–2011 Strategic Plan of the National Council of Churches builds on past efforts—such as peace-making and poverty-reducing initiatives and studies of church-dividing issues—to look forward to promoting a new vision of an authentic common life as an alternative to that prevalent in contemporary American culture, to nurturing more theologically based grass-roots justice initiatives around issues like racism, to developing ecumenical and interfaith education and life-long learning opportunities, and to collaborating more effectively with the international efforts of Church World Service.[20] The World Council of Churches is the broadest and most inclusive of all efforts for Christian unity. It asks its member churches to come together to "reflect, speak, act, worship and work together, challenge and support each other, share and debate with each other."[21] It has six major program areas, with opportunities for individual and church participation in promoting the ecumenical movement worldwide, exploring new dimensions of spirituality, challenging violence and economic injustice, addressing environmental destruction, furthering religious education, and stimulating inter-religious dialogue.[22]

There are also national organizations specifically for liberal Christians, like the Center for Progressive Christianity, founded in 1994,[23] and organizations committed to promoting liberal religion across traditions, like the Network of Spiritual Progressives, founded in 2006 and cochaired by Rabbi Michael Lerner, Dr. Cornel West, and Sister Joan Chittister.[24] Terrific books have been written by liberal Christians, and I've tried to include a number of them in my bibliography. The classic magazine for liberals is *The Christian Century*, which I mentioned above; its cover motto is "Thinking critically. Living faithfully." What used to be *Zion's Herald*, founded in 1823 and at the forefront of the nineteenth-century Social Gospel movement, was renamed *The Progressive Christian* in 2006; its motto is "Faith and the common good."[25] It was recognized as the best general interest magazine in its class in 2008 by the oldest American religious journalism group, the Associated Church Press, ahead of *The Christian Century* and *Sojourners Magazine*.[26] *Sojourners* is also very much worth reading. Founded in 1971 by Rev. Jim Wallis, who remains its editor, this magazine is evangelical in theology and liberal in the political implications it draws from Christianity. Its motto is "Faith, politics and culture," and its mission is "to articulate the biblical call to social justice, inspiring hope and building a movement to transform individuals, communities, the church, and the world."[27]

In fact, social justice, hope, and building a movement of transformation have always been at the center of liberal Christianity. A dramatic challenge has been posed to all of us, though, by the economic debacle that began on Wall Street in the fall of 2008 and has spread around the world. As we've heard many times, this is the worst financial crisis since the Great Depression, with most analysts predicting that it will get worse before it gets better. How exactly does the rubber hit the road for liberal Christians in responding to an epochal calamity like this?

I believe that this is especially a time that aches for what liberal Christianity has to offer. For this tradition has the ability to look ahead to a new social covenant, not just back to an old one. It puts rationality and openness to new ideas ahead of blind faith and dogma tied to the past. Criticized sometimes for not taking sin seriously enough, it points us to the classic Christian virtues of faith, hope, and love while at the same time struggling against vices like fear-mongering, greed, and anger. It reminds us that we're all equal in the sight of God. That makes a real difference when it comes to issues of wealth and class, just as much as with those of gender, sexual orientation, race, and other characteristics upon which humans have historically discriminated against each other. It asks us to look beyond personal salvation in the hereafter to help build community here and now. Reminding us of Jesus's words not to judge lest we be judged,[28] and not to throw stones at others since we sin ourselves,[29] liberal Christianity promotes tolerance and dialogue in areas of difference and conflict. What's needed now is nothing less than a new Christianity for America and the world—one that works respectfully and appreciatively, hand-in-hand, with Christians who don't affirm themselves as liberal, with people of other religious traditions, and with the nonreligious and the antireligious. Here's some of what that might mean during the global financial crisis.

The new Christian covenant cannot be wedded to classical liberalism. That is, Adam Smith's invisible hand of the free market has failed and cannot be allowed to remain an idol. No doubt the economic ideology of unfettered capitalism is one possible social and political implication of theological liberalism, as discussed in chapter 8. Yet, we're in a time that demands active partnership between the government and the private business sector. Business always has to keep its eye on the bottom line, profit; government at its best is concerned first and foremost with the common good. Robert McElvaine, in an October 2008 op-ed in the *Washington Post,* lamented the power of "economic fundamentalists" who have defied sensible government regulation of markets and businesses. Their reign must come to an end.[30] Although we certainly saw the ill effects of state ownership in the former Soviet Union and a number of its satellite countries, it's now become necessary partially to nationalize our banks. As the Vatican has proclaimed in its official newspaper, *L'Osservatore Romano,* the free market model has also "grown too much and badly in the past two decades" since the fall of European communism.[31]

It's poignant that former Federal Reserve chairman Alan Greenspan, the long-lionized free-marketer, found himself explaining to Congress that this crisis had "revealed a flaw in a lifetime of economic thinking and left him in a 'state of shocked disbelief.' "[32] Greenspan stated that he was mistaken in thinking that banks would do whatever was necessary to safeguard their shareholders and institutions. He described his error, rather cosmically, as "a flaw in the model...that defines how the world works." As he put it, "A critical pillar to market competition and free markets did break down. I still do not fully understand why it happened."[33]

My own (now deceased) father, for many years an investment advisor with a large private bank, used to instruct me that "greed and fear run the marketplace." I always wondered how that kind of marketplace could unambiguously lead to positive results. And how my devotedly Christian father could square that statement with Christian virtues of faith, hope, and love. A new liberal Christianity must generate a model for how the world works that sees human beings always in tension between the darkness and the light, a model or theology that takes vices seriously and provides an opening for Christian virtues.

After the financial crisis began, my local newspaper in California profiled an 82-year-old retired nuclear engineer, Ed Sayre, who explains that it's not so far-fetched to compare the 2008 economy to the beginnings of the Great Depression.[34] What he's most concerned about, though, is whether the role of the community will be as strong this time. Back then, he relates, neighbors pulled together to help each other out. Because the world is more disconnected now and many of us barely know our neighbors, Sayre doesn't "think we would be able to work together in that way today." This is, of course, what Christian churches should be all about: knowing each other, supporting each other, caring for each other, helping each other in very practical ways. This is how love gets realized in a concrete sense. That in turn generates hope. And ultimately it illuminates the faith that the universe is ordered and that the law of life includes compassion for others as surely as the instinct for self-preservation. This is Jesus reminding us to "Do to others as you would have them do to you."[35] And it's also Jesus saying that in order to enter the kingdom of God one must feed the hungry and welcome the stranger, attending to the least of our brothers and sisters as if they were Jesus himself.[36]

Yet, this can't be just a matter of charity. We read in the book of Acts that in the early Christian communities none were needy because "They would sell their possessions and goods and distribute the proceeds to all, as any had need."[37] But, the societal answer, for which liberal churches must now advocate, well beyond voluntary giving and mutual support in Christian communities, is legislation that covers each and every citizen equally as a matter of social justice. That should include, for example, protection for homeowners who received subprime loans in good faith, extension of unemployment benefits for those who have been laid off, health insurance for the uninsured, and decent benefits for those on Medicaid and Medicare. It also requires a progressive income tax system in which the rich pay a higher percentage of their income than the poor.

Ed Sayre remembers how frustrating it was that "during the Hoover administration, they just sat back and kind of watched it happen." With Roosevelt, though, there was some financial relief, but also enormous pride when local residents joined the Civilian Conservation Corps to work on projects to develop state and national parks, and when the Works Progress Administration began distributing money for countless public projects, providing improvements to roads, bridges, and other parts of the nation's infrastructure. As I write, it seems that this could happen again in ways appropriate to the twenty-first century. Federal Reserve chairman Ben Bernanke is backing a large stimulus package that would include spending on infrastructure projects, and there are indications of bipartisan support.

Sayre remembers how governmental investments like this during the Great Depression bolstered the country's infrastructure for much of the rest of the century. This time he'd like to see additional scope that could include initiatives like clean-energy initiatives and high-speed rail construction.

A new Christianity for America and the world must remind us that we're all in this together. What the apostle Paul says of the body of Christ that is the church, liberal Christians must say of the whole world: "The body does not consist of one member but of many...The eye cannot say to the hand, 'I have no need of you,' nor again the head to the feet, 'I have no need of you'...If one member suffers, all suffer together with it; if one member is honored, all rejoice together in it."[38] If there's any doubt that this economic disaster affects each and every one of us, here are headlines in my local newspaper for just one day in late October 2008:[39] "Mass firings to hit Wall Street," "Just scraping by: Small S.J. business owner hit hard as contract prices fall for scrap metal," "Foreclosures up over year-ago quarter," "Layoffs gathering steam, more to come," "8% of valley residents lack health coverage," "Grim economy hangs over teens applying to college." And these are the kinds of comments made by individuals interviewed in those articles: "We're getting slaughtered..." "Medicaid has really degraded...It's really bad..." "People are really scared..." There were other stories of financial woes for the public in that paper, like AT&T raising its rates for basic landline service by up to 25 percent, with this year's increases being the first in 14 years. "The timing is obviously wrong for a rate hike," noted a spokesperson for a nonprofit utility watchdog group.

It's in times of crisis like this, and like the terrorist attacks of September 11, 2001, that we're brought together in the consciousness of how deeply interlocked and interdependent we are. We're able to talk to each other—across all divisions of age and occupation and ethnicity and class—about our common plight and our vision of solutions for the common good. That happens in grocery stores, on the streets, in our neighborhoods, on the playing fields, on the subway, in school—wherever people gather outside of our normal insularity. How ironic, then, that words like "class warfare" were utilized during the 2008 presidential campaign, after the economic crisis began, with a predictably divisive effect.[40]

It's particularly important that a new Christianity work respectfully and collaboratively with non-Christians, both in the United States and around the world. Instead of asking who will be left behind in a coming apocalypse, and instead of trying to undermine candidates for public office by suggesting that there might be something wrong if they aren't Christian or the right kind of Christian, a new Christianity will affirm that everyone on the face of the earth is made in the image of God and are all equally God's children.[41] America itself must also be asked to practice the virtue of humility, as when it needed to follow, not lead, Europe in a global response to the financial crisis by beginning to nationalize its banks.[42] And it's particularly important that the richest nation on earth be constantly aware of how its actions affect poorer nations and peoples. It cannot save itself at the expense of those who have been economically downtrodden for so long. For "Woe to you," said Jesus, "... who are rich, for you have received your consolation."[43]

Finally, a new Christianity must convince us of the truth of Jesus's words that we cannot serve both God and wealth.[44] Money, or the fantasy of economic security, may always stand as the greatest temptation to violate the first of the Ten Commandments: "I am the Lord your God...you shall have no other gods before me. You shall not make for yourself an idol."[45] It's the golden calf that we risk bowing down to and worshipping every day. Jesus counseled us not to store up for ourselves "treasures on earth, where moth and rust consume and where thieves break in and steal."[46] To help us find freedom from material desires and material anxieties, he pointed us to the birds of the air and the lilies of the field: "Look at the birds of the air; they neither sow nor reap nor gather into barns, and yet your heavenly Father feeds them... Can any of you by worrying add a single hour to your span of life? And why do you worry about clothing? Consider the lilies of the field, how they grow; they neither toil nor spin, yet I tell you, even Solomon in all his glory was not clothed like one of these."[47]

Ultimately what matters most is love and community, including a commitment to social justice and careful stewardship of the earth's resources. There's where hope lies, regardless of how little or how much any one of us may possess materially. Liberal Christianity in the twenty-first century must lead the way through its firm commitment to progress, the essential goodness of humanity, tolerance, and freedom. Jesus came that we might have life, and have it abundantly. Jesus was a liberal.

ACKNOWLEDGMENTS

I am grateful to the students of Stanford University and to the congregation of the Stanford Memorial Church for all the help they have provided—known and unknown—over the last eight years as I have been thinking and writing about the role of liberal Christianity in America and the world today. Many of the sermons I have preached have inspired and have been inspired by the contents of this book. That is true as well for classes, lectures, dormitory talks, seminars, discussions, and other activities with which I have been involved at the university. My gratitude extends to many Stanford professors, staff, alumni, and local community members as well.

I owe special thanks to Senior Associate Dean for Religious Life Patricia Karlin-Neumann and Associate Dean Joanne Sanders; much of my understanding has been developed through our work together in university chaplaincy. Likewise, I am deeply appreciative of all members of the Office for Religious Life for their continuous support since I arrived at Stanford. There are also many members of the almost forty religious organizations on campus that constitute Stanford Associated Religions who have been dialogue partners over the years as I have worked out my ideas. And I am very grateful to President John Hennessy and Provost John Etchemendy for their backing and generous provision of sabbatical time to pursue this book.

A number of people have kindly donated their time to read some or all of this book in various drafts. I want to acknowledge them individually with my heartfelt thanks: Dan Clendenin, Brent Coffin, Bob Dealy, Elizabeth Ellis, Anita Farber-Robertson, Robert Jonas, Ned Kendrick, Naomi Lucks, Thomas Mikelson, Emma Pease, Allie Perry, Charlie Pillsbury, Ron Sanders, Gerson Schreiber, Garry Trudeau, Barry Svigals, Kate Wheeler, and Joe Wheelwright. I appreciate the encouragement and support of my sons, Dan and Will. I am also grateful for the careful attention paid to the manuscript by my editors at Palgrave Macmillan, especially Jake Klisivitch and Alan Bradshaw. Finally, though, it is my wife, Ellen, who has been my most constructive critic and most consistent supporter through the long incubation of this book. Her contribution has been incalculable, and my appreciation is far beyond words.

SUGGESTIONS FOR FURTHER READING

CHAPTER ONE   SOME LIBERAL PERSPECTIVES

Borg, Marcus J., and N. T. Wright. *The Meaning of Jesus: Two Visions*. San Francisco: HarperSanFrancisco, 1999.

Boswell, John. *Christianity, Social Tolerance and Homosexuality*. Chicago: University of Chicago Press, 1980.

Collins, Francis S. *The Language of God*. New York: Free Press, 2006.

Crossan, John Dominic. *Jesus: A Revolutionary Biography*. San Francisco: HarperSanFrancsico, 1994.

Kissling, Frances. *Prayerfully Pro-Choice: Resources for Worship*. Washington, D.C.: Religious Coalition for Reproductive Choice, 2001.

Roughgarden, Joan. *Evolution and Christian Faith*. Washington, D.C: Island Press, 2006.

Steffen, Lloyd H., ed. *Abortion: A Reader*. Cleveland: Pilgrim Press, 1996.

CHAPTER TWO   THE ESSENCE
OF LIBERAL CHRISTIANITY

hooks, bell. *All About Love: New Visions*. New York: Perennial, 2001.

King, Martin Luther Jr. *The Strength to Love*. Minneapolis: Augsburg Fortress, 1981.

Washington, James Melvin., ed. *A Testament of Hope: The Essential Writings of Martin Luther King Jr.* New York: HarperCollins, 1991.

CHAPTER THREE   GOD

Coffin, William Sloane, Jr. *Letters to a Young Doubter*. Louisville: Westminster/John Knox Press, 2005.

Happold, F. C. *Mysticism: A Study and an Anthology*. London: Penguin Books, 1991.

Jammer, Max. *Einstein and Religion: Physics and Theology*. Princeton, NJ: Princeton University Press, 1999.

Rucker, Rudy. *Infinity and the Mind: The Science and Philosophy of the Infinite*. Princeton, NJ: Princeton University Press, 1995.

CHAPTER FOUR   JESUS AND THE CHURCH

Borg, Marcus J. *Meeting Jesus Again for the First Time*. San Francisco: HarperSanFrancisco, 1994.

Clifford, Ann M. *Introducing Feminist Theology.* Maryknoll, NY: Orbis Books, 2001.
Pelikan, Jaroslav. *Jesus Through the Centuries: His Place in the History of Culture.* New York: Harper & Row, 1985.

CHAPTER FIVE   UNDERSTANDING THE BIBLE

Borg, Marcus J. *Reading the Bible Again for the First Time: Taking the Bible Seriously But Not Literally.* San Francisco: HarperSanFrancisco, 2001.
Buehrens, John A. *Understanding the Bible: An Introduction for Skeptics, Seekers and Religious Liberals.* Boston: Beacon Press, 2003.
Gomes, Peter. *The Good Book: Reading the Bible with Mind and Heart.* San Francisco: HarperSanFrancisco, 2002.
The HarperCollins Study Bible. New York: HarperCollins, 2006.

CHAPTER SIX   FAITH

Cracknell, Kenneth. *Wilfred Cantwell Smith: A Reader.* Oxford: OneWorld, 2001.
Fowler, James. *Stages of Faith: The Psychology of Human Development and the Quest for Meaning.* San Francisco: Harper & Row, 1981.
McLennan, Scotty. *Finding Your Religion: When the Faith You Grew Up With Has Lost Its Meaning.* San Francisco: HarperSanFrancisco, 1999.
Smith, Wilfred Cantwell. *Faith and Belief: The Difference Between Them.* Oxford: Oneworld, 1998.

CHAPTER SEVEN   TALKING TO ATHEISTS AND CHRISTIAN CONSERVATIVES

Dawkins, Richard. *The God Delusion.* Boston: Houghton Mifflin Company, 2006.
Dennett, Daniel. *Breaking the Spell: Religion as a Natural Phenomenon.* New York: Viking, 2006.
Harris, Sam. *The End of Faith: Religion, Terror, and the Future of Reason.* New York: W. W. Norton, 2004.
Hitchens, Christopher. *God Is Not Great: How Religion Poisons Everything.* New York: Twelve, 2007.
Hutcheson, Richard G., Jr., and Peggy Shriver. *The Divided Church: Moving Liberals and Conservatives from Diatribe to Dialogue.* Downers Grove, Ill.: InterVarsity Press, 1999.

CHAPTER EIGHT   THE GREAT SOCIAL ISSUES

Allen, Joseph L. *War: A Primer for Christians.* Dallas: Southern Methodist University Press, 2001.
Carson, Clayborne, and Martin Luther King, Jr. *The Autobiography of Martin Luther King, Jr.* New York: Warner Books, 1991.
De Vries, Barend A. *Champions of the Poor: The Economic Consequences of Judeo-Christian Values.* Washington, D.C.: Georgetown University Press, 1998.

Rauschenbusch, Walter. *Christianity and the Social Crisis*. San Francisco: HarperOne, 2008.
Rockefeller, Steven, and John Elder. *Spirit and Nature: Why the Environment Is a Religious Issue*. Boston: Beacon Press. 1992.

CHAPTER NINE   CHURCH AND STATE

Church, Forrest. *The American Creed: A Biography of the Declaration of Independence*. New York: St. Martin's Griffin, 2002.
Needleman, Jacob. *The American Soul: Rediscovering the Wisdom of the Founders*. New York: Tarcher/Putnam, 2002.
Wallis, Jim. *God's Politics: Why the Right Gets It Wrong and the Left Doesn't Get It*. San Francisco: HarperSanFrancisco, 2005.

CHAPTER TEN   CHRISTIAN DOCTRINE

Borg, Marcus. *The Heart of Christianity: Rediscovering a Life of Faith*. San Francisco: HarperSanFrancisco, 2003.
Chittester, Joan. *In Search of Belief*. Ligouri, MO: Ligouri/Trimph, 2006.

CHAPTER ELEVEN   THE CHURCH YEAR

Rickeman, Virginia. *The Well Is Deep: Prayers to Draw Up Living Water*. Cleveland: United Church Press, 1999.

EPILOGUE   RECLAIMING LIBERAL
CHRISTIANITY FOR ALL

Burklo, Jim. *Open Christianity: Home by Another Road*. Los Altos, Cal.: Rising Star Press, 2000.
Dionne, E.J. *Souled Out: Reclaiming Faith and Politics After the Religious Right*. Princeton, NJ: Princeton University Press, 2008.
Wallis, Jim. *The Great Awakening: Reviving Faith and Politics in a Post-Religious Right America*. San Francisco: HarperOne, 2008.

NOTES

PREFACE

1. Gary Vance, "Wasn't Jesus a Liberal?" www.commondreams.org/views04/1019–24.htm
2. Gary Vance, "Wasn't Jesus a Liberal? Part Two," www.commondreams.org/views05/1009–31.htm
3. See, for example, Matthew 5:21–22, 5:33–34.
4. Matthew 5:38–39.
5. Matthew 5:44; Luke 6:27, 35.
6. Matthew 26:28; Mark 14:24; Luke 22:20 (King James version).
7. 2 Corinthians 3:6.
8. See, for example, Matthew 12:10–13; Mark 3:1–5; Luke 6:6–10; 13:10–16.
9. Mark 2:27.
10. See, for example, Robert Wuthnow, "The Moral Minority," *American Prospect* (May 22, 2000); "Denomination/Denominationalism" in William H. Swatos Jr., *Encyclopedia of Religion and Society,* http://hirr.hartsem.edu/ency/denomination.htm; "Liberal Christianity," *Answers.com,* http://www.answers.com/topic/liberal-christianity?print=true
11. A. C. Gaebelein, "The Present-Day Apostasy," as cited in George M. Marsden, *Fundamentalism and American Culture* (New York: Oxford University Press, 1980), p. 127.
12. Richard Dawkins, *The God Delusion* (Boston: Houghton Mifflin, 2006).
13. Sam Harris: *The End of Faith: Religion, Terror, and the Future of Reason* (New York: W. W. Norton, 2004).
14. Daniel C. Dennett, *Breaking the Spell: Religion as a Natural Phenomenon* (New York: Viking, 2006).
15. Christopher Hitchens, *God Is Not Great: How Religion Poisons Everything* (New York: Twelve, 2007).
16. See the 2006 Baylor Institute for the Studies of Religion Survey, conducted by Gallup and called by *USA Today* (September 12, 2006) "by far the most comprehensive national religion survey to date." Fourteen percent of all Americans self-identified as "theologically liberal" and 9 percent called themselves "seekers." Demographically it was found that mainline Protestants and Catholics constituted 22 percent and 21 percent respectively of the American population, so the total numbers of liberal Christians may actually be considerably higher than 20 percent. The U.S. population reached 300 million in October 2006.
17. Ann Coulter, *Godless: The Church of Liberalism* (New York: Three Rivers Press, 2007), p. 4.
18. Wayne A. Meeks, "Introduction to the *HarperCollins Study Bible* (San Francisco: HarperOne, 2006), p. xiii.

CHAPTER 1

1. Ralph Waldo Emerson, "The Divinity School Address," in Conrad Wright, *Three Prophets of Religious Liberalism: Channing, Emerson, Parker* (Boston: Beacon Press, 1961), pp. 96–97.
2. Matthew 5:1–7:29,
3. Richard Dawkins, *The God Delusion* (Boston: Houghton Mifflin, 2006), p. 97.

4. *HarperCollins Dictionary of Religion* (San Francisco: HarperSanFrancisco, 1995), pp. 769, 833. See also dating of New Testament books in the *HarperCollins Study Bible* (New York: HarperCollins, 1993) and the *Oxford Bible Commentary* (Oxford University Press, 2001).

5. N. T. Wright, "Knowing Jesus: Faith and History," in Marcus J. Borg and N. T. Wright, *The Meaning of Jesus: Two Visions* (San Francisco: HarperSanFrancisco, 1999), p. 22.

6. John Dominic Crossan, *Jesus: A Revolutionary Biography* (San Francisco: HarperSanFrancisco, 1994), p. xii.

7. For example, Marcus J. Borg, *Meeting Jesus Again for the First Time* (San Francisco: HarperSanFrancisco, 1994), p. 40.

8. Crossan, *Jesus*, p. 103; Marcus J. Borg, "Seeing Jesus: Sources, Lenses and Method," in Borg and Wright, *Meaning of Jesus*, p. 8.

9. N. T. Wright, "The Mission and Message of Jesus," in Borg and Wright, *Meaning of Jesus*, p. 31.

10. Ibid., p. 51.

11. Jaroslav Pelikan, *Jesus Through the Centuries: His Place in the History of Culture* (New York: Harper & Row, 1985), pp. 14–17; see also Mark 6:4 and 6:15; Matthew 21:11 and 21:46; Luke 4:24, 7:16, and 13:33; and John 4:19, 4:44, 6:14, and 9:17.

12. Wright, "Mission and Message," p. 33.

13. Marcus Borg, "Jesus Before and After Easter: Jewish Mystic and Christian Messiah," in Borg and Wright, *Meaning of Jesus*, p. 59.

14. Luke 3:23,

15. Wright, "Mission and Message," pp. 33–35.

16. Crossan, *Jesus*, pp. 67–71.

17. Borg, "Jesus Before and After Easter," p. 75.

18. Ibid, pp. 58–59, 65.

19. Crossan, *Jesus*, p. 131.

20. Mark 11:15–19, Matthew 21:12–17, Luke 19:45–48, John 2:13–25.

21. Crossan, *Jesus*, p. 130–133, 152.

22. Ibid., p. 82.

23. Borg, "Jesus Before and After Easter," p. 67.

24. N. T. Wright, "The Truth of the Gospel and Christian Living," in Borg and Wright, *Meaning of Jesus*, p. 222.

25. Wright, "Mission and Message," p. 40.

26. Borg, "Jesus Before and After Easter," pp. 68–70.

27. Luke 6:20, 36–77.

28. Jesus does so in John 9:35–37, 10:36, 11:4. In Matthew 27:43 it is also reported by his enemies, mocking him on the cross, that he called himself the Son of God. And the angel in Luke 1:35 tells Mary, before Jesus's birth, that he will be called Son of God.

29. Romans 8:14.

30. Gunther Bornkamm, "Jesus Christ," *Encyclopedia Britannica* (Chicago: 1978), vol. 10, p. 154.

31. See Borg, *Meeting Jesus,* and Borg, "Jesus Before and After Easter," pp. 59–64; also, Wright, "Mission and Message," p. 35.

32. Luke 4:18.

33. Mark 1:10.

34. Borg, *Meeting Jesus*, p. 35.

35. Ibid., pp. 9–10.

36. Genesis 1:1–2:4.

37. Matthew 4:7.

38. Christopher Hitchens, *God Is Not Great: How Religion Poisons Everything* (New York: Twelve, 2007), p. 4.

39. Ibid, p. 5.

40. Ibid,, pp. 64–65.

41. "Admissions," Liberty University, http://www.liberty.edu/admissions

42. Jerry Falwell, *Listen, America!* (New York: Bantam, 1981), as quoted in John C. Bennett, "Assessing the Concerns of the Religious Right," *Christian Century*, October 14, 1981, p. 1018.

43. Cornelia Dean, "Believing Scripture but Playing by Science's Rules," *New York Times* (February 12, 2007).

44. "The Clergy Letter" of the Evolution Weekend project, http://www.butler.edu/clergy-project/Christian_Clergy/ChrClergyLtr.htm

45. David Van Biema, "God vs. Science," *Time*, November 2, 2006.
46. Francis S. Collins, *The Language of God* (New York: Free Press, 2006), pp. 89, 96.
47. Charles Darwin, *On the Origin of Species by Means of Natural Selection, or the Preservation of Favoured Races in the Struggle for Life* (London: John Murray, 1859).
48. Biema, "God vs. Science."
49. Phillip E. Johnson, *Darwin on Trial* (Washington, D.C.: Regnery Gateway, 1991).
50. See Collins, *The Language of God*, pp. 186–93.
51. See Ibid., pp. 193–94.
52. Biema, "God vs. Science."
53. Ibid.
54. Ibid.
55. "The Clergy Letter" of the Evolution Weekend project.
56. Collins, *The Language of God*, p. 147.
57. Joan Roughgarden, *Evolution and Christian Faith* (Washington, D.C.: Island Press, 2006), pp. 7–8.
58. Collins, *The Language of God*, pp. 233–34.
59. David Batstone, "God-talk and Moral Values," *SoJoMail*, November 9, 2004. See also Jim Wallis, "The Religious Right Era is Over," *Sojourners Magazine*, October 2004; and the words of Diane Kippers from the National Association of Evangelicals, in CNN's "Fight Over Faith," October 25, 2004, http://transcripts.cnn.com/TRANSCRIPTS/0410/25/cp.01.html
60. "Democrats in Defeat Ponder 'Values Gap,'" *The Christian Century*, November 30, 2004, p. 12.
61. Scotty McLennan, "Endurance," a sermon delivered in the Stanford Memorial Church on November 14, 2004, p. 3.
62. Luke 1:46–55.
63. Matthew 1:19–20.
64. Luke 1:28, 42.
65. Luke 1: 35.
66. Luke 1:38.
67. Daniel Schiff, *Abortion in Judaism* (New York Cambridge University Press, 2002), pp. 2, 28.
68. Rachel Biale, "Abortion in Jewish Law," in Lloyd Steffen, ed., *Abortion: A Reader* (Cleveland, Ohio: Pilgrim Press, 1996), pp. 190–93.
69. See Paul D. Simmons, "Personhood, the Bible, and the Abortion Debate," in *Prayerfully Pro-Choice: Resources for Worship* (Washington, D.C.: Religious Coalition for Reproductive Choice, 2001), p. 116; Charles W. Braughman, "The Breath of Life: What Does the Bible Say in the Crucial Question in the Abortion Debate: When Does Human Life Begin?" *Christian Social Action* 9, no. 3 (1996), pp. 30–34; Mary Anne Warren, "The Moral Significance of Birth," *Hypatia* 4, no. 3 (1989), pp. 46–65. For other passages referencing the breath of life, see Genesis 6:17; Psalm 104:29–30; Job 33:4 and 34:14–15; Habakkuk 2:19.
70. See Reform Rabbinate statement (1975) and Conservative Rabbinate Statement (1983) in *Prayerfully Pro-Choice*, p. 47. For orthodox position, see Schiff, *Abortion in Judaism*.
71. As quoted in B. A. Robinson, "Abortion: Ancient Christian Beliefs" (ReligiousTolerance.org, 2004), www.religioustolerance.org/abo_hist.htm
72. Robinson, "Abortion."
73. *Roe v. Wade*, 410 U.S. 113, 132 (1973).
74. Ibid., 160.
75. F. M. Sturtevant, Letter to the editor, *Wall Street Journal* (November 14, 1994), as quoted in Tibor R. Machan, *The Passion for Liberty* (New York: Rowan & Littlefield, 2003), pp. 181–82.
76. Katherine Hancock Ragsdale, "Faithful Witness for Choice" (1997), in *Prayerfully Pro-Choice*, p. 28.
77. George F. Johnston, *Abortion from the Religious and Moral Perspective: An Annotated Bibliography* (Westport, CT: Praeger, 2003).
78. *Skinner v. Oklahoma*, 316 U.S. 535, 541 (1942).
79. John 2:1–11.
80. *Perez v. Sharp*, 32 Cal.2d 711 (1948).
81. "Miscegenation Statute in California," *Nation*, vol. 167 (October 16, 1948), p. 415.
82. *Loving v. Virginia*, 388 U.S. 1, 87 S.Ct. 1817 (1967).
83. *Loving v. Virginia*, 87 S.Ct. 1817, 1819 (1967).

84. "Miscegenation Statute," *Nation*, p. 415.
85. Citing Acts 17:26 (King James version).
86. See Genesis 19:1–11.
87. See Leviticus 18:22 and 20:13.
88. For a more thorough explanation of homosexuality in the context of the Jewish Holiness Code, see Peter J. Gomes, *The Good Book: Reading the Bible with Mind and Heart* (New York: Avon, 1996), pp. 153–55.
89. Romans 1:26–27; 1 Cor. 6:9–10; 1 Timothy 1:9–11.
90. See John Boswell, *Christianity, Social Tolerance and Homosexuality* (Chicago: University of Chicago Press, 1980).
91. See, for example, Luke 6:17–26; Matthew 5:1–12.
92. *The New Interpreter's Bible*, vol. 9 (Nashville: Abingdon Press, 1995), p. 143.
93. E.g., Matthew 19:19.
94. E.g., Luke 6:27.
95. 1 Cor. 13:1, 4–7.
96. See, for example, Matthew 7:15, 24:11, 24:24; Mark 13:22; Luke 6:26.
97. *Perez v. Sharp*, 32 Cal.2d 711, 720 (1948).
98. Luke 6:21.
99. Luke 6:37.
100. See Camille Ricketts, "Panel Discusses Gay Marriage," *Stanford Daily* (February 4, 2004), pp. 1, 10.
101. Ibid., p. 1.
102. Ephesians 6:5.
103. As cited in Peter Gomes, *The Good Book: Reading the Bible with Mind and Heart* (San Francisco: HarperSanFrancisco, 2002), pp. 100–101.

CHAPTER 2

1. Huston Smith, *The World's Religions* (San Francisco: HarperSanFrancisco, 1991), pp. 330–35.
2. *Interpreter's Bible*, vol. 8 (New York: Abingdon Press, 1952), p. 625.
3. John 10:10.
4. Luke 2:10.
5. Luke 2:11.
6. See *New Interpreter's Bible*, vol. 6 (Nashville: Abingdon Press, 2001), p. 121.
7. Isaiah 9:6.
8. Luke 2:5–7.
9. Luke 2:12.
10. Matthew 27:29,37.
11. William Wordsworth, "The World Is Too Much with Us," in B. J. Whiting, et al., *The College Survey of English Literature*, vol. 2 (New York: Harcourt, Brace & World, 1942), p. 67.
12. Luke 2:14 (King James version).
13. Spartacus Educational, "John Haynes Holmes," at http://www.spartacus.schoolnet.co.uk/USAholmesJH.htm
14. John Haynes Holmes, "To Live a Life--Not Merely a Season," quoted in Carl Seaburg, ed., *Celebrating Christmas: An Anthology* (Boston: Unitarian Universalist Ministers Association, 1983), p. 127.
15. Matthew 5:39, 5:44, 6:12, 25:35, and 7:12.
16. "Prayer," *The HarperCollins Dictionary of Religion* (San Francisco: HarperSanFrancisco, 1995), pp. 852–53.
17. Judith S. Levey and Agnes Greenhall, eds., *The Concise Columbia Encyclopedia* (New York, Columbia University Press, 1983), pp. 743, 884.
18. Song of Solomon 4:9–11; 5:10–11, 13–16; 8:7.
19. bell hooks, *All About Love: New Visions* (New York: Perennial, 2001).
20. bell hooks, *Salvation: Black People and Love* (New York: William Morrow, 2001).
21. hooks, *All About Love*, pp. 183–84.
22. Ibid., p. 184.

23. Ibid., p. 152.
24. Ibid., pp. 157–158.
25. Ibid., pp. 179, 187.
26. Thomas Merton, as quoted in ibid., pp. 187–88.
27. John 13:34.
28. *The Jerome Biblical Commentary* (Englewood Cliffs, N.J.: Prentice-Hall, 1968), p. 67.
29. Leviticus 19:18.
30. Matthew 22: 34–40; also Mark 12: 28–34 and Luke 10: 25–28.
31. Leviticus 19: 10–11,13–18.
32. See Matthew 16:18.
33. John 15:12–13.
34. John 12:13.
35. Matthew 21:12–13.
36. Matthew 21:14.
37. Matthew 23:13,23.
38. Matthew 25:31–46.
39. Martin Luther King, Jr., "I See the Promised Land," sermon delivered April 3, 1968, at Bishop Charles Mason Temple, Memphis, Tenn., reproduced in James Melvin Washington, ed., *A Testament of Hope: The Essential Writings of Martin Luther King, Jr.* (San Francisco: Harper & Row, 1986), pp. 281–82, 284–86.
40. Martin Luther King Jr., *The Strength to Love* (1963), excerpted in Washington, *Testament of Hope*, p. 513.
41. "Damon and Pythias," in William J. Bennett, ed., *The Book of Virtues* (New York: Simon & Schuster, 1993), pp. 306–11.
42. See Matthew 10:39 and 16:25; Mark 8:35; Luke 9:24; John 12:25.
43. Osama bin Laden, translation of taped remarks aired on the Al-Jazeera television network on October 7, 2001, *San Jose Mercury News* (October 8, 2001), p. 16A.
44. Franklin D. Roosevelt, "First Inaugural Address," March 4, 1933 (Franklin D. Roosevelt Library & Digital Archives, www.fdrlibrary.marist.edu).
45. King, *The Strength to Love*, pp. 509–10.
46. Ibid., p. 512.
47. Ibid.
48. Ibid.
49. Ibid., pp. 510–11.
50. Ibid., pp. 513–14.
51. Ibid., p.515.
52. Ibid., p. 516.
53. King, "I See the Promised Land," p. 284.
54. John 16:33.
55. *The New Interpreter's Bible*, vol. 9 (Nashville: Abingdon Press, 1995), p. 785.
56. 1 John 4:18.
57. Robert S. Graetz, *Montgomery: A White Preacher's Memoir* (Minneapolis: Fortress Press, 1991), p.93.
58. Paraphrasing the last paragraph of King, "I See the Promised Land," p. 286.

CHAPTER 3

1. Exodus 4:21.
2. Deuteronomy 20:1–17; Joshua 6:21.
3. Genesis 22:1–14.
4. Theodosius Dobzhansky, *Mankind Evolving: The Evolution of the Human Species* (New Haven: Yale University Press, 1962).
5. Theodosius Dobzhansky, *The Biology of Ultimate Concern* (New York: New American Library, 1967), p. 1.
6. Ibid., p. 63.
7. See, for example, Ernest Nagel and James R. Newman, *Gödel's Proof* (New York: New York University Press, 1958).

8. See Frederic B. Fitch, "A Complete and Consistent Modal Set Theory," *Journal of Symbolic Logic* 32, no.1 (March 1967), pp. 93–103. Also, "A Theory of Logical Essences," *The Monist* 51, no. 1 (Jan. 1967), pp. 104–9.

9. See, for example, Rudy Rucker, *Infinity and the Mind: The Science and Philosophy of the Infinite* (Boston: Birkhauser, 1982), pp. 6–9.

10. The next section is adapted from my Yale senior thesis, "Finite Man—Infinite Mind" (May 1, 1970).

11. Tobias Dantzig, *Number: The Language of Science* (New York: Macmillan, 1935), p. 139.

12. That is, the Babylonian equivalent of decimal places. For discussion of the Babylonian number system, see pp. 17–27 in Otto Neugebauer, *The Exact Sciences in Antiquity* (Princeton, N.J.: Princeton University Press, 1952).

13. Neugebauer, *Exact Sciences*, pp. 34, 47, and Derek John de Solla Price, *Science Since Babylon* (New Haven, CT: Yale University Press, 1961), pp. 13–14.

14. Edward Kasner and James Newman, *Mathematics and the Imagination* (New York: Simon & Schuster, 1940), p. 35.

15. Georg Cantor, *Contributions to the Founding of the Theory of Transfinite Numbers* (London: Open Court Publishing Company, 1915), p. 1.

16. Dantzig, *Number*, p. 112.

17. David Hilbert, "On the Infinite" in Jean van Heijenoort, *From Frege to Gödel* (Cambridge, MA: Harvard University Press, 1967).

18. Georg Cantor, "On Linear Aggregates," *Mathematische Annalen,* XXI (1883), p. 52.

19. E. T. Bell, *Men of Mathematics* (New York: Simon & Schuster, 1937), p. 570.

20. Kasner and Newman, *Mathematics*, pp. 61–62.

21. Raymond L. Wilder, *Introduction to the Foundations of Mathematics* (New York: John Wiley, 1965), pp. 202–3.

22. Abraham Robinson, "Formalism 64," in *Proceedings of the 1964 International Congress for Logic, Methodology and Philosophy of Science* (Jerusalem), p. 230.

23. Bell, *Men of Mathematics*, p. 398.

24. Georg Cantor, *Gesammelte Abhandlungen* (1932), p. 378, as cited in Rucker, *Infinity and the Mind*, p. 9.

25. See Rucker, *Infinity and the Mind*, pp. 44–51.

26. Peter L. Berger, A *Rumor of Angels: Modern Society and the Rediscovery of the Supernatural* (Garden City, N.Y.: Doubleday, 1969), p. 58.

27. Charles Darwin, *On the Origin of Species by Means of Natural Selection, or the Preservation of Favoured Races in the Struggle for Life* (London: John Murray, 1859).

28. Dobzhansky, *Mankind Evolving*, p. xi.

29. As cited in Max Jammer, *Einstein and Religion: Physics and Theology* (Princeton, N.J.: Princeton University Press, 1999), p. 48.

30. Ibid., p. 51.

31. Ibid., pp. 43–44.

32. "My Credo" (speech to the German League of Human Rights, Berlin, 1932), reproduced in Michael White and John Gribbin, *Einstein: A Life in Science* (London: Simon & Schuster, 1993), pp. 262–63.

33. Prinz Hubertus zu Lowenstein, *Towards the Further Shore* (London: Victor Gollancz, 1968), p. 156, as cited in Jammer, *Einstein and Religion*, p. 97.

34. Daniel Dennett, *Breaking the Spell: Religion as a Natural Phenomenon* (New York: Viking, 2006), p. 245.

35. Ibid., p. 215.

36. August 7, 1941, remarks as cited in Jammer, *Einstein and Religion*, p. 97.

37. Richard Dawkins, *The God Delusion* (Boston: Houghton Mifflin, 2006), p. 19.

38. M. Pearlman, *Ben Gurion Looks Back* (London: Weidenfeld & Nicholson, 1965), p. 217, as cited in Jammer, *Einstein and Religion*, p. 96.

39. Einstein, "My Credo," p. 263.

40. As quoted from Einstein's 1930 essay "Religion and Science" in Jammer, *Einstein and Religion*, p. 114.

41. F. C. Happold, *Mysticism: A Study and an Anthology* (London: Penguin Books, 1970), pp. 16, 19, 20.

42. Sam Harris, *The End of Faith: Religion, Terror, and the Future of Reason* (New York: W. W. Norton, 2004), p. 40.

43. Jammer, *Einstein and Religion*, p. 126.

44. William Wordsworth, "Lines Composed a Few Miles above Tintern Abbey on Revisiting the Banks on the Wye During a Tour. July 13, 1798," as collected in B. J. Whiting et al., *College Survey of English Literature* (New York: Harcourt, Brace & World, 1942), vol. 2, p. 53.

45. This is reported in detail in my earlier book, *Finding Your Religion: When the Faith You Grew Up With Has Lost Its Meaning* (San Francisco: HarperSanFrancisco, 1999), pp. 64, 207–209.

46. Aldous Huxley, *The Doors of Perception* (London: Chatto & Windus, 1960), p. 12.

47. Ibid., p. 19.

48. Aldous Huxley, *Heaven and Hell* (London: Chatto & Windus, 1960), p. 121.

49. Ibid., pp. 127–28.

50. Huxley, *Doors of Perception*, p. 62.

51. Huxley, *Heaven and Hell*, pp. 128–129.

52. Mohandas K. Gandhi, *Collected Works,* as cited in Stephen Hay, ed., *Sources of Indian Tradition* (New York: Columbia University Press, 1988), vol. II, pp. 251–52. (These quotations from this anthology are as close as I can come to reconstructing those priestly readings in India.)

53. Ibid., p. 252.

54. Ibid., p. 270.

55. Martin Luther King Jr., "The Most Durable Power," in James Melvin Washington, ed., *A Testament of Hope: The Essential Writings of Martin Luther King, Jr.* (San Francisco: Harper & Row, 1986), p. 11.

56. Paul Tillich, "The Idea of a Personal God," *Union Review* 2 (1940), pp. 8–10.

57. Many of the lessons taught in that seminar have been collected and reworked in William Sloane Coffin's last book, *Letters to a Young Doubter* (Louisville: Westminster/John Knox Press, 2005).

58. See William Sloane Coffin, *The Courage to Love* (New York: Harper & Row, 1982), p. 35.

59. An excellent biography is Warren Goldstein, *William Sloane Coffin: A Holy Impatience* (New Haven, CT: Yale University Press, 2004).

60. Coffin, *Courage to Love*, p. 1.

61. Coffin, *Letters*, p. 25. See also William Sloane Coffin, *Credo* (Louisville: Westminster/John Knox Press, 2004), pp. 1–28.

62. Coffin, *Credo*, p. 22.

63. Coffin, *Letters*, p. 185.

64. Dawkins, *The God Delusion*, p. 19.

65. See the account in Goldstein, *William Sloane Coffin*, pp. 307–11.

66. This sermon is reproduced in its entirety, as preached, in Coffin, *Courage to Love*, pp. 93–98.

67. Coffin, *Letters*, p. 42.

CHAPTER 4

1. See, for example, Mark 16, Matthew 28, Luke 24, John 20–21, and Acts 1:1–11.

2. Acts 9:1–19, 22:6–16, 26:12–18.

3. Marcus J. Borg, *Meeting Jesus Again for the First Time: The Historical Jesus and the Heart of Contemporary Faith* (San Francisco: HarperSanFrancisco, 1995), p. 11.

4. "Arius," *Encyclopedia Britannica* (Chicago: 1978), vol. I, p. 518.

5. "Nicaea, councils of," *Encyclopedia Britannica*, vol. VII, p. 319.

6. Harry Lismer Short, "Unitarians and Universalists," *Encyclopedia Britannica*, vol. 18, pp. 859–62.

7. See "The Beloved Community of Martin Luther King, Jr." (Atlanta: The King Center, 2004), www.thekingcenter.org/prog/bc/ which cites his books *Stride Toward Freedom* (1958) and *Strength to Love* (1963) as sources for the development of this concept.

8. 1 Corinthians 12:26.

9. 1 Corinthians 12:23–25.

10. Henri Nouwen, *Can You Drink the Cup?* (Notre Dame, Ind.: Maria Press, 1996), p. 58, as collected in Robert A. Jonas, ed., *Henri Nouwen* (Maryknoll, NY: Orbis Books, 1998), pp. 96–97.

11. Romans 12:10,13,16,18.

12. Michael Goldberg, *Theology and Narrative: A Critical Introduction* (Nashville: Abingdon, 1982), p. 244.
13. Jaroslav Pelikan, *Jesus Through the Centuries: His Place in the History of Culture* (New York: Harper & Row, 1985), p. 2.
14. Albert Schweitzer, *The Quest of the Historical Jesus* [1906] (New York: Macmillan, 1961), p. 4.
15. Pelikan, *Jesus Through the Centuries*, p. 58.
16. *Merriam-Webster's Collegiate Dictionary*, 10th ed. (Springfield, MA: Merriam-Webster, Inc., 1997), p. 686.
17. Pelikan, *Jesus Through the Centuries*, p. 57. See Alfred North Whitehead, *Science and the Modern World* (New York: Mentor Books, 1952), p. 13.
18. Ibid., p. 64.
19. Ibid., pp. 188–193.
20. Ibid., p. 194.
21. Ibid., pp. 197–198.
22. See Robert Bruce Mullin, *Miracles and the Modern Religious Imagination* (New Haven, CT: Yale University Press, 1996), especially pages 1–27.
23. All Emerson quotations in this section come from his "Divinity School Address," as reprinted in Conrad Wright, *Three Prophets of Religious Liberalism: Channing, Emerson, Parker* (Boston: Beacon Press, 1961), pp. 98–102.
24. Galatians 3:28, 5:1.
25. Pelikan, *Jesus Through the Centuries*, p. 209.
26. Ibid., p. 218.
27. Gustavo Gutierrez, *A Theology of Liberation* (Maryknoll, NY: Orbis Books, 1988).
28. Leonardo Boff and Clodovis Boff, "A Concise History of Liberation Theology," from their book, *Introducing Liberation Theology* (Maryknoll, NY: Orbis Books, 1987).
29. Luke 6:20,24.
30. Boff and Boff, "A Concise History of Liberation Theology."
31. Mary Daly, *Beyond God the Father: Toward a Philosophy of Women's Liberation* (Boston: Beacon Press, 1973).
32. Peter J. Gomes, *The Good Book: Reading the Bible with Mind and Heart* (New York: Avon Books, 1996), p. 120. Gomes's account of the walkout is on pp. 120–21. Mary Daly's own account of it is in Mary Daly, "Sin Big," *New Yorker*, Feb. 26, 1996, p. 76.
33. For overviews on feminist theology, see Ann M. Clifford, *Introducing Feminist Theology* (Maryknoll, NY: Orbis Books, 2001), and Janet Martin Soskice and Diana Lipton, eds., *Feminism and Theology* (Oxford: Oxford University Press, 2003). For feminist biblical scholarship, see Carol A. Newsom and Sharon H. Ringe, eds., *Women's Bible Commentary* (Louisville: Westminster/John Knox Press, 1998), and Elisabeth Schussler Fiorenza, *Searching the Scriptures*, 2 vols. (New York: Crossroad, 1993 and 1994).
34. Marcus J. Borg, *The God We Never Knew: Beyond Dogmatic Religion to a More Authentic Contemporary Faith* (San Francisco: HarperSanFrancisco, 1997), p. 70.
35. Ibid.
36. David Von Drehle, "Catholics Divided on Role of Laity," *Washington Post*, April 10, 2005, p. A1.
37. Phyllis Trible, "Feminist Hermeneutics and Biblical Studies," reprinted in Ann Loades, ed., *Feminist Theology: A Reader* (Louisville: Westminster/John Knox Press, 1990), p. 23.
38. Clifford, *Introducing Feminist Theology*, p. 76.
39. See, for example, Elisabeth Schussler Fiorenza, "Women in the Pre-Pauline and Pauline Churches," *Union Seminary Quarterly Review* 33 (3 and 4), 1978, reprinted in Soskice and Lipton, *Feminism and Theology*.
40. Luke 8: 1–3.
41. Clifford, *Introducing Feminist Theology*, p. 78.
42. Teresa Okure, "The Significance Today of Jesus' Commission to Mary Magdalene," *International Review of Mission*, LXXXI, no. 322, reprinted in Soskice and Lipton, *Feminism and Theology*, p. 314.
43. Jane Schaberg, "New Testament: The Case of Mary Magdalene," in Phyllis Trible et al., *Feminist Approaches to the Bible* (Washington, D.C.: Biblical Archaeology Society, 1995), pp. 82–83.
44. Schaberg, "Mary Magdalene," p. 83.
45. Letty M. Russell and J. Shannon Clarkson, *Dictionary of Feminist Theologies* (Louisville: Westminster/John Knox Press, 1996), p. 207.

46. Galatians 3:27–28.
47. Clifford, *Introducing Feminist Theology*, p. 2.
48. Schussler Fiorenza, "Women in the Pre-Pauline and Pauline Churches," p. 207.
49. Ibid., p. 211.
50. Elisabeth Schussler Fiorenza, "Missionaries, Apostles, Co-workers: Romans 16 and the Reconstruction of Women's Early Christian History," in Loades, ed., *Feminist Theology*, pp. 61–64.
51. I Corinthians 14:34–35.
52. Schussler Fiorenza, "Women in the Pre-Pauline and Pauline Churches," pp. 212, 219.
53. Clifford, *Introducing Feminist Theology*, pp. 2, 135.
54. Schussler Fiorenza, "Women in the Pre-Pauline and Pauline Churches," p. 203.
55. Clifford, *Introducing Feminist Theology*, p. 46.
56. Elizabeth Cady Stanton, *Woman's Bible*, cited in Clifford, *Introducing Feminist Theology*, p. 48.
57. Newsom and Ringe, eds., *Women's Bible Commentary* (Louisville: Westminster/John Knox Press, 1998).
58. Schussler Fiorenza, *Searching the Scriptures*.
59. Clifford, *Introducing Feminist Theology*, p. 49.
60. Loades, ed., *Feminist Theology*, p. 15.
61. David Robinson, *The Unitarians and the Universalists* (Westport, CT: Greenwood Press, 1985), p. 219.
62. *American Heritage Dictionary of the English Language*, Fourth Edition (New York: Houghton Mifflin, 2007).
63. "Ordination of Women" at wikipedia.org/wiki/Ordination_of_women
64. Clifford, *Introducing Feminist Theology*, pp. 141, 153–154.
65. Ibid., p. 154.
66. Ibid., p. 140.
67. William Sloane Coffin, *Credo* (Louisville: Westminster/John Knox Press, 2004), p. 137.
68. Henri Nouwen, *Reaching Out: The Three Movements of Spiritual Life* (Garden City, NY: Doubleday, 1966), p. 110, in Robert A. Jonas, ed., *Henri Nouwen* (Maryknoll, NY: Orbis Books, 1998), p. 99.
69. Henri Nouwen, *Letters to Marc About Jesus* (San Francisco: Harper & Row, 1988), p. 76, in Jonas, ed., *Henri Nouwen*, p. 103.
70. Martin Luther King, Jr., "Paul's Letter to American Christians" (sermon delivered at Dexter Avenue Baptist Church, Nov. 4, 1956), reprinted in Clayborne Carson, ed., *The Papers of Martin Luther King Jr.*, vol. III (Berkeley: University of California Press, 1997), pp. 414–20.
71. Martin Luther King Jr., "An Experiment in Love" (1958), in James Melvin Washington, ed., *A Testament of Hope: The Essential Writings of Martin Luther King Jr.* (San Francisco: Harper & Row, 1986), p. 17.
72. Coffin, *Credo*, p. 138.
73. Ibid., p. 144.
74. Ibid., p. 139.
75. Ibid., p. 139.
76. John Dominic Crossan, *Jesus: A Revolutionary Biography* (San Francisco: HarperSanFrancisco, 1994), p. 200.

CHAPTER 5

1. "Judaism (authoritative texts and their interpretation)," in Jonathan Z. Smith, ed., *The HarperCollins Dictionary of Religion* (San Francisco: HarperSanFrancisco, 1995), pp. 576–77.
2. See Huston Smith, *The World's Religions* (San Francisco: HarperSanFrancisco, 1991), pp. 346–56.
3. *HarperCollins Dictionary of Religion*, p. 1011.
4. The *Revised Common Lectionary* is now used by the majority of mainline Protestant churches and Roman Catholic churches (with some variations) in the United States and Canada. Eastern Orthodox churches generally use a different lectionary, based on a

one-year cycle. See the *Online Revised Common Lectionary*, a project of the Vanderbilt Divinity Library at http://divinity.library.vanderbilt.edu/lectionary/

5. Reginald H. Fuller, *Preaching the Lectionary* (Collegeville, Minn.: The Liturgical Press, 1984), p. ix.
6. Marcus J. Borg, *The Heart of Christianity: Rediscovering a Life of Faith* (San Francisco: HarperSanFrancisco, 1989), pp. 43, 47.
7. N. T. Wright, *Simply Christian: Why Christianity Makes Sense* (San Francisco: HarperSanFrancisco, 2006), p. 173.
8. From an average of Gallup polls in 2005–2007 as reported by Frank Newport, "One-Third of Americans Believe the Bible is Literally True" (Gallup, Inc.: 2008), http://www.gallup.com/poll/27682/OneThird-Americans-Believe-Bible- Literally-True.aspx
9. Richard G. Hutcheson Jr. and Peggy Shriver, *The Divided Church: Moving Liberals and Conservatives from Diatribe to Dialogue* (Downers Grove, Ill.: InterVarsity Press, 1999), p. 67.
10. Borg, *Heart of Christianity*, pp. 7–8.
11. Ibid., p. 9.
12. Ibid., p. 13.
13. Ibid., pp. 53–54.
14. Ibid., p. 55.
15. Ibid., p. 51.
16. Ibid., pp. 15–16.
17. See I Corinthians 12:12–31.
18. Hutcheson and Shriver, *Divided Church*, pp. 37, 39, 41.
19. Wright, *Simply Christian*, pp. 180–81.
20. Ibid., p. 181.
21. Ibid., p. 191.
22. N. T. Wright, "The Transforming Reality of the Bodily Resurrection," in Marcus J. Borg and N. T. Wright, *The Meaning of Jesus: Two Visions* (San Francisco: HarperSanFrancisco, 1998), pp. 114–15, 120, 124.
23. Daniel 1:1–2.
24. 2 Kings 18:21.
25. Matthew 7:1.
26. Matthew 5:43–48.
27. Matthew 5:38–39.
28. Matthew 25:31–46.
29. Matthew 11:19.
30. Wright, *Simply Christian*, p. 186.
31. Luke 24:44–45.
32. *The New Interpreter's Bible,* vol. 9 (Nashville: Abingdon Press, 1995), p. 486.
33. *The Oxford Bible Commentary* (Oxford: Oxford University Press, 2001), p. 925.
34. Peter J. Gomes, *The Good Book: Reading the Bible with Mind and Heart* (New York: Avon Books, 1996), pp. 29–30.
35. Marcus J. Borg, *Reading the Bible Again for the First Time: Taking the Bible Seriously But Not Literally* (San Francisco: HarperSanFrancisco, 2001), p. 3.
36. Gomes, *Good Book*, p. 31.
37. Ibid., p. 34.
38. *New Interpreter's Bible*, vol. 1, pp. 1–2.
39. Ibid., p. 104.
40. Ibid., p. 5.
41. Gomes, *Good Book*, p. 41.
42. *New Interpreter's Bible*, vol. 1, p. 5.
43. John 8:12.
44. John 15:1.
45. 1 Peter 2:6.
46. John 6:48.
47. John 10:16.
48. Matthew 9:15.
49. John 1:29.
50. Revelation 1:8.
51. John 1:1.

52. John 14:6.
53. Borg, *Heart of Christianity,* p. 49.
54. Gomes, *Good Book*, p. 6.
55. Ibid., p. 8.
56. Borg, *Reading the Bible Again*, pp. 13–18.
57. Ibid., pp. 22–23.
58. Borg, *Heart of Christianity*, p. 7.
59. *The HarperCollins Study Bible* (New York: HarperCollins, 1993).
60. Gomes, *Good Book*, p. xi.
61. Borg, *Heart of Christianity,"* p. 57.
62. Ibid., pp. 57–59.
63. Borg, *Reading the Bible Again*, p. 32.
64. Samuel Longfellow, "Light of Ages and of Nations," Hymn # 189 in *Singing the Living Tradition* (Boston: Beacon Press, 1993).
65. Matthew 5:45.
66. Mark 4: 35–41.
67. Matthew 27:46 (King James version).
68. Job 38–41.
69. Job 1:1.
70. See Job 1:2–5; 2:9–10.
71. Job 1:3.
72. What follows in this paragraph and the next is from the first chapter of Job.
73. See Job, chapter 2.
74. *Jerome Biblical Commentary* (Englewood Cliffs, N.J.: Prentice-Hall, 1968), pp. 511–512.
75. Job 3:1–4, 11–12.
76. Job 3:23.
77. Peter Calvocoressi, *Who's Who in the Bible* (London: Penguin Books, 1999), p. 87.
78. Job 6:4, 15; 7:11, 19.
79. Job 9:15–16, 32–33; 10:7.
80. Job 38:1–4, 8–10.
81. Job 40: 1–2.
82. Job 40: 3–5.
83. Job 40: 7–9.
84. Job 42: 2–6.
85. Job 42:7.
86. Job 42:8.

CHAPTER 6

1. Sam Harris, *The End of Faith: Religion, Terror, and the Future of Reason* (New York: W. W. Norton, 2004), p. 65.
2. Psalm 14:1–4.
3. Kenneth Cracknell, *Wilfred Cantwell Smith: A Reader* (Oxford: One World, 2001), pp. 5, 9.
4. Wilfred Cantwell Smith, *Faith and Belief* (Princeton, NJ: Princeton University Press, 1979).
5. Smith, *Faith and Belief,* pp. 3–13. 20; Wilfred Cantwell Smith, *Towards a World Theology: Faith and the Comparative History of Religion* (Philadelphia: Westminster Press, 1981), p. 168.
6. For example: Albert Camus, *The Stranger* (New York: Vintage Books, 1988), pp. 8, 37, 41, 69, 114, 121.
7. Ibid., p. 114.
8. James Fowler, *Stages of Faith: The Psychology of Human Development and the Quest for Meaning* (San Francisco: Harper & Row, 1981); Sharon Parks, *The Critical Years: The Young Adult Search for a Faith to Live By* (San Francisco: Harper & Row, 1986); Sharon Parks, *Big Questions, Worthy Dreams: Mentoring Young Adults in Their Search for Meaning, Purpose, and Faith* (San Francisco: Jossey-Bass, 2000); Fritz Oser and George Scarlett, eds., *Religious Development in Childhood and Adolescence* (San Francisco: Jossey-Bass, 1991); Fritz Oser and Paul Gmunder, *Religious Judgment: A Developmental Approach* (Birmingham, Ala., Religious Education Press, 1991).

9. For a fuller treatment of this, see, Scotty McLennan, *Finding Your Religion: When the Faith You Grew Up With Has Lost Its Meaning* (San Francisco: HarperSanFrancisco, 1999).
10. See the conclusions in Fritz K. Oser, W. George Scarlett, and Anton Bucher, "Religious and Spiritual Development Throughout the Life Span," in William Damon and Richard M. Lerner, *Handbook of Child Psychology,* vol. 1 (New York: John Wiley, 6th ed., 2006), pp. 942–98: For example, "Stage theory is indispensable for defining religious and spiritual development, and it provides possibilities for guiding interventions designed to support religious and spiritual development. In addition, a stage-structural approach can provide ways to explain universals in religious and spiritual development." (p. 991).
11. Fowler, *Stages of Faith*, p. 197, quoting Paul Ricoeur.
12. McLennan, *Finding Your Religion*, pp. 20–27.
13. Richard Dawkins, *The God Delusion* (Boston: Houghton Mifflin, 2006), p. 166.
14. Ibid., p. 31.
15. Ibid., pp. 58–59.
16. Ibid., p. 349.
17. Ibid., p. 348.
18. Ibid., p. 349.
19. Ibid., p. 350.
20. Ibid., p. 38.
21. Ibid., p. 19.
22. Daniel C. Dennett, *Breaking the Spell: Religion as a Natural Phenomenon* (New York: Viking, 2006), p. 245.
23. Ibid., p. 10.
24. Ibid., p. 210.
25. Harris, *End of Faith,* p, 67.
26. Sam Harris, *Letter to a Christian Nation* (New York: Alfred A. Knopf, 2006), p. 67.
27. Dawkins, *The God Delusion*, p. 5.
28. Smith, *Faith and Belief*, p. 116.
29. Ibid., pp. 123, 184.
30. Ibid., p. 122.
31. Ibid., p. 118.
32. Ibid., p. 144.
33. Ibid.
34. Ibid., pp. 144–45.
35. Ibid., p. 120.
36. Ibid., pp. 124.
37. Ibid., pp. 14, 57; see also Dennett, *Breaking the Spell*, p. 224.
38. Smith, *Faith and Belief*, p. 159.
39. Harris, *End of Faith*, p. 67.
40. See similar statements in two published sets of conversations with the Dalai Lama, edited by Daniel Goleman: *Healing Emotions* (Boston: Shambhala, 1997), p. 3, and *Destructive Emotions* (New York: Bantam Books, 2003), p. 41.
41. Smith, *Faith and Belief*, p. 168.
42. Smith, *World Theology*, pp. 11–14.
43. Ibid., p. 15.
44. "Devil," *Encyclopedia Britannica* (Chicago: 1978), pp. 502–3.
45. The oral tradition of the Garden of Eden story was likely put into written form around 900 B.C., according to biblical scholar Marcus J. Borg in *Reading the Bible Again for the First Time* (San Francisco: HarperSanFrancisco, 2001), p. 63.
46. Smith, *World Theology*, p. 44.
47. Ibid., pp. 101, 126.
48. Ibid., p. 180.
49. Ibid., p. 192–93.
50. Ibid., p. 152.
51. See ch. 4, "Objectivity and the Humane Sciences" in Smith, *World Theology*, pp. 56–80.
52. Salwa Ferahian, "W. C. Smith Remembered" (1997), http://www.lib.umich.edu/area/Near.East/sferah.htm
53. Hilary Putnam et al., "Wilfred Cantwell Smith: In Memoriam," a minute of the Harvard Faculty of Arts and Sciences, *Harvard University Gazette* (November 29, 2001).
54. Ferahian, "W. C. Smith."

55. Ibid.
56. Smith, *World Theology*, p. 103.
57. Ibid., p. 112.
58. Ibid., p. 97.
59. Lloyd Stone, "This is My Song," in *Singing the Living Tradition* (Boston: Beacon Press, 1993), 159.

CHAPTER 7

1. Richard Dawkins, *The God Delusion* (Boston: Houghton Mifflin, 2006), p. 12.
2. Daniel C. Dennett, *Breaking the Spell: Religion as a Natural Phenomenon* (New York: Viking, 2006), p. 303.
3. Sam Harris, *The End of Faith: Religion, Terror, and the Future of Reason* (New York: W.W. Norton, 2004), p. 232.
4. Ibid., p. 45.
5. Dennett, *Breaking the Spell*, pp. 299, 301.
6. See especially Chapter 3, "In the Shadow of God," in Harris, *The End of Faith*, pp. 80–107.
7. Sam Harris, *Letter to a Christian Nation* (New York: Alfred A. Knopf, 2006), p. 13.
8. 2 Thessalonians 1:6–9.
9. Luke 12:49, 51, 53.
10. Matthew 10:34–36.
11. Harris, *Letter to a Christian Nation*, p. 57.
12. *The Interpreter's Bible*, vol. 7 (Nashville: Abingdon Press, 1952), p. 235.
13. Ibid., p. 374.
14. Sabine Baring-Gould, "Onward, Christian Soldiers" (1864).
15. Julia Ward Howe, "The Battle Hymn of the Republic" (1861).
16. See, for example, James Carroll, *Constantine's Sword: The Church and the Jews: A History* (Boston: Houghton Mifflin, 2001).
17. Ibid., p. 250.
18. See Scotty McLennan, "Declaring War on the Wicked," sermon in the Stanford Memorial Church, Feb. 2, 2003.
19. George W. Bush, "State of the Union Address," Jan. 28, 2003.
20. The next two paragraphs are adapted from Scotty McLennan, *Finding Your Religion: When the Faith You Grew Up With Has Lost Its Meaning* (San Francisco: HarperSanFrancisco, 1999), pp. 133–34.
21. John Kelsay et al., "Religion and the Roots of Conflict," *Religion and Human Rights* (New York: Project on Religion and Human Rights, 1994), p. 10.
22. Ibid., pp. 3–6.
23. Harris, *End of Faith*, p. 73.
24. *Interpreter's Bible*, vol. 7, p. 373. See also, Marcus J. Borg, "An Appreciation of Albert Schweitzer," in Albert Schweitzer, *The Quest of the Historical Jesus* (Minneapolis: Fortress Press, 2001), pp. vii–viii.
25. Matthew 5:5,7,9,39,44; 6:14;7:1,3,12.
26. Matthew 5:38.
27. *Interpreter's Bible,* vol. 8, p. 235; vol. 7, p. 373.
28. Harris, *End of Faith*, pp. 78–9.
29. Harris, *Letter to a Christian Nation*, pp. 88–90.
30. Harris, *End of Faith*, pp. 64, 221.
31. Ibid., p.227.
32. Ibid., pp. 234–35.
33. Dennett, *Breaking the Spell,* p. 230, quoting Richard Dawkins.
34. Ibid., pp. 13, 203, 298.
35. William Sloane Coffin, *Credo* (Louisville, Westminster/John Knox Press, 2004), p. 157.
36. Ibid., p. 145.
37. Mark 12:30; Luke 10:27; Matthew 22:37.
38. Deuteronomy 6:5.
39. Judith S. Levey and Agnes Greenhall, eds., *The Concise Columbia Encyclopedia* (New York: Columbia University Press, 1983), p. 380.

40. Hillel, *M. 'Abot 2.6,* as cited in *The New Interpreter's Bible* (Nashville: Abingdon Press, 1995), p. 228.
41. I am grateful to Charles Pillsbury for providing this insight about the New Testament gospels' addition to the Shema. He in turn learned it from a sermon by Union Theological Seminary Professor Barbara Lunblad on the occasion of Sister Margaret Farley's retirement from the Yale Divinity School on April 15, 2005.
42. Dennett, *Breaking the Spell,* p. 250.
43. Ibid., p. 254.
44. Ibid.
45. Ibid., p. 268.
46. Ibid., p. 233.
47. Ibid., p. 297.
48. Ibid.
49. Ibid., pp. 272, 276.
50. Ibid., p. 285.
51. Thomas J. S. Mikelson, "Wake, Now, My Senses," in *Singing the Living Tradition* (Boston: Beacon Press, 1993), 298.
52. Dawkins, *The God Delusion,* pp. 1–3.
53. Richard Dawkins, *Unweaving the Rainbow: Science, Delusion and the Appetite for Wonder* (London: Penguin Press, 1998), p. ix.
54. John Keats, "Lamia" (1820), as cited in Dawkins, *Unweaving the Rainbow,* p. 16.
55. Dawkins, *The God Delusion,* p. 12.
56. Ibid., p. 166.
57. Ralph Waldo Emerson, "The Divinity School Address" (1838), in Conrad Wright, *Three Prophets of Religious Liberalism: Channing, Emerson, Parker* (Boston: Beacon Press, 1961), pp. 96, 102.
58. Dawkins, *The God Delusion,* p. 286.
59. Ibid., p. 284.
60. Scotty McLennan, "Intelligent Design," sermon in Stanford Memorial Church on Jan, 8, 2005.
61. Genesis 1:4, 10, 12, 18, 21, 25, 31.
62. Genesis 15:5.
63. Psalm 19:1.
64. Luke 12:27.
65. Carl Sagan, *Pale Blue Dot,* cited in Dawkins, *The God Delusion,* p. 12.
66. Albert Einstein, cited in Dawkins, *The God Delusion,* pp. 9, 19.
67. Dawkins, *The God Delusion,* p. 19.
68. William Blake, "Auguries of Innocence" (1803), cited in Dawkins, *Unweaving the Rainbow,* p. 17.
69. Dawkins, *Unweaving the Rainbow,* p. 17.
70. Ibid., p. 9.
71. *Concise Columbia Encyclopedia* (New York: Columbia University Press), p. 324.
72. Dawkins, *Unweaving the Rainbow,* p. 15.
73. William Wordsworth, *Lyrical Ballads* (1802), cited in Dawkins, *Unweaving the Rainbow,* p. 39.
74. Dawkins, *Unweaving the Rainbow,* p. ix.
75. Ibid., p. 6.
76. Alan Wolfe, "The Opening of the Evangelical Mind," *Atlantic Monthly* (digital edition at http://www.theatlantic.com/issues/2000/10/wolfe.htm), p. 2.
77. Quoted at ibid.
78. Wolfe, "Opening," p. 2.
79. Ibid., p. 4; Richard Mouw, "Ultimately Everything Holds Together," *Atlantic Monthly* (digital edition sidebar to Wolfe article), p. 1; Mark Noll, "Serious Faith…Careful Learning," *Atlantic Monthly* (digital edition sidebar to Wolfe article).
80. Wolfe, "Opening," part 4, p. 3.
81. Jim Burklo, *Open Christianity: Home by Another Road* (Los Altos, CA: Rising Star Press, 2000), pp. ix–x.
82. Ibid., pp. 250, 256.
83. I Corinthians 10:17.
84. Marcus J. Borg and N. T. Wright, *The Meaning of Jesus: Two Visions* (San Francisco: HarperSanFrancisco, 1999), pp. vii, x–xi.

CHAPTER 8

1. Gary Vance, "Wasn't Jesus a Liberal?" www.commondreams.org/views04/1019–24.htm
2. Ann Coulter, *Godless: The Church of Liberalism* (New York: Three Rivers Press, 2007), back cover.
3. "Liberalism, theological," *Encyclopedia Britannica,* vol. 11 (Chicago: 1978), pp. 195–96.
4. Ibid.
5. Richard W. Buliet, ed., *The Columbia History of the Twentieth Century* (New York: Columbia University Press, 1998), p. 87.
6. Martin Luther King Jr., "Pilgrimage to Nonviolence," *Christian Century* (April 13, 1960), reprinted in James Melvin Washington, ed., *A Testament of Hope: The Essential Writings of Martin Luther King Jr.* (San Francisco: Harper & Row, 1986), pp. 37–38.
7. Quoted in "Seven Days," http://www.sourdoughrecords.com/pope/sevendays.html
8. Matthew 19:16–30; Mark 10: 7–31; Luke 18:18–30.
9. Amos 5:7, 11.
10. Mark 10:21.
11. Matthew 19:22.
12. Matthew 19:29; Mark 10:29–30; Luke 18:29–30.
13. Matthew 19:24; Mark 10:25; Luke 18:25.
14. Mark 10:27.
15. *New Interpreter's Bible,* vol. 8 (Nashville: Abingdon Press, 1995), p. 649.
16. See the U.S. Conference of Catholic Bishops' pastoral letter, "Economic Justice for All: Catholic Social Teaching and the U.S. Economy," *Origins* 16 (November 27, 1986).
17. *New Interpreter's Bible,* vol. 8, p. 649; Jonathan Z. Smith, ed., *The HarperCollins Dictionary of Religion* (San Francisco: HarperSanFrancisco, 1995), p. 367; Judith S. Levery and Agnes Greenhall, eds., *The Concise Columbia Encyclopedia* (New York: Columbia University Press, 1983), p. 303.
18. Matthew 6:31,33.
19. Luke 12:48.
20. Rebecca M. Blank, *It Takes a Nation: A New Agenda for Fighting Poverty* (Princeton, N.J.: Princeton University Press, 1997), p. 56.
21. Barend A. de Vries, *Champions of the Poor: The Economic Consequences of Judeo-Christian Values* (Washington, D.C.: Georgetown University Press, 1998), p. 21.
22. "The Bush Tax Cut" (Dean for America, 2003), www.bushtax.com
23. Citizens for Tax Justice, "Year-by-Year Analysis of the Bush Tax Cuts…" (June 12, 2002), www.ctj.org/html/gwb0602.htm
24. "The President's Agenda for Tax Relief" (White House web page 2004), www.white-house.gov/news/reports/taxplan.html
25. De Vries, *Champions,* p. 268.
26. Ibid., p. 2.
27. Amos 5:24.
28. William Sloane Coffin, *Credo* (Louisville: Westminster/John Knox Press, 2004), p. 62.
29. U.S. Census Bureau, press release, August 28, 2007, http://www.census.gov/Press-Release/www/releases/archives/income_wealth/010583.html
30. U.S. Department of Health and Human Services, "The 2008 Poverty Guidelines," http://aspe.hhs.gov/poverty/08Poverty.shtml
31. Coffin, *Credo*, p. 155.
32. Ibid., pp. 64–5.
33. William Sloane Coffin, *The Heart Is a Little to the Left* (Hanover, NH: University Press of New England, 1999), p. 16.
34. Martin Luther King Jr., "Letter from Birmingham City Jail," in James Melvin Washington, ed., *A Testament of Hope: The Essential Writings of Martin Luther King, Jr.* (San Francisco, Harper & Row, 1986), p. 298.
35. Stephen B. Oates, *Let the Trumpet Sound: The Life of Martin Luther King Jr.* (New York: New American Library, 1982), pp. 60, 64.
36. Ibid., p. 65.
37. Ibid.
38. Washington, *A Testament of Hope,* p. 289.
39. King, "Letter," pp. 296–297.
40. Ibid., p. 297.

41. Ibid., pp. 289, 302.
42. Ibid., p. 298.
43. Ibid., p. 299.
44. Ibid., p. 290.
45. Ibid., p. 290.
46. Ibid., p. 292.
47. Ibid., pp. 294–95.
48. Ibid., p. 294.
49. Joseph L. Allen, *War: A Primer for Christians* (Nashville: Abingdon Press, 1991), p. 16.
50. Ibid., p. 31; Judith S. Levey and Agnes Greenhall, eds., *The Concise Columbia Encyclopedia* (New York: Columbia University Press, 1983), p. 194.
51. Allen, *War*, p. 8.
52. Scotty McLennan, "Declaring a Just War?" *San Francisco Chronicle* (February 10, 2003), p. A20.
53. Thom Shanker, "Gates Endorses Pause in Iraq Troop Withdrawals," *New York Times*, Feb. 12, 2008.
54. David M. Herszenhorn, "Estimates of Iraq War Cost Were Not Close to Ballpark," *New York Times*, March 19, 2008.
55. A. H. Alkhuzai, I. J. Ahmad, M. J. Hweel, T. W. Ismail, et al. (2008), "Violence-Related Mortality in Iraq from 2002 to 2006," *New England Journal of Medicine* 358(2):484–93.
56. Gilbert Burnham, Riyadh Lafta, Shannon Doocy, and Les Roberts, "Mortality after the 2003 Invasion of Iraq: A Cross-sectional Cluster Sample Survey," *The Lancet*, Oct. 11, 2006.
57. Associated Press, "U.N.: More than 4 Million Iraqis Displaced," June 5, 2007.
58. Psalm 22:16–20.
59. George W. Bush, "State of the Union Address," Jan. 28, 2003.
60. George W. Bush, quoted in David Remnick, "Hearts and Minds," *New Yorker*, May 17, 2004.
61. Dana Priest and R. Jeffrey Smith of the *Washington Post*, "Memo: Torture 'may be justified' in some cases," *San Jose Mercury News*, June 8, 2004, p. 9A.
62. Ibid.
63. Ibid.; See also Michael Hirsh, John Barry, and Daniel Klaidman, "A Tortured Debate," *Newsweek*, June 21, 2004, pp. 50–53; and Angie Cannon, "Time Bombs in the Files," *U.S. News and World Report*, June 21, 2004, p. 67.
64. Matthew 27:46; Mark 15:34.
65. Psalm 22:1.
66. Psalm 22:24.
67. Luke 8:26–39.
68. Joseph R. Des Jardins, *Environmental Ethics: An Introduction to Environmental Philosophy* (Belmont, CA: Wadsworth Publishing Co., 1993), p. viii.
69. Lynn White Jr., "The Historical Roots of Our Ecological Crisis," *Science*, vol. 155 (March, 1967), pp. 1203–1207.
70. Genesis 1:27–28.
71. White, "Historical Roots," p. 1205.
72. Ibid.
73. From Elizabeth Roberts and Elias Amidon, *Earth Prayers from Around the World* (San Francisco: Harper, 1991), p. 10.
74. See Luke 10: 25–37.
75. White, "Historical Roots," p. 1206.
76. Ibid., pp. 1206–7.
77. See, for example, Steven Rockefeller and John Elder, *Spirit and Nature: Why the Environment Is a Religious Issue* (Boston: Beacon Press, 1992).
78. Deuteronomy 30:9.
79. Deuteronomy 29:23.
80. St. Francis of Assisi, "All Creatures of Our God and King," set to a melody from *Geistliche Kirchengesang*, Cologne (1623).
81. Rockefeller and Elder, *Spirit and Nature*, pp. 159–60.
82. Ibid., p. 162.
83. Ibid., p. 163.
84. From Roberts and Amidon, *Earth Prayers*, p. 57.

CHAPTER 9

1. "Conversation on Religion in American Life," Scott Simon speaks with Morris Fiorina and Alain De Boton on *Weekend Edition*, Nov. 13, 2004, www.npr.org/templates/story/story.php?storyId=4168707
2. Pat Robertson, *AP/Fox News*, Jan. 2, 2004, cited in *Sojourners,* Oct. 2004, p. 35.
3. Jerry Falwell, *New York Times,* July 16, 2004, cited in *Sojourners,* Oct. 2004, p. 35.
4. Cited by John Buchanan in "Poor Priorities," *Christian Century,* Nov. 2, 2004, p. 3.
5. Jim Wallis, *God's Politics: Why the Right Gets It Wrong and the Left Doesn't Get It* (San Francisco: HarperSanFrancisco, 2005).
6. Jim Wallis, *The Great Awakening: Reviving Faith and Politics in a Post-Religious Right America* (San Francisco: HarperOne, 2008).
7. "God is Not a Republican or a Democrat," *Sojourners,* Oct. 2004, p. 35. Also see bumper sticker advertisement and Election 2008 Issues Guide in *Sojourners,* Nov. 2008, pp. 29–32, 45.
8. *Sojourners,* Nov. 2008, pp. 29–32.
9. Ibid., pp. 30, 32.
10. National Association of Evangelicals, "For the Health of the Nations: An Evangelical Call to Civic Responsibility" (last revised, Sept. 9, 2004).
11. Isaiah 65:17, 19.
12. Luke 21: 12–17.
13. Luke 21:19.
14. Isaiah 65:18, 21, 25.
15. Matthew 22:21 (King James version); see also Mark 12:17 and Luke 20:25.
16. Peter Calvocoressi, *Who's Who in the Bible* (London: Penguin, 1999), p. 149.
17. Ibid., pp. 63–64.
18. *The New Interpreter's Bible,* vol. 8 (Nashville: Abingdon Press, 1995), p. 420.
19. *Merriam-Webster's Collegiate Dictionary* (Springfield, Mass.: Merriam-Webster, 1997), p. 308.
20. *New Interpreter's Bible,* vol. 8, p. 674.
21. Matthew 22:21 (King James version).
22. Matthew 22:37–40.
23. *Oxford Bible Commentary* (Oxford: Oxford University Press, 2001), p. 873.
24. Matthew 12:14.
25. See, for example, Matthew 14:5; 21:11; 21:46.
26. Luke 4:18.
27. Luke 4: 24.
28. Matthew 25:35–36, 40.
29. See, for example, James Luther Adams, *The Prophethood of All Believers* (Boston: Beacon Press, 1986), pp. 255–56.
30. Lawrence Tribe, quoted at a New York conference in 1984 (cited in Oct.14, 1984, sermon by Scotty McLennan, "Why the Church Should Be in Politics").
31. Pat Robertson, comments made on NBC *Today,* Oct. 30, 1988.
32. Jerry Falwell, comments made on NBC *Today* Oct. 30, 1988.
33. Tribe, at conference, 1984.
34. Text of the Williamsburg Charter at www.religioustolerance.org/wil_burg.htm
35. Katherine Lee Bates, "America the Beautiful" (1895) in *Services of Religion* (Boston: Beacon Press, 1937), 383.
36. Samuel Francis Smith, "My Country, 'Tis of Thee" (1832), in *Services of Religion,* p. 384.
37. Wallis, *God's Politics,* p. xiv.
38. Forrest Church, *The American Creed: A Biography of the Declaration of Independence* (New York: St. Martin's Griffin, 2002), p. 105.
39. Alexis de Tocqueville, *Democracy in America* (New York: Knopf's Everyman's Library, 1994), vol. II, p. 6.
40. Church, *American Creed.* pp. 141–2.
41. Ibid., pp. xii-xiv.
42. Calvin Coolidge, Vice-Presidential Nomination Speech, 1920, cited in Church, *American Creed,* p. 35.
43. Martin Luther King Jr., "Letter from Birmingham City Jail," in James M. Washington, ed., *A Testament of Hope* (San Francisco: Harper & Row, 1986), p. 293.

44. Abraham Lincoln, Second Inaugural Address, in Church, *American Creed*, pp. 55–56.
45. "Declaration of Sentiments," Seneca Falls, NY, 1848, in Church, *American Creed*, p. 63.
46. John F. Kennedy, Inaugural Address, 1961, in Church, *American Creed*, p. 109.
47. Church, *American Creed*, p. 121.
48. Ibid., p. 122.
49. George W. Bush, *New York Times*, Feb. 2002, p. A1.
50. Emma Lazarus, "The New Colossus" (1883)
51. Jacob Needleman, *The American Soul: Rediscovering the Wisdom of the Founders* (New York: Tarcher/Putnam, 2002), p. 46.
52. Ibid., p. 3.
53. John Gardner, "Foreword" to Brian O'Connell, *Civil Society: The Underpinnings of American Democracy* (Medford, Mass.: Tufts University, 1999), pp. xiv–xvi.

CHAPTER 10

1. Arthur Blessit, "How Far Did Jesus and Mary Walk?" www.blessit.com/jesuswalked.html
2. Matthew 28: 18–19.
3. *The HarperCollins Study Bible* (New York: HarperCollins, 1993), p. 1721.
4. *The New Interpreter's Bible,* vol. 8 (Nashville: Abingdon Press, 1995), p. 504.
5. *The HarperCollins Dictionary of Religion* (San Francisco: HarperSanFrancisco, 1995), p. 1100.
6. *Merriam-Webster's Collegiate Dictionary* (Springfield, Mass.: Merriam-Webster, 1997), p. 1265.
7. "The Nicene Creed," *The Book of Common Prayer* (New York: The Church Hymnal Corporation), pp. 326–327.
8. See citations from Joseph Priestley's 1792 book, *A History of the Corruptions of Christianity*, quoted in David Robinson, *The Unitarians and the Universalists* (Westport, CT: Greenwood Press, 1985), pp. 22–23.
9. Conrad Wright, *Three Prophets of Religious Liberalism: Channing, Emerson, Parker* (Boston: Beacon Press, 1961), p. 17.
10. Ralph Waldo Emerson, "The Divinity School Address" (1838), in Wright, *Three Prophets*, pp. 96–98, 102, 108, 112.
11. Mark 10: 17–18.
12. Matthew 23:9.
13. Matthew 26:39. See also Mark 14:36, Luke 22:42.
14. See note in *The HarperCollins Study Bible* (San Francisco: HarperOne, 2006), p. 1702.
15. Luke 22:42.
16. *Jerome Biblical Commentary* (Englewood Cliffs, NJ: Prentice-Hall, 1968), p. 159.
17. See, for example, I John 4:7–12; John 3:16; Romans 8:35–39. For a comparative religion perspective, see Huston Smith, *The World's Religions* (San Francisco: HarperSanFrancisco, 1991), pp. 325–27.
18. Matthew 3:16–17.
19. John 14:26.
20. 2 Corinthians 13:13.
21. Daniel L. Migliore, *Faith Seeking Understanding: An Introduction to Christian Theology* (Grand Rapids, Mich.: William B. Eerdmans Publishing, 1991), p. 59.
22. Ibid., pp. 63, 70–71.
23. Scotty McLennan, *Finding Your Religion: When the Faith You Grew Up With Has Lost Its Meaning* (San Francisco: HarperSanFrancisco, 1999), pp. 111–12.
24. Words by Reginald Heber, 1826.
25. *Jerome Biblical Commentary*, p. 255.
26. 1 Corinthians 11:23–25.
27. *Encyclopedia Britannica,* vol. 3 (Chicago: 1978), p. 46.
28. See William Morris, ed., *American Heritage Dictionary of the English Language* (Boston: Houghton Mifflin, 1973), pp. 268–70.
29. 1 Corinthians 10:17.

30. *HarperCollins Dictionary of Religion*, p. 820.
31. Jim Burko, *Open Christianity* (Los Altos, CA: Rising Star Press, 2000), pp. 163–64.
32. 1 Corinthians 11:20; see *Interpreter's Dictionary of the Bible,* vol. 3 (Nashville: Abingdon Press, 1982), p. 158.
33. *Interpreter's Dictionary*, vol. 2, p. 179; vol. 3, p. 158.
34. Ibid., vol. 2, p. 179.
35. Luke 22:19; 1 Corinthians 11:23–24; see also the accounts of Jesus feeding the multitudes in Matthew 15:36, Mark 14:23, Luke 22:17,19.
36. *New Interpreter's Bible*, vol. 10, p. 934.
37. 1 Corinthians 11:21.
38. 1 Corinthians 11:22.
39. *New Interpreter's Bible,* vol. 10, p. 934.
40. 1 Corinthians 11:28.
41. 1 Corinthians 11:33.
42. 1 Corinthians 11:23–26.
43. See, for example, Matthew 9:10–13.
44. See Matthew 15:32–38; Mark 8:1–9; John 6:1–14.
45. John 6:11.
46. Matthew 25:35–36.
47. Henri Nouwen, *Writings Selected with an Introduction by Robert A. Jonas* (Maryknoll, NY: Orbis Books, 1998), p. 95.
48. See Carl Scovel, "Soul Food," *The Unitarian Universalist Christian*, vol. 57 (2002), pp. 90–92.
49. Ibid., p. 91.
50. Ibid., p. 92
51. 2003 Gallup poll as reported at http://speakingoffaith.publicradio.org/programs/ 2005/01/27_godsofbusiness/galluppoll.shtml; 2001 Barna poll as reported at www.adherents.com/misc/BarnaPoll.html
52. *New Interpreter's Bible*, vol. 9, p. 554.
53. John Stott, *Evangelical Truth* (Downers Grove, Ill.: InterVarsity Press, 1999), pp. 88–90.
54. John 3:2.
55. *Jerome Biblical Commentary,* p. 429.
56. John 3:3.
57. John 3:5.
58. *Jerome Biblical Commentary*, pp. 429–30; *Oxford Bible Commentary* (Oxford: Oxford University Press, 2001), p. 966.
59. Romans 6:4.
60. *New Interpreter's Bible*, vol. 9, p. 550.
61. John 3:5.
62. John 3:6.
63. *Jerome Biblical Commentary,* p. 430.
64. Stott, *Evangelical Truth,* pp. 90–91.
65. John 3:8.
66. John 3:16.
67. John Cheever, "The Housebreaker of Shady Hill," in *The Stories of John Cheever* (New York: Ballantine Books, 1985), pp. 300–20.
68. Ibid., pp. 318–19.
69. Isaiah 64:1
70. Mark 13:24–26.
71. *The Concise Columbia Encyclopedia* (New York: Columbia University Press, 1983), p. 694.
72. Advertising copy for Tim LaHaye and Jerry B. Jenkins, 10th anniversary limited edition of *Left Behind: A Novel of the Earth's Last Days*, http://www.leftbehind.com/channelbooks.asp?pageid=1102&channelID=30
73. "Are We Living in the End Times?" http://www.leftbehind.com/channelbooks.asp?channelID=131
74. Walter Wink sermon at the Stanford Memorial Church on November 6, 2005 (these actual words are taken from an October 17, 2001, article in *The Christian Century*, but are very similar to what he said in his 2005 sermon).
75. As cited in Reginald Stackhouse, *The End of the World? A New Look at an Old Belief* (New York: Paulist Press, 1997).

76. *HarperCollins Dictionary of Religion*, p. 55.
77. *Encyclopedia Britannica*, vol. 1, pp. 445–46.
78. Marcus J. Borg, "An Appreciation of Albert Schweitzer," in Albert Schweitzer, *The Quest of the Historical Jesus* (Minneapolis: Fortress Press, 2001), p. vii.
79. Mark 13:30–31.
80. Mark 9:1.
81. Luke 21:32; Matthew 24: 34.
82. Matthew 4:17.
83. Borg, "Appreciation of Schweitzer," p. viii.
84. Ibid., p. ix.
85. *Interpreter's Bible*, vol. 7 (Nashville: Abingdon Press, 1951), p. 774.
86. 2 Peter 3:8.
87. "Are We Living in the End Times?" http://www.leftbehind.com/channelbooks. asp?channelID=131
88. Leon Festinger, Henry W. Reicken, and Stanley Schacter, *When Prophecy Fails* (Minneapolis: University of Minnesota Press, 1956).
89. Leon Festinger, *A Theory of Cognitive Dissonance* (Stanford, CA: Stanford University Press, 1957).
90. Festinger et al, *When Prophecy Fails*, pp. 12–23.
91. *The Concise Columbia Encyclopedia* (New York: Columbia University Press, 1983), p. 8.
92. See *Interpreter's Dictionary of the Bible*, vol. 3, p. 23.
93. Luke 13:18–19.
94. Mark 4:26–28.
95. Luke 17:20–21.
96. George Fox, as quoted by the Philadelphia Society of Friends Yearly Meeting at www. pym.org (1997)
97. See, for this language, the purposes and principles of the Unitarian Universalist Association, adopted as a bylaw by the 1984 and 1985 General Assemblies.
98. Matthew 5:39,42,44; 6:14,19,21; 7:1,12.
99. Matthew 6:10 (King James version).
100. John 9:1–17.
101. John 5:1–18; 7:21–24.
102. Matthew 12:9–14; Mark 3:1–6; Luke 6:6–11.
103. Luke 13:10–17; 14:1–6.
104. Exodus 20:8–10; see also Deuteronomy 5:12–14.
105. Hosea 6:6 as cited by Jesus in Matthew 12:7.
106. *HarperCollins Study Bible*, p.1355.
107. Amos 5:21,24.
108. *HarperCollins Dictionary of Religion*, pp. 838–39; Peter Calvocoressi, *Who's Who in the Bible* (London: Penguin, 1999), p. 149.
109. *New Interpreter's Bible*, vol. 8, pp. 559–60, 277–78.
110. Deuteronomy 5:14–15.
111. *New Interpreter's Bible*, vol. 8, pp. 277–78.
112. Luke 13:15–17.
113. Luke 14:5–6.
114. *New Interpreter's Bible*, vol. 8, p. 278.
115. Harold Kushner, *To Life! A Celebration of Jewish Being and Thinking* (New York: Warner, 1993), pp. 95–97; see also Abraham Joshua Heschel, *The Sabbath* (New York: Farrar, Straus & Giroux, 1975).
116. Exodus 20:8–10; see also Deuteronomy 5:12–14.
117. Psalm 23:1–3.

CHAPTER 11

1. Richard Dawkins, *The God Delusion* (Boston: Houghton Mifflin, 2006), p. 59.
2. Dawkins, *God Delusion*, p. 94; for a contrary view, see N. T. Wright, "Born of a Virgin?" in Marcus J. Borg and N. T. Wright, *The Meaning of Jesus* (San Francisco: HarperSanFrancisco, 1999), pp. 176–77.

3. Sam Harris, *The End of Faith: Religion, Terror, and the Future of Reason* (New York: W. W. Norton, 2004), pp. 94–95; John Dominic Crossan, *Jesus: A Revolutionary Biography* (San Francisco: HarperSanFrancisco, 1994), pp. 16–18. See also Matthew 1:20–23 and Luke 1:31–35.

4. N. T. Wright, "The Transforming Reality of the Bodily Resurrection," in Borg and Wright, *Meaning of Jesus*, pp. 120, 122; Marcus Borg, "The Truth of Easter" in Borg and Wright, *Meaning of Jesus*, p. 131.

5. From the Apostles' Creed. See, for example, *The Book of Common Prayer, According to the Use of the Episcopal Church* (New York: The Church Hymnal Corporation, 1979), pp. 53–54.

6. Isaiah 9:2.

7. Luke 2: 10.

8. Matthew 2:13–18.

9. E.g., John 8:12; 9:5.

10. *HarperCollins Dictionary of Religion* (San Francisco: HarperSanFrancisco, 1995), p. 580.

11. Ibid., p. 649.

12. "Ceremonial and Ritualistic Objects," *Encyclopedia Britannica* (Chicago:1978), vol. 3, p. 1177.

13. Carl Seaburg, ed., *Celebrating Christmas* (Boston: Unitarian Universalist Ministers Association,1983), pp. 4, 6.

14. Ibid,, p. 6.

15. The first three lines of the third verse are "Hail, the heaven-born Prince of Peace:/ hail, the Sun of Righteousness./ Light and life to all he brings." Charles Wesley, "Hark the Herald Angels Sing," www.oremus.org/hymnal/h/h078.html

16. Seaburg, *Celebrating Christmas*, p. 6,7.

17. Jo Clare Hartsig and Walter Wink, "Light in Montana: How One Town Said No to Hate," *Civic Participation and Community Action Sourcebook* (New England Literacy Resource Center, 1995), http://hub1.worlded.org/docs/vera/montana.htm

18. Peter Yarrow, "Light One Candle," *Singing the Living Tradition* (Boston: Beacon Press, 1993), #221.

19. Hartsig and Wink, "Light in Montana."

20. Luke 21:34.

21. Jeremiah 33:15.

22. *Encyclopedia Britannica,* vol. 1 (1978), p. 104.

23. From Isaiah 9:6.

24. Albert Nerenberg, "Laugh 'Til It Stops Hurting," *The Gazette* (Montreal), March 1, 2008, citing Norman Cousins, *Anatomy of an Illness as Perceived by the Patient: Reflections on Healing and Regeneration* (New York: Norton, 1979), www.canada.com/montrealgazette/story.html?k=34744&id=3860b4ee-58e5-4950-9c94-a2ffd1ce6754

25. Virginia Rickeman, *The Well Is Deep* (Cleveland: United Church Press, 1999), pp. 4–5; see also Malinda Elizabeth Berry, "Blessed Assurance," *Sojourners*, Dec. 2006, p. 48.

26. Rickeman, *The Well Is Deep*, pp. 4–5

27. Vanessa Rush Southern, "Advent," in *This Piece of Eden* (Boston: Skinner House Books, 2001). Reprinted with the permission of Skinner House Books. *This Piece of Eden* by Vanessa Southern is available at (800) 215–9076 or www.uua.org/bookstore.

28. 1 Corinthians 15:14,19.

29. Borg and Wright, *Meaning of Jesus*, p. 129.

30. Luke 24:15,31.

31. John 20:19.

32. Acts 22:6–11.

33. Mark 12:25.

34. John 20:11–18.

35. Luke 24:13–31.

36. 1 Corinthians 15:5–8.

37. Acts 7:55–56.

38. Phillip H. Wiebe, *Visions of Jesus* (Oxford: Oxford University Press, 1997), pp. 16–21.

39. William Sloane Coffin, *Living the Truth in a World of Illusions* (San Francisco: Harper & Row, 1985), p. 73.

40. Marcus J. Borg, *The God We Never Knew* (San Francisco: HarperSanFrancisco, 1997), p. 93.

41. Marcus J. Borg, *The Heart of Christianity* (San Francisco: HarperSanFrancisco, 2003), p. 54.
42. Luke 23:34.
43. Luke 24:36; John 20:21,26.
44. See Matthew 22:34–40 and Luke 10:25–28.
45. Matthew 5:44.
46. 1 Corinthians 13:7.
47. 1 John 4:16.
48. See, for example, Luke 5:17–26.
49. See. For example, Acts 3:1–10.
50. Matthew 6:24–34; Luke 12:22–31.
51. David O. Rankin, *Portraits from the Cross* (Boston: Unitarian Universalist Association, 1978), p. 17.
52. Clarke Dewey Wells, "Hope Again," in *Singing the Living Tradition* (Boston: Beacon Press, 1993), 624. Reprinted with the kind permission of Reverend Barbara Carlson.
53. Title of hymn written by Frederick Lucian Hosmer (270 in *Singing the Living Tradition).*
54. Bob Lepine, "The Passion of the Christ," The Family Room at http://www.familylife.com/familyroom
55. Dennis Prager, "The Passion: Jews and Christians Are Watching Different Films," http://www.townhall.com/columnists/dennisprager/printdp20031028.shtml
56. Ibid.
57. Luke 10:29–37.
58. John 4:3–30.
59. Matthew 26:52; Luke 22:51.
60. Luke 23:34, 43.
61. Luke 4:18.
62. Matthew 21:5–9; See also Mark 11:1–10; Luke 19:28–40; John 12:125.
63. Luke 20:47 and 21:2–4; Mark 12:40–44.
64. Matthew 25:35–36.
65. John 15:13.

EPILOGUE

1. John M. Buchanan, "Mislabeled," *Christian Century*, Oct. 7, 2008, p. 3.
2. http://en.wikipedia.org/wiki/Christian_Century, citing Linda-Marie Delloff, "Charles Clayton Morrison: Shaping a Journal's Identity," *Christian Century* (Jan. 18, 1984, centennial edition); see also http://wikipeidia.org/wiki/Christianity_Today, citing Christian Smith, *American Evangelicalism: Embattled and Thriving* (Chicago: University of Chicago Press, 1998).
3. Buchanan, "Mislabeled."
4. Mitt Romney, speech to the Republican Convention, Associated Press, Sept. 3, 2008.
5. Ibid.
6. www.answers.com/topic/michael-dukakis
7. Peter Baker, "Obama and the L-Word," *Washington Post*, Feb. 7, 2008, http://voices.washingtonpost.com/the-trail/2008/02/07/obama_and_the_lword_1.html
8. Buchanan, "Mislabeled."
9. "Liberalism," *Encyclopedia Britannica,* vol. 10 (Chicago: 1978), p. 846.
10. Deuteronomy 34:10.
11. Exodus 17:3.
12. Exodus 17:7.
13. Exodus 17:4.
14. Matthew 21:23–32.
15. Matthew 21:31–32.
16. *Webster's New Collegiate Dictionary* (Springfield, Mass.: G. & C. Merriam, 1961), p. 484.
17. Buchanan, "Mislabeled."
18. Job description for "Dean for Religious Life" (Stanford University, 2000).
19. See note 15 to the Preface. Also see "U.S. Religious Landscape Survey" released Feb. 25, 2008, by the Pew Forum on Religion and Public Life (http://religions.pewforum.org). It

found that 18 percent of Americans are members of mainline Protestant churches. Although not all of those would identify as theologically liberal, 24 percent of Americans are members of Roman Catholic Churches, and a percentage of them would also identify as theologically liberal. Another indicator may be that 19 percent of Protestants and 29 percent of Catholics conceive of God as an "impersonal force" rather than a "personal God." Moreover, of the 63 percent of Americans who believe that scripture represents the word of God, almost half say it should not be taken literally. On the other hand, more than a quarter of the American population (which includes 5 percent who are members of non-Christian faiths) states that their faith's sacred texts are not the word of God but are written by people, and 15 percent of Protestants self-identify as politically liberal, as do 18 percent of Catholics (34 percent of Protestants call themselves "moderate," as do 38 percent of Catholics, while the figures for political conservatives are 44 percent and 36 percent respectively).

20. "2007–2011 Strategic Plan,." National Council of the Churches of Christ in the United States of America, www.ncccusa.org/pdfs/NCCstrategicplan.html
21. "Who Are We?" World Council of Churches, www.oikoumene.org/en/who-are-we.html
22. "Programmes," World Council of Churches, www.oikoumene.org/?id=1635
23. See www.tcpc.org.
24. See www.spiritualprogressives.org.
25. "About Us," *The Progressive Christian* website, www.tpcmagazine.org/about.html
26. "ACP 'Best of the Christian Press' Awards," Associated Church Press website, www.theacp.org/news/news08/awards08.htm
27. *Sojourners*, June 2008, p. 6.
28. Matthew 7:1; Luke 6:37.
29. John 8:7.
30. Robert McElvaine, cited in *The Week*, Oct.10, 2008, p. 4.
31. "Pope denounces greed," *The Week*, Oct. 17, 2008, p. 9.
32. Martin Crutsinger and Marcy Gordon, "Greenspan: 'Shocked disbelief': Ex-Fed Chief admits 'mistake' in trusting banks' self-interest," *San Jose Mercury News*, Oct. 24, 2008, p. 1E.
33. Ibid., p. 4E.
34. Chris O'Brien, "Fighting Depression," *San Jose Mercury News* (October 22, 2008), p. 1C.
35. Luke 6:31.
36. Matthew 25:35.
37. Acts 2:45.
38. 1 Corinthians 12:14,21,26.
39. *San Jose Mercury News*, Oct. 24, 2008.
40. John McCain stated during the third presidential debate on Oct. 15, 2008, "The whole premise behind Senator Obama's plans are class warfare, let's spread the wealth around." http://elections.nytimes.com/2008/president/debates/transcripts/third-presidential-debate.html
41. General Colin Powell's comment near the end of the 2008 presidential campaign was particularly important in this respect. When he was endorsing Barack Obama on Oct.19 on NBC's "Meet the Press" with Tom Brokaw, he said, "I'm also troubled by, not what Senator McCain says, but what members of the party say. And it is permitted to be said such things as, 'Well, you know that Mr. Obama is a Muslim.' Well, the correct answer is, he is not a Muslim; he's a Christian. He's always been a Christian. But the really right answer is, 'What if he is?' Is there something wrong with being a Muslim in this country? The answer's no, that's not America."
42. "Nationalizing banks: Europe shows the way," *The Week*, Oct. 24, 2008.
43. Luke 6:24.
44. Matthew 6:24; Luke 16:13.
45. Exodus 20:2–4.
46. Matthew 6:19.
47. Matthew 6:26–29.

INDEX